More Praise for
Epic Content Marketing

"Joe Pulizzi has made me a content believer! Starting today, we will start to develop our business content with a devoted discipline to behave more like a great media company."

KATHERINE BUTTON BELL,
Vice President & Chief Marketing Officer,
Emerson

"Joe Pulizzi may know more about content marketing than any person alive. He proves it in these pages."

JAY BAER,
New York Times Bestselling Author
of *Youtility: Why Smart Marketing
Is About Help Not Hype*

"The future of successful brand building, and especially the art of solidifying the emotional connection between people and brands, will require expertise in Content Marketing. *Epic Content Marketing* gives all the details practitioners need without overcomplicating."

PROFESSOR JOANN SCIARRINO,
Knight Chair
Digital Advertising and Marketing,
University of North Carolina–Chapel Hill

"Joe Pulizzi is the godfather of our burgeoning profession of Content Marketing. He lays out the objectives, principles, and core strategies of our field in a way that's easy-to-understand, inspiring, and entertaining. If your company doesn't yet realize that it's a media company, with all the challenges and advantages that implies, you're missing the most powerful way to connect with your customers."

JULIE FLEISCHER,
Director of Media & Consumer Engagement,
Kraft Foods

EPIC
CONTENT
MARKETING

HOW TO TELL A DIFFERENT STORY, BREAK THROUGH THE CLUTTER, AND WIN MORE CUSTOMERS BY MARKETING LESS

JOE PULIZZI

New York   Chicago   San Francisco   Athens   London   Madrid
Mexico City   Milan   New Delhi   Singapore   Sydney   Toronto

9 0   QFR/QFR   1 9 8 7 6 5

ISBN   978-0-07-181989-3
MHID   0-07-181989-4

e-ISBN   978-0-07-181991-6
e-MHID   0-07-181991-6

Library of Congress Cataloging-in-Publicatino Data
Pulizzi, Joe.
    Epic content marketing : how to tell a different story, break through the clutter, & win more customers by marketing less / by Joe Pullizzi.
    pages cm
ISBN 978-0-07-181989-3 (alk. paper) — ISBN 0-07-181989-4 (alk. paper)
1. Marketing—Social aspects.   2. Social media.   3. Internet marketing.   4. Target marketing.   I. Title.
HF5415.P756   2014
658.8—dc23

                                                                    2013024374

McGraw-Hill Education books are available at special quantity discounts to use as premiums and sales promotions or for use in corporate training programs. To contact a representative, please visit the Contact Us pages at www.mhprofessional.com.

For Adam and Joshua . . . do or do not, there is no try!

Phil. 4:13

PART I
Content Marketing—There and Back Again

PART II
Defining Your Content Niche and Strategy

PART III
Managing the Content Process

PART IV
Marketing Your Stories

PART V
Making Content Work

Foreword

Have you heard of SAP? If you are a business professional, then you probably have heard of us. You might know that we are German-based. Maybe you even know that we sell business software that powers the financial and accounting systems of large companies. But we are much more than a German-based software company. And we are much less known to the average consumer.

I bet you didn't know that 80 percent of our customers are actually small or medium-sized businesses. Our software powers 74 percent of the world's transaction revenue and 97 percent of the 1.8 billion text messages sent every day across the globe. Our customers distribute 78 percent of the world's food supply, 76 percent of the world's health and beauty products, 82 percent of the coffee and tea we drink each day, 79 percent of the chocolate, and 77 percent of the beer we drink.

As you can see from the illustrative examples above, our communications challenge is solved through stories. Stories not about what we sell but stories that explain what we do for our customers. We believe that the power of stories lies in making the reader and the consumer part of the story. We believe in *Epic Content Marketing*.

Stories are nothing new. They've been around for as long as we have. The earliest humans gathered around the campfire and figured out that effective storytelling was the best way to pass on the information that was vital for survival. They knew that truly connecting with their audience in an emotional way was a matter of life and death.

Fast-forward 10,000 years or so and we see that the emergence of the web, mobile accessibility, and social media have changed some of the ways we tell stories. It has allowed anyone to become a publisher of content. It allows us to tell stories in as little as 140 characters and six-second videos.

The world is now swimming in content and information. While content consumers are having fun creating and consuming all of this content that moves around the world in milliseconds, marketers and businesses are struggling in a growing battle for customer attention.

The era of one-way, single-threaded, brand-directed mass communications is officially over. And yet most of the content and the messages coming out of businesses today are firmly stuck in the good old days. As marketing tactics have become less and less effective, businesses have responded by creating more and more promotional content that no one wants, no one likes, and no one responds to.

Businesses are responding to a world with too much content by creating more content. And as each piece lands on their websites and in social streams, they send the same message to their audience: we only care about ourselves.

We care about telling you "who we are" and "what we do." We talk about the big-name logos of our customers. We invite you to spend an hour with us so we can tell you how smart we are. We create content about us, for us because we think that is what we are supposed to do.

The problem: no one is listening, reading, or acting on this content. E-mail open rates, banner click-through rates, telephone contact rates—all going down!

The only way to reach your audience in today's information-drenched, content-saturated world is through *Epic Content Marketing* that emotionally connects with the people you are trying to reach.

I met Joe Pulizzi at a conference just a few short years ago. I was so thrilled to meet him because I heard him talking about how content marketing is nothing new but that it is still a young and immature discipline at many brands. I heard Joe show examples from some of the greatest brands in the world like John Deere, Procter & Gamble, and Red Bull.

I could relate to the content marketing challenges Joe discussed. And so after one of his talks, I walked up to him, introduced myself, and asked him how a business-to-business brand could accomplish the same as these well-known consumer brands.

Joe's advice was simple and straightforward. He suggested I create a content marketing mission statement, to start with a small pilot that connects with our brand's "higher purpose," and to start highlighting for our team those companies that are creating epic content: content that is truly worth creating.

And so that is how we got started. We realized that we were creating too much promotional and product-specific content that wasn't being downloaded, read, or acted upon. We ran reports on our websites that showed us that we were reaching the few who wanted product information and were ignoring the many who were not even sure that there was a technology solution to their problem. In short, we had a content gap.

We are trying to highlight that gap to the various groups across our company that create content. But content production comes from a great number of sources across the company. It is not just marketing but also communications and PR. Sales support. Customer Service. Product development and technical engineers. All these groups and more are creating content.

We have found that the biggest obstacle is in the "why?"—helping our teams to understand that if we think and act like a publisher, we will create more of the content our customers are looking for. And *less* of the content they ignore. One of the biggest challenges in content marketing is to put the needs of our customers ahead of our own and to tell stories that connect with people.

To help our teams, we identified our potential customers' top questions and search terms. We are documenting the questions about how technology and innovation can help a business with its biggest problems: how to grow, how to reduce costs, how to beat the competition, how to gain loyal customers.

We are also meeting with teams across the organization to walk them through the step-by-step process of how to answer those questions using the content types and channels that our customers are using.

At a minimum we are trying to show them how to be helpful. Ideally, we hope not to just educate our future customers but also to entertain them. To help them become successful in their careers. We know that if we do this, they will not only know who we are and what we do but also that we are a partner for their business.

At SAP, our customers have a lot of questions. And we are doing our best to answer them. We are staying focused on them and their needs. On telling stories that connect. But we have a long journey ahead.

Not all of our content is epic yet. But we're working on it. Creating *Epic Content Marketing* is a long process . . . but the first step is to just accept that we have to market differently today to survive and flourish.

Wherever you are in your content marketing journey, this book that you either physically have in your hands, have displayed on your tablet, or possibly are listening to while you are working out can make all the difference for your business, your department, your career. Heed Joe's

advice like we did and watch your customers start to look at you differently . . . less like someone trying to sell them something, and more like
a true resource and informational expert.

Isn't that what all marketers and business owners want?

Today, no matter how big you are or what budget you have, this is
achievable. Are you ready?

MICHAEL BRENNER
Vice President of Marketing and Content Strategy
SAP

Acknowledgments

There are so many people who were instrumental in making this book happen.

First and foremost, thanks to my friend and mentor Jim McDermott, who reviewed each chapter along the way, and was a true source of inspiration.

Second, to Robert Rose, my friend and CMI's chief strategist and my coauthor on *Managing Content Marketing*. Much of the thinking in this book comes either from him or our collaboration.

And I can't forget Mr. Joe Kalinowski (bum bum), my creative director, who put together all the charts and images you'll find in this resource.

A big thanks goes to the entire Content Marketing Institute team, for picking up much of the slack while I prepared the manuscript for this book . . . and as you'll see, there are so many areas of this book that were inspired by them: Michele Linn, Pam Kozelka, Jodi Harris, Peter Loibl, Laura Kozak, Clare McDermott, Angela Vannucci, Lisa Murton Beets, Kelley Whetsell, Cathy McPhillips, Amanda Subler, Shelley Koenig, and Mark Sherbin.

The other contributors to this book you'll find throughout each chapter. A book is a true collaboration . . . and this book holds true to that.

And finally, to my family: my parents Terry and Tony Pulizzi, my sister Lea, and my brother Tony. But especially to Pam, my best friend and soul mate. I love you.

Introduction

Greatness is won, not awarded.

GUY KAWASAKI FROM *HOW TO DRIVE YOUR COMPETITION CRAZY*

$39,400.

What is the total amount of money we have spent on advertising our company, the Content Marketing Institute (CMI), since we launched in April 2007? Just $39,400.

During that time we've been recognized as the fastest-growing start-up in northern Ohio and the ninth fastest-growing private media company by *Inc.* magazine in 2012 (just two places behind Facebook). We accomplished these feats in one of the worst economic environments since the Great Depression, and with far fewer resources than our competitors.

I tell you these things not to boast, but because I believe there is a better way—a better way to market. And there's a much better marketing model for business owners and marketers to attract and retain customers.

Advertising is not dead, but content marketing is the driver that leading companies now use to capture the hearts and minds of their customers.

THE SECRET

I began to use the term *content marketing* in 2001. (You'll hear a lot about content marketing in this book.) I started work in the industry (what we now call the "content marketing industry") a year before then at a large business-to-business (B2B) media company called Penton Media, headquartered in Cleveland, Ohio.

For 13 years (7 at Penton and 6 at CMI) I had the opportunity to work with some of the best global brands in every industry from financial services to retail to transportation, many having marketing budgets that would make you blush. I've also worked with hundreds of the smallest companies, from heating and air conditioning to accounting to landscaping, who barely had two nickels to rub together.

All chief marketing officers to the small business owners believed they had different problems and challenges. But they didn't really. It was always the same with them as it is with my own company. Do you want to know the secret? Here it is:

Your customers don't care about you, your products, or your services. They care about themselves.

Before you go any farther in this book, you have to accept this truth as the first step. Most of us feel we have something wonderful and revolutionary to offer people. We really don't . . . at least not anything more than customers can probably find elsewhere. If that's really true, how do we get customers to pay attention to us, to trust us, to ultimately buy something from us, and to keep coming back for more?

WHY EPIC?

There are many definitions of the word *epic*. According to Dictionary .com, the sixth of six definitions cites *epic* as "of heroic or impressive proportions; an epic voyage." This is the definition I want you to focus on for this book.

In North America, nine in ten businesses (of any size in any industry) use content marketing (Figure I.1). Content marketing is not new, but it is getting cluttered—contaminated, if you will.

A search for, say, "content marketing" in Google will render over 500 million results. How do we break through this clutter?

We need to be epic with our content marketing. We need to do it better. We need to focus more on our customers and less on our products. Yes, you heard that right: to sell more, we need to be marketing our products and services less.

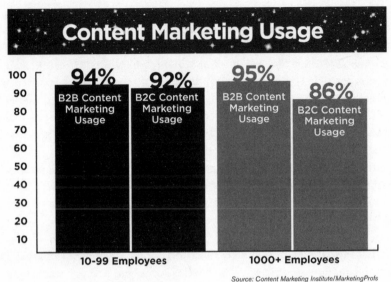

Figure I.1 Organizations of all shapes and sizes are using content marketing to attract and retain customers.

CHANGE YOUR STARS

I'm a big fan of the movie *A Knight's Tale* featuring the late Heath Ledger. In that movie, the actor's character transforms himself from peasant to nobility by "changing his stars," advice given to him by his father when he was very young.

This may sound corny, but my goal for you, as it pertains to this book, is to *change your stars*. You need to both think differently about marketing and then act differently about how you go to market.

Everything I have learned from working with hundreds of companies and then growing CMI through the art and science of content marketing is in this book. You have given me a gift by buying this book. I will return the favor and make sure it is not a waste of your time.

HOW TO READ THIS BOOK

People often ask me how long their blog posts or newsletter articles should be. My answer is always this: "as long as it needs to be." And that's exactly what you'll find in this book. Some chapters are very short; others not so much. Regardless, each one will provide some insight to help you think differently about your business or give tangible advice on developing your own content marketing process.

In many of my speeches, I bring up the Jack Palance character, Curly, from the movie *City Slickers*. Remember, the "one thing"? You know, that one thing that is the secret of life? My goal for every speech I give, as well as this book, is for you to take away that one thing that will make a difference in your business.

Some of the ideas and concepts in this book will be new. Some will be familiar, which you may want to skip. Please feel free to jump around. Find the "one thing" that will help you grow your company and create either more or better customers.

GROW

Whether you are a CMO at a Fortune 500 company or own the smallest of small businesses, this book is for those who want to grow their business. Size is not an issue. Whatever your title or role, if you are part of the marketing process to generate revenue (to help make or sustain a sale), this book is for you.

Each chapter includes the following for your reference:

- **Epic thoughts.** These are issues to keep in mind. To help you think differently about your marketing. Concepts that will help *change your stars*.
- **Epic resources.** This book is made up of literally thousands of books, articles, blog posts, movies, and comments from friends and influencers. Any of those resources that helped that specific chapter come together will be included at the end of each chapter.

Good luck, and thank you for deciding to take this epic journey with me.

Patience, persistence and perspiration make an unbeatable combination for success.

NAPOLEON HILL

PART I

Content Marketing—There and Back Again

CHAPTER 1

What Is Content Marketing?

You do not lead by hitting people over the head—that's assault, not leadership.

DWIGHT D. EISENHOWER

In March 2007 I left a six-figure executive position at the largest independent business media company in North America to bootstrap a start-up. Many of my friends and mentors actively went out of their way to tell me I was making a mistake. Don't let anyone tell you it's not fun to start a business!

For the previous seven years I had worked with brands from around the world helping them publish and distribute their own stories to attract and retain customers. By 2001, it was easy to see that effective marketing was starting to look more and more like publishing. Large brands were seeing amazing results by creating their own content, similar to what media companies had been doing since the dawn of time, rather than paying to advertise around other people's content. It was that year that I started to slip the phrase "content marketing" into my discussions with marketing executives.

What if more businesses of all sizes did this type of activity, focusing not on their products in marketing, but on the informational needs of their target customer first?

Then I asked myself, "What if I could launch a business using this model as the basis for starting and growing a business?"

That's exactly what we did when we launched our company, Content Marketing Institute (CMI), with very little money and an idea back in 2007. This year, we will exceed over $4 million in revenues. Next year, we'll be at $6 million. To achieve this type of growth with little to no traditional advertising, we had to develop a new business model around content creation and distribution.

Even while this idea of content marketing is now a recognized industry term (see Figure 1.1), most business owners have no playbook to do this properly. I talk to people every day from businesses that waste an incredible amount of time on social media tactics without first having the content marketing strategy to make it work for the business.

CONTENT MARKETING: A COLLECTION OF DEFINITIONS

The marketing strategy goes by many names: custom publishing, custom media, customer media, customer publishing, member media, private media, content strategy, branded content, corporate media, brand journalism, native advertising, inbound marketing, contract publishing, branded storytelling, corporate publishing, corporate journalism, and branded media.

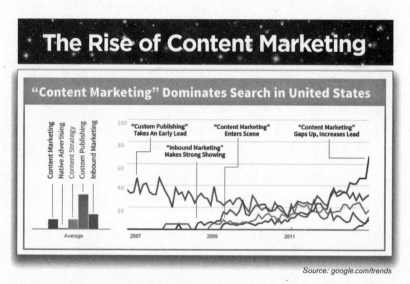

Figure 1.1 In 2013, *content marketing*, as a term, surpassed every other industry phrase as a percentage of Google searches.

Perhaps nothing says it better than *content marketing*. But what exactly is content marketing?

CONTENT MARKETING: THE FORMAL DEFINITION

Content marketing is the marketing and business process for creating and distributing valuable and compelling content to attract, acquire, and engage a clearly defined and understood target audience—with the objective of driving profitable customer action.

A content marketing strategy can leverage all story channels (print, online, in-person, mobile, social, and so on); be employed at any and all stages of the buying process, from attention-oriented strategies to retention and loyalty strategies; and include multiple buying groups.

FROM *MANAGING CONTENT MARKETING*

Content marketing is a strategy focused on the creation of a valuable experience. It is humans being helpful to each other, sharing valuable pieces of content that enrich the community and position the business as a leader in the field. It is content that is engaging, eminently shareable, and, most of all, focused on helping customers discover (on their own) that your product or service is the one that will scratch their itch.

CONTENT MARKETING: LESS FORMAL DEFINITION

Content marketing is *owning* media as opposed to *renting* it. It's a marketing process to attract and retain customers by consistently creating and curating content in order to change or enhance a consumer behavior.

CONTENT MARKETING: ELEVATOR PITCH

Traditional marketing and advertising is telling the world you're a rock star. Content marketing is showing the world that you are one.[*]

CONTENT MARKETING: FOR PRACTITIONERS

Content marketing is about delivering the content your audience is seeking in all the places they are searching for it. It is the effective combination of created, curated, and syndicated content.[†]

Content marketing is the process of developing and sharing relevant, valuable, and engaging content to a target audience with the

[*]Robert Rose, Lead Strategist, Content Marketing Institute.
[†]Michael Brenner, Senior Director, Global Marketing, SAP.

goal of acquiring new customers or increasing business from existing customers.*

CONTENT MARKETING: FOR NONBELIEVERS

Your customers don't care about you, your products, or your services. They care about themselves, their wants, and their needs. Content marketing is about creating interesting information your customers are passionate about *so they actually pay attention to you.*

This last definition is my favorite (with kudos to bestselling author David Meerman Scott for helping to popularize this), and the hardest for marketers and business owners to deal with. So often we marketers believe that our products and services are so special—so amazing—and we think that if more people knew about them, all of our sales problems would be solved.

MARKETING BY SELLING LESS

Basically, content marketing is the art of communicating with your customers and prospects without selling. It is noninterruption marketing. Instead of pitching your products or services, you are delivering information that makes your buyers more intelligent or perhaps entertaining them to build an emotional connection. *The essence of this strategy is the belief that if we, as businesses, deliver consistent, ongoing valuable information to buyers, they ultimately reward us with their business and loyalty.*

Don't get me wrong, there is a time for sales collateral, feature and benefit marketing, and customer testimonials about why you are so awesome. If you are like most companies, you have plenty of that content. The problem with that type of content is that it is only critical when your prospect is ready to buy. What about the other 99 percent of the time when your customers aren't ready to buy? Ah, that is where content marketing pays its dues.

> Ecclesiastes assures us . . . that there is a time for every purpose under heaven. A time to laugh . . . and a time to weep. A time to mourn . . . and there is a time to dance. *And there was a time for this law, but not anymore.*
> KEVIN BACON (REN) IN *FOOTLOOSE* (1984)

*Amanda Maksymiw, Content Marketing Manager, Lattice Engines.

There was a time when paid media was the best and most effective way to sell our products and services, but not anymore.
JOE PULIZZI

INFORM OR ENTERTAIN

Anyone who tries to make a distinction between education and entertainment doesn't know the first thing about either.
MARSHALL MCLUHAN

Ten years ago I had the opportunity to have lunch with Kirk Cheyfitz, CEO of Story Worldwide, a global content agency. His words at that lunch have always stuck with me.

"Inform or entertain," Cheyfitz said. "What other options do brands have when communicating with their customers and prospects? Brands serve their customers best when they are telling engaging stories."

Actually you have four choices. You can inform and help your customers live better lives, find better jobs, or be more successful in the jobs they have now. You can also choose to entertain and begin to build an emotional connection with your customers. These two choices help you build a following (like a media company does . . . but more on that later).

Your third choice is to develop lackluster content that doesn't move the needle. This is content that could be self-serving and promotional. It could also be content that you want to be useful or entertaining, but because of quality, consistency, or planning issues, is ignored by your customers.

Your fourth choice is to spend money on traditional marketing, such as paid advertising, traditional direct mail, and public relations. Again, there's nothing wrong with these activities, but this book will show you a better way to use those advertising dollars.

CONTENT MARKETING VS. SOCIAL MEDIA MARKETING: WHAT'S THE DIFFERENCE?

Toby Murdock, CEO, KaPost

As I meet with brands and agencies, I still come across people who are totally unfamiliar with the term "content marketing." And as I begin to explain it, they often respond, "Oh, brands publishing content? You mean social media marketing."

Indeed, content marketing heavily involves social media. And, of course, in social media, marketers use content to get their messages across. But although there is plenty of overlap between content marketing and social media marketing, they are actually two distinct entities, with different focal points, goals, and processes. To help clear the confusion, let's look at the major ways in which they differ.

CENTER OF GRAVITY

In social media marketing, the center of gravity—the focus of the marketing activity—is located within the social networks themselves. When marketers operate social media campaigns, they are operating inside of Facebook, Twitter, Google+, and so on. As they produce content, they place it inside of these networks.

In contrast, the center of gravity for content marketing is a brand website (your ultimate platform; see Chapter 19 for more), whether it be a branded web address, such as AmericanExpress.com, or a microsite for a brand's specific product, such as Amex's OPEN Forum. Social networks are vital to the success of content marketing efforts, but in this case, Facebook, Twitter, and Google+ are used primarily as a distributor of links back to the content on the brand's website, not as containers of the content itself.

TYPES OF CONTENT

In social media marketing, content is built to fit the context of the chosen social platform: short messages in the 140 characters range for Twitter; contests, quizzes, and games for Facebook; and so on. *With this type of marketing, brands model their behavior after that of the individuals using the social networks.*

On the other hand, in content marketing, the context of websites permits much longer forms of content. Brands can publish blog posts, videos, infographics, and e-books, just to name a few formats. *With this type of marketing, brands model their behavior after that of media publishers.*

OBJECTIVES

While both social media marketing and content marketing can be used for a multitude of purposes, social media marketing generally tends to focus on two main objectives. First, it is used for brand awareness: generating activity and discussion around the brand. Secondly, it is used for customer retention and satisfaction; brands can use social channels as an open forum for direct dialogues with customers, often around issues or questions that consumers have.

In contrast, content marketing's website-based center of gravity enables it to focus more on demand (or lead) generation. As quality content brings prospects to a brand's site, that brand can develop a relationship with the prospects and nurture them toward a lead conversion or purchase.

EVOLUTION OF ONLINE MARKETING

We need to think of social media marketing and content marketing less as two isolated options and more as interrelated parts of marketing's ongoing evolution. The Internet has unleashed a revolutionary ability for every brand to communicate directly with its customers—without the need for a media industry intermediary.

Social media marketing is the natural first step in this process: access to users is direct (users spend lots of time on social networks), and content is generally formatted into shorter chunks, which makes the publishing process relatively easy.

But as brands become more familiar with their new role as publisher, the natural progression is to move toward content marketing. Yes, the bar here is higher: in content marketing, brands must produce longer-form, higher-quality content and build audiences on their own sites—they must become true media publishers. But the rewards and results are arguably more powerful. Brands can engage more deeply with their customers through content marketing efforts. And by driving consumers to its own website, a brand has a greater opportunity to gain leads and move them down the conversion funnel.

As we all pioneer this new strategy of content marketing, a shared definition of what we do relative to approaches like social media marketing is invaluable.

THE NEW WORLD OF CONTENT-MARKETING

Let's take a look at the first content marketing definition one more time, but this time remove the "valuable and compelling."

> Content marketing is the marketing and business process for creating and distributing content to attract, acquire, and engage a clearly defined and understood target audience—with the objective of driving profitable customer action.

That's the difference between content marketing and the other informational garbage you get from companies trying to sell you "stuff."

Companies send out information all the time; it's just that most of the time informational garbage is not very compelling or useful (think: *spam*). That's what makes content marketing so intriguing in today's environment of thousands of marketing messages per person per day. *Good content marketing makes a person stop, read, think, and behave differently.*

THE DIFFERENCE BETWEEN *CONTENT* AND *CONTENT MARKETING*

Not a day goes by that some marketer somewhere around the world doesn't try to figure this out. Here's the answer.

Some experts say that content is any word, image, or pixel that can be engaged with by another human being. In the context of this book, content is *compelling content that informs, engages, or amuses.*

What makes content marketing different from simple content is that content marketing must do something for the business. It must inform, engage, or amuse *with the objective of driving profitable customer action.*

Your content may engage or inform, but if it's not accomplishing your business goals (for example, customer retention or lead generation), it's not content marketing. The content you create must work directly to attract and/or retain customers in some way.

CONTENT MARKETING NEXT

According to the Roper Public Affairs, 80 percent of buyers prefer to get company information in a series of articles versus an advertisement. Seventy percent say content marketing makes them feel closer to the sponsoring company, and 60 percent say that company content helps them make better product decisions. Think of this: What if your customers looked forward to receiving your marketing? What would it be like if, when they received it via print, e-mail, website, social media, or mobile device, they spent 15, 30, or 45 minutes with it? What if you actually sold more by marketing your products and services less?

Yes, you really can create marketing that is anticipated and truly makes a connection! You can develop and execute "sales" messages that are needed, even requested, by your customers. Content marketing is a far cry from the interruption marketing we are bombarded with every minute of every day. Content marketing is about marketing for the present and the future.

EPIC THOUGHTS

- Content is just ... content, unless it's driving behavior change in your customers and prospects. Then it's called "content marketing."
- Your marketing needs to be anticipated, loved, and wanted. This is the new world we live in today.
- Your content marketing strategy comes before your social media strategy—yesterday, today, and always.

EPIC RESOURCES

- Google Trends, "content marketing" search, http://www.google.com/trends/explore#q=%22content%20marketing%22.
- *Footloose* (1984), starring John Lithgow and Kevin Bacon.
- Robert Rose and Joe Pulizzi, *Managing Content Marketing*, Cleveland: CMI Books, 2011.
- Roper Public Affairs & Corporate Communications, "Consumers' Attitude Toward Custom Content," March 2011, http://www.ascend integratedmedia.com/sites/default/files/research/63402297 -Consumers-Attitude-Towards-Custom-Content-2011.pdf.

CHAPTER 2

The History of Content Marketing

History will be kind to me for I intend to write it.
WINSTON CHURCHILL

THE STORY OF JOHN

There once was a struggling blacksmith named John. John was young, broke, and in desperate need to provide for his young family in Vermont. In 1836, John made the tough decision to leave his family, with all of $73 in his pocket, to make his way west in the hope of finding fortune . . . or at least a job.

After two weeks of travel, John decided to set up camp in Grand Detour, Illinois. It was there he put out his blacksmith shingle.

Day after day, John would hear the tales of farmers from the Northeast struggling to push their plows through the sticky Illinois soil. Where their iron plows used to easily slide through the New England sediment, the Midwest sod seemed quite the challenge. The farmers became frustrated, having to clean the mud off the iron plows every few yards.

John believed that if he could mold the outside of the plow in steel, the mud and dirt would not stick. So in 1837 John built the first polished plow using a broken saw blade.

During the days and months that passed, John would work with the farmers and listen to their problems; he would continue to refine the plow for many years. John would go on to become one of the greatest inventors and businessmen of his time.

That man was John Deere.

CONTENT MARKETING IN THE NINETEENTH CENTURY

Even though John Deere passed away in 1886, his values of listening and teaching live on through the company he built. Deere & Company, arguably the most famous agricultural company in the world, launched, created, and distributed *The Furrow* magazine in 1895 (see Figure 2.1). Deere leveraged *The Furrow*, not to sell John Deere equipment directly (as a catalog would do), but to educate farmers on new technology and how they could be more successful business owners and farmers (thus, content marketing).

Source: John Deere

Figure 2.1   *The Furrow* from Deere & Company is now the largest circulated magazine to farmers in the world.

From the beginning, *The Furrow* was not filled with promotional messages and self-serving content. It was developed by thoughtful journalists, storytellers, and designers, and covered topics that farmers cared about deeply. The goal of the content was to help farmers become more prosperous and, of course, profitable.

Now, 120 years later, *The Furrow* is still going strong. It is the largest circulated farming magazine in the world, delivered monthly to over 1.5 million farmers, in 12 languages to 40 different countries.

John Deere is often given credit for being the first to leverage content marketing as part of a long-term business process.

A GLORIOUS PAST

And John Deere was just the beginning:

- **1900: Michelin develops** *The Michelin Guide.* This 400-page guide, now with its iconic red cover, helps drivers maintain their cars and find decent lodging. In its first edition, 35,000 copies were distributed for free.
- **1904: Jell-O recipe book pays off.** Jell-O distributes free copies of a recipe book that contributes to sales of over $1 million by 1906.
- **1913: Burns & McDonnell Engineering launch** *BenchMark.*This Kansas City engineering and consulting firm still produces its award-winning *BenchMark* magazine (see Figure 2.2) to this day.
- **1922: Sears launches World's Largest Store radio program.** The station helped keep farmers informed during the deflation crisis with content supplied by Sears's Roebuck Agricultural Foundation.
- **1930s: Procter & Gamble (P&G) begins foray into radio serial dramas.** This extremely successful initiative, featuring brands such as Duz and Oxydol detergents, marked the beginning of the "soap opera."

UNDERSTANDING HISTORY

As mentioned in Chapter 1, content marketing, as an industry, is taking off, but it's important to realize where brands have been. Brands have been telling stories for centuries. That endeavor started when they had just a few channels, and it continues today, even as they can choose from literally hundreds of media channels for marketing.

Telling a quality story to the right person at the right time always cuts through the clutter. There will be another new channel tomorrow,

Source: Burns & McDonnell

Figure 2.2 Engineering firm Burns & McDonnell has been publishing its customer magazine for over 100 years.

and another one the next day. It's easy to be seduced by the new. As smart content marketers, we need to keep in mind that channels come and go, but good stories (and storytelling) last forever.

EPIC THOUGHTS

- Content marketing is not new. Brands have been telling epic stories for centuries. The difference? It's more critical than ever to get it right.
- *The Furrow* magazine is the largest circulated magazine to farmers in the world. Could you be the leading provider of information for your customers?

EPIC RESOURCES

- Deere & Company, "The History of John Deere," accessed April 6, 2013, http://www.deere.com/wps/dcom/en_US/corporate/our_company/about_us/history/history.page.
- *The Furrow*, accessed April 6, 2013, http://www.deere.com/wps/dcom/en_US/industry/agriculture/our_offerings/furrow/furrow.page.
- Rex Hammock, "The History of Media: Brands Have Been Publishers Since the 19th Century," *RexBlog.com*, May 19, 2011, http://www.rexblog.com/2011/05/19/23189.
- Joe Pulizzi, "The History of Content Marketing" (Infographic), ContentMarketingInstitute.com, February 22, 2012, http://contentmarketinginstitute.com/2012/02/history-content-marketing-infographic/.

CHAPTER 3

Why Content Marketing?

It isn't uncommon for managers at senior levels of large organizations to be so out of touch with customer or production reality that they don't know just how broken some of their business processes are.

MICHAEL HAMMER AND JAMES CHAMPY,

REENGINEERING THE CORPORATION

When you have a question or a problem, where do you go for the answer? Most likely a search engine such as Google.

When you are browsing through your favorite social networking site, what do you tend to share? Perhaps interesting stories or clever images?

When you are working out, do you possibly listen to interesting podcasts or to the latest business audiobook?

When you are doing research to purchase a hotel room or perhaps buy some new business software, what do you look for? Perhaps testimonials or ratings for the hotel? Maybe a research or comparison report for the software?

In each case, it's content that solves our problems, makes us laugh or gives us the idea for our next journey. Jon Wuebben, author of *Content Is Currency*, states that "through content, you connect. Content is the currency that powers the connection. It speaks to us, makes us want to share it, and motivates people to buy."

Simply put, all those wonderful social media channels we have today are useless without epic content.

THERE AND BACK AGAIN

In 2008, I partnered with Newt Barrett to write *Get Content Get Customers* (McGraw-Hill). Two paragraphs toward the beginning of the book are still relevant, now five years later:

> Marketing organizations are now realizing that they can create content whose quality is equal to or better than what many media companies are producing. Moreover, they are seeing that they can deliver tangible benefits to prospects and customers by offering relevant content that helps produce solutions to some of the toughest problems their prospective buyers are facing.
>
> By delivering content that is vital and relevant to your target market, you will begin to take on an important role in your customers' lives. This applies to your online, print, and in-person communications. And this is the same role that newspapers, magazines, TV, radio, conferences, workshops, and Web sites have played in the past. Now it's time for your organization to play that role.

CUTTING THROUGH THE CLUTTER

Today, we have the same opportunity we had five years ago, but the stakes are higher. Yankelovich, a marketing research firm, states that consumers, once exposed to 500 marketing messages per day in the 1970s, nowadays are bombarded with as many as 5,000 or more.

But consumers aren't tuning out—they are becoming highly selective. According to Google's *Zero Moment of Truth* research, in 2010 the average consumer engaged with 5 pieces of content before making a buying decision. In 2011, that number doubled to more than 10.

Google is projecting that this number will continue to increase as consumers engage in even more media. Of course it will. According to comScore, in November 2012 the penetration of smartphones moved beyond the 50 percent mark in both the United States and most of Europe. That means the majority of us have content-gathering tools with us as all times.

And let's face it: we have a relationship problem with our phones. According to a 2012 *Time* magazine study of 5,000 international cell phone or smartphone owners:

- Eighty-four percent said that they could not go a single day without their cell phones.
- Fifty percent of Americans sleep with their phone next to them, including 80 percent of 18- to 24-year-olds.
- Twenty percent check their phone every 10 minutes.

And according to a 2012 Pew Internet Survey, over 50 percent of cell phone owners engage in content on their cell phones *while* they watch video or television content. This means that even though your customers are being inundated with content 24/7, *they can and do let messages through that they want and need.*

THE CASE FOR CONTENT MARKETING

Not a day goes by that I don't get a question from someone asking why content marketing is taking off like it is.

How long will content marketing last?
Is *content marketing* a buzzword?
When will the party end?

A CORRECTION PERIOD

If you follow the stock market at all, then you understand what a correction is. Technically, a correction in the stock market happens when stocks (as a whole) decline at least 10 percent over a relatively short period of time, usually after a good run-up in stocks (called a "bull market").

Over the last 50 years, we've seen (for the most part), a bull market in paid media. The majority of marketing programs have revolved around paid media of some kind. Even today, many marketing campaigns on the consumer side center around the 30-second spot. Heck, CBS received approximately $4 million for each Super Bowl advertisement in 2013. Not a bad day's work, if you can get it.

When I worked at Penton Media in the early 2000s, I had the opportunity to discuss marketing budgets with a number of business-to-business (B2B) marketing executives. There was lots of investment in trade show exhibits, print advertising, and sponsorships. The remaining dollars went to public relations. The pennies on the floor went to owned media (content marketing).

It was clear back then and it is even clearer today that most brands were (and are) overweight in paid media and underweight in owned media. The movement (make that: the *revolution*) of content marketing is a necessary correction in the marketplace.

Even with content marketing's rise (see Figure 3.1), the majority of marketing budgets still reside outside of content creation and distribution.

REASONS FOR THE SHIFT

There are many reasons for this correction. Here are a few to chew on.

No technology barriers. In the past, the publishing process was complex and expensive. Traditionally, media companies spent hundreds of thousands of dollars on complex content management and production systems. Today, anyone can publish for free online in five minutes (seconds?) or less.

Talent availability. Journalists are no longer wary of working for nonmedia companies. In 2012, CMI performed a workshop for 13

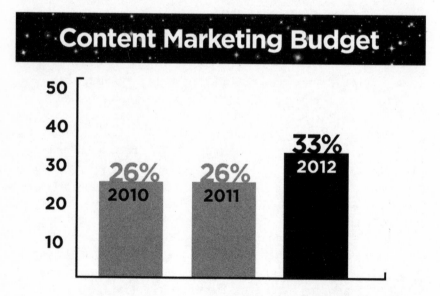

Source: Content Marketing Institute/MarketingProfs

Figure 3.1 Content marketing budgets continue to increase. Now, one in three marketing dollars are spent on content creation and distribution.

technology companies. Each tech company had an open position for an in-house journalist, managing editor, or content marketing director. Today, these positions are being filled by journalists who have made the move from the traditional media side. This trend is just getting started.

Content acceptance. You don't have to be the *Wall Street Journal* to have engaging content that is shared. Consumers are making a decision on the spot as to what is credible and what is not. According to a 2012 Edelman study, Millennials, now between the ages 19 to 34, actually expect brands to develop content for them, with 80 percent wanting to be directly entertained through content marketing.

In addition, Sally Hogshead, author of the book *Fascinate*, says that a company has as little as nine seconds to capture the attention of its customers. That goes for both media and nonmedia companies. Helpful and compelling content cuts through the clutter. Everything else gets ignored, skipped, or disregarded.

Social media. Social media won't work for most brands without valuable, consistent, and compelling information creation and distribution. If brands want to be successful in social media, they need to tell compelling stories first. According to the 2013 CMI/MarketingProfs Content Marketing Benchmarks Study, almost 90 percent of businesses leverage social media to communicate with customers. This type of penetration means that more organizations are trying to figure out what kind of content to put into those social media channels.

Google. Google's most recent major algorithm (how Google determines its search engine rankings) updates, Penguin and Panda, show that the company is putting more and more importance on content sharing. From what Google will tell us, content shared from credible sources is key to being found in search. So if you want to be found in search engines today, it's almost impossible to game the system (sometimes called "black hat search engine optimization") without a solid content marketing strategy.

Don't get me wrong, I'm not a traditional marketing hater. I believe that an integrated program of paid, earned, and owned media works best. But, simply put, most of us are still overweight in paid media. Until we see more substantial resources shift to the owned media side of the house, the correction will continue.

YOUR CONTENT RESPONSIBILITY

Media companies often make the case that their content is different because they take an unbiased stance on their content creation. When that case is presented, I generally bring up media organizations such as MSNBC (liberal) and Fox News (conservative). Every company, no matter what it sells, has an inherent bias in one direction or another, whether that bias is known to the organization or not.

Does that mean that we'll be seeing nonmedia companies start to cover industry news? Well, yes. In fact, that is already happening. Adobe, one of the largest software and analytics companies in the world, runs a content site called CMO.com (see Figure 3.2). CMO.com is a daily news

Source: CMO.com

Figure 3.2 CMO.com is the content platform from Adobe, targeting senior marketing executives with daily stories around digital marketing.

source for marketing executives, covering topics from social media to marketing leadership. Many times, it covers news about the industry and includes interviews with the leading CMOs and cutting-edge reports, even though it isn't an "unbiased" source.

Tim Moran, editor-in-chief of Adobe's CMO.com, believes that CMO.com fills an important need for both Adobe and the marketing community. "Yes, CMO.com is a marketing initiative for Adobe, but it's much more than that," states Tim. "We believe that Adobe should have a strong industry voice, and that it's our responsibility to cover the marketplace, providing helpful and relevant content for our customers and prospects. The more our readers know and understand, the better for them and for Adobe."

And Tim knows the value of helpful content, serving as editor for major media companies such as United Business Media and CMP for over 20 years. Tim believes as long as Adobe is transparent the content is coming from it, its customers, prospects, and readers appreciate the value that the company is bringing to the table.

To companies such as Adobe and John Deere, content marketing is not just a nice to have but an integral part of the organization's culture and communication strategy. Content marketing is part of how they go to market.

DOES TRADITIONAL MEDIA HAVE A FUNDING PROBLEM?

At the beginning of 2013, the IAB (Interactive Advertising Bureau) held a one-day event on the state of the media business as it pertained to content marketing. During the event, one publisher stood up and announced, "We simply do not have the resources that our advertisers have. We cannot hire the quality journalists and do the amount of research necessary for the amount of funding (advertising) we get. But at least all my journalist friends who were terminated for budget reasons are finding homes on the brand side."

According to *Advertising Age*, P&G (Procter & Gamble) was the largest spender of advertising in 2011 at a clip of $5 billion. Just for perspective, the New York Times company's properties, which includes the *New York Times* and the *Boston Globe*, did $2 billion in total revenue in 2012. That means P&G, all by itself, spent two and a half times more on advertising (just advertising!) than the *New York Times* collects in a year. To further the point, as of February 2013 Apple had $137 billion in cash sitting in the bank. Apple could buy the *New York Times* and it would still have enough cash to do, well, pretty much whatever it wanted.

Tom Foremski, a technology reporter for ZDNet, believes that content marketing (corporate media) could be the answer to the funding problems of real journalism. Mr. Foremski contends that special interests have so much money and are so influential, the gatekeepers traditionally involved in media and the creation of "real" journalism are all but gone.

In particular, Mr. Foremski highlights the recent takeover attempt of Australia's Fairfax Media. "Take a look at Australia, where multibillionaire mining magnate Gina Rinehart has been trying to acquire Fairfax Media, publisher of top newspapers, in a bid to counter antimining forces. We'll see more of that as newspapers and other traditional media continue to weaken."

Simon Sproule, head of global marketing for Nissan, has been building up his content marketing team for years, working to position Nissan as a trusted information provider for his customers and prospects. At the same time, he's hesitant to invest in paid media. "I don't have the confidence that traditional news organizations will be able to survive the transition to the new business models," he says. "Why should I invest large amounts of money over the next few years in a failing enterprise?"

The point is this: traditional media outlets, where consumers used to get the majority of their information, simply do not have the resources that nonmedia companies have to compete over the long term. The same goes for smaller businesses that want to compete with their niche blog, all the way up to the SAPs and Oracles of the world. Brands like Nissan are jumping on this opportunity.

HUNTING AN AUDIENCE

Hopefully, by now you have figured out that publishing is not dead. Far from it; in fact, publishing has never been stronger. What is dying is the business model of ad-supported content. This leaves an opportunity for you—if, and only if, you put the processes in place to tell valuable and helpful stories for your customers and prospects.

Brand publishers (nonmedia companies such as Intel, DuPont, or the local heating and air-conditioning company) and media companies actually have the same goal. That goal is to build an audience, one that loves your content so much that it leads to subscription. That, in turn, leads to finding ways to monetize that audience.

Brand publishers are challenged with trying to get found in search engines, drive leads, and figure out social media. At the center of making all that happen is storytelling. It's all about brands creating helpful, valuable, and compelling stories that position them as trusted experts in their fields. That content, if worthy, will convert casual, passersby readers into loyal ones. In turn, those loyal readers may then be converted into loyal customers.

Media companies are trying to do the same thing—*exactly the same thing*. The only difference is how the money is generated from the content (more on this in the next chapter).

Robert Rose, my coauthor in *Managing Content Marketing*, states that "to succeed today, we need to use content to continually engage our audiences—from the first time we meet them, continuing throughout the entire customer life cycle. In short, the job of marketing is no longer to create customers, it is (to paraphrase Peter Drucker) to create *passionate subscribers* to our brand."

An underlying theme throughout this book is about attracting and keeping an audience. Once the audience is built, that is when the magic happens. That is when marketers see long-term return. Content marketing without a loyal audience is not content marketing at all. Your content can't accomplish much without an engaged audience. And even though this book presents some thoughts about how media companies are competing with you for the same audience, they can be powerful partners to help you grow and sustain your audience.

EPIC THOUGHTS

- Your customers are exposed to over 5,000 marketing messages per day. Are your messages cutting through the clutter and making impact?
- In the past, entering the content creation and distribution business was filled with all kinds of barriers. Today, all the barriers to entry are gone . . . paving the way for you (if you choose).
- The future of media is not the media; it's brands like yours. Like it or not, your competitors are starting to wake up to this fact.

EPIC RESOURCES

- Jon Wuebben, *Content Is Currency*, Nicholas Brealey Publishing, 2012.
- Joe Pulizzi and Newt Barrett, *Get Content Get Customers*, McGraw-Hill, 2009.
- Google, *Zero Moment of Truth*, http://www.zeromomentoftruth.com/.
- Jason Gilbert, "Smartphone Addiction: Staggering Percentage of Humans Couldn't Go a Day without Their Phone," *Huffington Post*, August 16, 2012, http://www.huffingtonpost.com/2012/08/16 /smartphone-addiction-time-survey_n_1791790.html.
- Content Marketing Institute and Marketing Profs, "B2B Content Marketing Benchmarks, Budgets and Trends," October 24, 2012, http://contentmarketinginstitute.com/2012/10/2013-b2b-content -marketing-research/.
- Sally Hogshead, *Fascinate*, HarperBusiness, 2010.
- Aaron Smith and Jan Lauren Boyles, "The Rise of the Connected Viewer," Pew Internet, July 17, 2012, http://www.pewinternet.org /Reports/2012/Connected-viewers.aspx.
- Adobe, CMO.com, accessed on March 1, 2013.
- "The Evolving Role of Brands for the Millennial Generation," Edelman Insights, December 4, 2012, http://www.slideshare.net /EdelmanInsights/the-evolving-role-of-brands-for-the-millennial -generation.
- Tom Foremski, "Is the Future of Serious Journalism in the Hands of Corporate Media?" ZDNet, November 5, 2012, http://www.zdnet .com/is-the-future-of-serious-journalism-in-the-hands-of-corporate -media-7000006929/.
- "100 Leading National Advertisers 2012 Edition Index," AdAge .com, June 25, 2012, http://adage.com/article/datacenter-advertising -spending/100-leading-national-advertisers/234882/.
- Douglas A. McIntyre, Ashley C. Allen, Michael A. Sauter, Samuel Weigley, and Lisa Uible, "Buy It Now! America's Biggest Advertisers," *NBCNews.com*, July 16, 2012, http://www.nbcnews.com/business /buy-it-now-americas-biggest-advertisers-887754.
- Daniel Gross, "Apple Has $137 Billion in Cash, Shareholders Aren't Pleased," *The Daily Beast*, February 8, 2013, http://www.thedaily beast.com/articles/2013/02/08/apple-has-137-billion-in-cash-share holders-aren-t-pleased.html.

CHAPTER 4

The Business Model of Content Marketing

People get into a rhythm that makes them resistant to change. To understand the mind-set, try switching hands when you brush your teeth in the morning.

GARY GESME, DEERE & COMPANY

There have been many examples of content marketing throughout the years. Yes, John Deere sells tractors to farmers, but John Deere is also a publisher. Deere creates and distributes content just like any media company in the agricultural space. But the business model behind it is very different from others.

SHOW ME THE MONEY

There is only one thing that separates the content developed by a media company and content developed by brands such as Intel, John Deere, or Walmart: *how the money comes in.*

For a media company, content is created in order to make money directly from the creation of content through *paid content sales* (direct purchase of content, like a subscription) or *advertising sales* (someone sponsors the content that is created, similar to what we see in newspapers and magazines or a Super Bowl commercial).

For a nonmedia company, content is created, not to profit from the content, but to attract and retain customers (to sell more or create more opportunities to sell more). *Content supports the business* (see Figure 4.1), but it is not *the* business model (meaning that nonmedia companies are not required to make revenues directly off the content itself).

In all other respects, the content creation activities in both types of companies are generally the same. This is important to understand. Nonmedia brands compete with traditional media for attention and retention, just as you compete with the regular competitors in your field.

Content Marketing Goals

Organizational Goals for B2B Content Marketing

Goal	Percentage
Brand Awareness	79%
Customer Acquisition	74%
Lead Generation	71%
Customer Retention/Loyalty	64%
Thought Leadership	64%
Engagement	63%
Website Traffic	60%
Lead Management/Nurturing	45%
Sales	43%

Source: Content Marketing Institute/MarketingProfs

Figure 4.1 Organizations can leverage content marketing to accomplish a number of marketing and business objectives.

THE BASIC MEDIA BUSINESS MODEL

Our company, the Content Marketing Institute (CMI), profits directly from the production of content. Although we position ourselves as an education and training organization, we leverage a media business model.

- **Daily web content.** We develop how-to, educational posts about content marketing online every day (even on the weekends). The content on that site is monetized through direct advertising and sponsorship from companies such as Salesforce.com and PR Newswire. This is similar to any media company, such as Mashable.com, *Huffington Post*, *Fast Company*, or the leading trade publisher in any industry.
- **Monthly webinars.** CMI creates one-hour educational webinars on topics from marketing automation to content curation. Each webinar we produce is sponsored (paid for) by another company.
- **In-person events.** CMI produces daylong paid workshops or large international events such as Content Marketing World, our annual event in Cleveland, Ohio. In these cases, we produce in-person content that attendees pay to get access to (paid content) and that sponsors support to interact with their prospects (the attendees).
- **Print advertising.** *Chief Content Officer* magazine is the official publication of CMI and is distributed to more than 20,000 marketing executives in North America and around the world. Each quarterly issue is supported by a number of sponsors who pay for access to our subscriber base and to be associated with our brand.

Although CMI employs a number of content marketing tactics (which will be discussed later), we are, in a business model sense, a media company.

HOW LEGO'S CONTENT SUPPORTS THE BUSINESS

In the 1980s and 1990s, LEGO faced a tremendous threat from competing construction toys. After all, the very simplicity of LEGO's building blocks also made them very easy to duplicate, both by small-scale copycats as well as established toy companies. LEGO unsuccessfully tried to block Tyco Toys, Inc., from selling the Super Blocks series after LEGO's patent ran out in 1983. The company knew it needed to build a powerhouse brand and

develop an integrated marketing approach to compete against a
growing set of building-block imitators.

CLARE MCDERMOTT, CHIEF EDITOR,

CHIEF CONTENT OFFICER MAGAZINE, APRIL 2011

Most people don't realize this, but LEGO is a content giant, at times
more closely resembling a media company than a toy company. Here's a
rundown of its integrated content marketing program.

MICROSITES

Each LEGO storyline has a dedicated microsite with plot and character
explanations, online games, movies, polls and quizzes, and of course
retail links. Some great examples: LEGO *Star Wars* and LEGO Ninjago.

LEGO MINISERIES

For each storyline release, LEGO produces a serial-style movie that runs
both on cable and then eventually through the LEGO website. Most
recently, LEGO released its LEGO Chima series with a new cartoon
through a partnership with the Cartoon Network.

LEGO CLICK

LEGO Click is a community platform that encourages fans and fanatics
alike to share their LEGO creation photos and videos, download apps,
and explore LEGO themes through online games and storylines.

MY LEGO NETWORK

There is a LEGO social network designed especially for children (with a
high level of safety and parental controls). Members can create their own
personal pages, win rewards, meet other LEGO fans and battle them in
game modules, and watch LEGO TV.

LEGO MAGAZINE

LEGO Club magazine is customized by local market and by age. LEGO
originally released it as *Brick Kicks* magazine back in 1987 (see Figure
4.2).

Source: LEGO

Figure 4.2 LEGO has been producing various content initiatives since launching *Brick Kicks* magazine for LEGO loyalists back in 1987.

LEGO ID

LEGO asks users to sign up for a free online ID that allows them to play multiplayer games, contribute to LEGO galleries, and set up a personal page on My LEGO Network.

LEGOLAND

LEGO partnered with Merlin Entertainments Group to develop LEGOLAND parks around the world (now six full parks and multiple discovery centers).

LEGO CLUB MEETINGS

LEGO holds meetings for "club" members around the world, where boys and girls can imagine together (and usually persuade their parents to buy something at the end of the meeting).

Believe it or not, this is just a portion of its content marketing tactics. Yes, LEGO has a fantastic product. That must come first. But the company has literally dominated the competition through multimedia storytelling. As a toy company, no one comes close to what LEGO has been able to accomplish.

Although LEGO generates direct revenues from its content (licensing fees for LEGOLAND, LEGO cartoons, books, and games like LEGO *Lord of the Rings*), the majority of content is created to support the business model (which is to sell more LEGO product).

LEGO shows us that, like it or not, we are all media companies today—we all have the opportunity to communicate directly with our audience. It's how we choose to use that privilege that makes all the difference.

THEY WILL NEVER BE AS FAST OR AS STRONG AS YOU

I've seen an agent punch through a concrete wall; men have emptied entire clips at them and hit nothing but air; yet, their strength, and their speed, are still based in a world that is built on rules. Because of that, they will never be as strong, or as fast, as you can be.

MORPHEUS, *THE MATRIX* (1999)

The Matrix is one of my favorite movies of all time. In the film, the "hero," Neo, discovers that he has the ability to defeat the "enemy," the Agents inside the Matrix, because he is not governed by the same rules as they are. He can be stronger and do things that the enemy cannot do, which is why, in the end, Neo wins.

The defining moment in the movie is not that Neo has discovered some new powers; it is that he begins to believe in himself.

You need to do the same. Thus begins your story. For you to make epic content marketing work for you, you first need to understand the truth—that regardless of any barriers you "think" are in the way, it is possible for you and your brand to become the go-to informational resource for your customers and prospects.

LIMITED RESOURCES

No matter how tight you believe your marketing budgets are, *most media companies do not have the money, resources, or flexibility that you have.* For the past decade, the majority of media companies have cut out their research departments entirely. In a recent direct e-mail, serial entrepreneur Jason Calacanis pronounced: "Sadly, the news sites that cover our space are underfunded and staffed by folks who are desperate to get traffic. That desperation results in low-quality content paired with stupid link-baiting headlines that are insulting to anyone with half a brain."

Journalists and storytellers are moving to the brand side; for example, General Electric hired a *Forbes* editor to run its GE Experts program. The rules of publishing that made it possible for media companies to gain power are, simply put, vanishing.

ON EQUAL FOOTING

Publishing used to be very exclusive, highly intensive, and costly. This is not the case anymore.

In February 2013, there was a feud between a *New York Times* reporter/reviewer and Tesla Motors, an electronic automobile start-up. Basically, the *New York Times* reviewer posted a negative review that Elon Musk, Tesla's CEO, did not agree with. As a result of the *New York Times* article, "Musk says that Tesla has lost about $100 million in sales and canceled orders due to the *Times* story, which said the sedan ran out of battery power sooner than promised during a chilly winter test drive from Washington, D.C., to Boston."

Tesla decided to fight back in a different way than what was done in the past by developing and distributing a series of blog posts on the Tesla website. Dan Frommer, founder of *City Notes* and SplatF, says:

> Even a few years ago, something like this probably would have required finding a rival newspaper—the *Wall Street Journal*, perhaps—to collaborate on a takedown [counterstrike against the other paper]. Or maybe an expensive full-page ad campaign in the top five papers, which would have looked defensive and seemed less convincing. But now that every smart company has a regularly updated blog . . . brands can speak for themselves very powerfully.

A *Time* magazine follow-up article stated that "by becoming its own publisher, Tesla recast its bad press on its own terms. This could be a model for unfairly maligned subjects to defend themselves—or for companies to misleadingly data-dump their way out of trouble. Either way, expect companies to take notice."

ONE AUDIENCE, NOT TWO

> There are two types of customers that exist in our world and must be satisfied: the audience of one and the advertiser. Without either of these two, we're sunk before we leave port.
> SAMIR "MR. MAGAZINE" HUSNI

Publishers have two audiences: the advertiser and the reader. All publishers will say that if you satisfy the reader, ultimately the advertiser will be happy. But the truth is, advertisers pay most of the bills, and often publishers do what they believe is right to get cash in the door.

Just ask the *Atlantic* about it. Like most media companies, the *Atlantic* sells sponsored content opportunities to advertisers (called "advertorials"). In one particular case in January 2013 (see Figure 4.3), the *Atlantic* ran a story sponsored by the Church of Scientology called "David Miscavige Leads Scientology to Milestone Year." Normally, the publisher will do two things with sponsored content promotions like this: first, it will work with the sponsor to make sure the content is somewhat credible, and second, it will clearly label the piece as advertising so as not to confuse the audience that the content doesn't come directly from the fine journalists at the *Atlantic*.

Unfortunately, in this instance neither was done to an acceptable standard. What ensued was a firestorm of criticism directed toward the *Atlantic*. Adding fuel to the fire, the *Atlantic* staff started to moderate comments (that is, delete negative comments) from the article on TheAtlantic.com website, making it appear as if the magazine were trying to cover up its mistake. The *Atlantic* removed the content from its site and stated that it was re-reviewing its sponsored content policies.

Even though many publishers derive revenues directly from the readers (through paid subscriptions), most media companies rely on advertising *and* sponsorship. They have two masters—the reader and the money person—and sometimes (and it's becoming more frequent) the content suffers.

The brand, on the other hand, doesn't have to deal with two audiences. Your readership and your cash-funding source are one and the same. *If you supply amazing, epic content for your readers consistently*

Source: theatlantic.com

Figure 4.3 The *Atlantic* publishes sponsored content from the Church of Scientology.

over time, they tend to reward you with new or repeat business. And here's another equally important lesson for content creators: *follow your own version of the Hippocratic oath—do no harm!*

SEVEN WAYS TO TAKE THE MEDIA WORLD BY STORM

These seven tips will create a powerful concoction that will be hard for any company, including media companies and your direct competitors, to compete with. (More detail to follow later on.)

1. **Make mobile your top channel strategy.** Remember when eBay was the online auctions king? Well, today, online auctions are just 10 percent of eBay's total business—its payment and mobile business is half the company. The online marketplace is betting its entire future on mobile, and it's winning. And right now 32 percent of *Wall Street Journal* website traffic comes from a mobile device (60 percent from a smartphone and 40 percent from a tablet device).

   Most media companies either have legacy systems in print or digital. Yes, digital, as in desktop publishing, is becoming a legacy system. Responsive design has helped. (Responsive design basically takes your "desktop" content and makes it perfectly readable on a mobile device.) But it is a Band-Aid, in my opinion. You need to plan, right now, for the inevitability that the majority of the traffic to your content marketing will come from a mobile device in two to five years. This means thinking mobile first as part of your channel strategy.

   Because of how media companies are built and the content processes and staffing they have in place, you can move faster than they can to a mobile-first strategy.

2. **Hire professional journalists and writers.** Companies such as GE, Avaya, and Monetate have all filled key marketing positions with journalists and editors from media companies. This is now the rule and not the exception. Why shouldn't you do the same?

3. **Repurpose all your content.** Todd Wheatland, vice president of thought leadership at Kelly Services (the global staffing firm), doesn't create content every day, but when the company does have a story to tell, it maximizes it. Todd's goal is to create 20 pieces of content (such as SlideShare presentations, videos, blog posts, and white papers) all from one story idea. So, the next time you begin a story concept for your content marketing program, set your heights on Kelly's model. (Read more on the 10-to-1 content method in Chapter 22.)

4. **Develop rent-to-own content strategies.** As a content marketer, your goal is to own your media channels, just as publishers do. A strategy that never fails is the "rent-to-own" model. This means partnering with media companies through webinars and sponsored content opportunities to get your content in front of those companies' audiences. The goal is to "convert" these prospect readers into your readers. With publishing models crumbling, most media companies are happy to partner with you on any number of rent-to-own strat-

egies. Just don't do what the Church of Scientology did with the *Atlantic*. Make the content helpful, not self-serving.

5. **Develop professional editorial practices.** Many brands today are leveraging employees and outside influencers as part of their content marketing programs. While I believe this is good, I see a gaping void in the editorial arena. Simply put, brands are not investing enough in editorial and proofreading as part of their processes. Every piece of content you create should have at least two sets of additional eyes on the content. In addition, your employees may have the stories, but they may not be storytellers. Assign an editor to help them tell a story that works for your content marketing program. See more on the content marketing process in Chapter 15.

6. **Buy a media company.** Do an analysis on the media companies in your industry. Have a team discussion about which ones are the best fit for your content marketing program. Consider purchasing that media company. (Do so even if yours is a small business.)

7. **Make the reader your number one priority.** As a media company, we at Content Marketing Institute do everything we can to commit to the reader experience. That said, most of the company's bills are paid by its sponsors. It's a challenging juggling act. As a brand, *you don't have this issue*. Leverage it. Commit your stories to one epic concept—what's in it for them, your readers (that is, your customers). This is your critical advantage, where you can and should focus all your attention.

If you choose to, you can be the leading "media company" in your industry. The only thing holding you back is you. Make the choice.

EPIC THOUGHTS

- The business model for content creation between media and non-media companies is almost the same . . . except for how the money comes in. This means that nonmedia companies have the advantage.
- Could it be that LEGO is actually a media company that happens to sell colored bricks?
- Media companies will never have the kind of resources and flexibility that you have.

EPIC RESOURCES

- "Idea Garage," *Chief Content Officer*, accessed July 9, 2013, http://www.nxtbook.com/nxtbooks/junta42/201104na_cco/index.php#/26.
- GE Stories, accessed July 9, 2013, http://www.ge.com/stories.
- Ryan Grenoble, "New York Times, Tesla's Elon Musk Reach End of Road in Spat over 'Model S,' Supercharging Stations," *Huffington Post*, February 20, 2013, http://www.huffingtonpost.com/2013/02/20/nyt-vs-tesla-feud-reaches-end-of-road_n_2720770.html.
- Matthew Ingham, "Tesla, The New York Times and the Levelling of the Playing Field,"*paidContent*,February 15,2013, http://paidcontent.org/2013/02/15/tesla-the-new-york-times-and-the-levelling-of-the-media-playing-field/.
- Jim Edwards, "Here's the Scientology-Sponsored Content Story That The Atlantic Doesn't Want You to See," Business Insider, January 15, 2013, http://www.businessinsider.com/heres-the-scientology-sponsored-content-story-that-the-atlantic-doesnt-want-you-to-see-2013-1.
- "David Miscavige Leads Scientology to Milestone Year," *The Atlantic*, January 14, 2013, in *Business Insider*, http://www.businessinsider.com/document/50f5611269beddba58000019/120420141-the-atlantic-14-january-2013-david-miscavige-leads-scientology-to-milestone-year.pdf.
- JP Mangalindan, "eBay Is Back!," *CNNMoney*, February 7, 2013, http://tech.fortune.cnn.com/2013/02/07/ebay-donahoe-comeback/.
- Sarah Marshall, "32% of WSJ Traffic coming from Mobile," Journalism.co.uk, February 19, 2013, http://www.journalism.co.uk/news/-dms13-32-of-wsj-traffic-coming-from-mobile/s2/a552137/.
- James Poniewozik, "Charged Debate. A Tesla Review Sparks a Battle between Data and News," *Time*, March 4, 2013.

CHAPTER 5

The Business Case for Content Marketing

If the facts don't fit the theory, change the facts.
ALBERT EINSTEIN

Even though content marketing is not new by any stretch, it's a fairly young discipline. That means there are a number of marketers and business owners who need to be persuaded into trying content marketing for the first time.

Robert Rose, lead author of *Managing Content Marketing*, makes the argument that the content marketing business case takes on the same components as a proper business plan.

1. **What's the need?** What do you hope to accomplish with your content marketing?
2. **How big a need is it?** Is the need big enough to build an entire plan around it?
3. **What's the business model?** How does it work? What do you have to do?
4. **What's your differentiating value?** Why is this initiative more important than other things on which you're spending resources?
5. **What are the risks?** What's in the way of success—or what happens if you fail?

What's not included in this list should be obvious: the cost and the return on investment (ROI), or what I call "return on objective" (ROO). Those topics will be covered extensively in Chapter 24. For now, you just need to make sure the boat is in the water and headed in the right direction.

MAKING THE CASE

For the past three years, we at Content Marketing Institute have looked at executive buy-in for content marketing as part of our annual research. Every year, those marketers who self-diagnosed themselves as "ineffective" almost always have many issues getting executive buy-in.

So what can a marketer do to educate and justify to the executive team the value of content marketing? The following thoughts are from a number of CMI contributors on what the value of content marketing is and how they would explain content marketing to someone who better understands the ways of traditional marketing.

> Content marketing is *thinking about the target audience's needs first*. Even hidebound execs must instinctively feel this is a good thing. But the real proof, of course, is in the pudding. *Show them the data from a content marketing campaign versus a typical product-driven campaign. Then stand back.*
>
> DOUG KESSLER (@DOUGKESSLER)

> More than anything, marketers want to engage with customers. *One of the disadvantages of traditional advertising was the one-way aspect of the conversation*: sales was one of your only measurements to see if engagement was really happening. *With content marketing, you can have a two-way conversation with your customers and use varied tools to measure engagement.* Watching your customers interact with your brand makes social media and content marketing fun and exciting. And, if you see that you're not getting the results you want, you can quickly change track without a major investment of printing, ad space, and production costs.
>
> AHAVA LEIBTAG (@AHAVAL)

> The value of content marketing lies in the engagement between the customer and your company. *Traditional advertising shouts at prospect customers whereas content marketing talks with them.* Essentially, it is about the creation and participation in mean-

ingful conversations and development of relationships. Content marketing can benefit your company by increasing sales leads and positioning your company/brand as a thought leader, in addition to increasing the number of visitors to your website.

AMANDA MAKSYMIW (@AMANDAMAKSYMIW)

When you're talking to any level of management about a content marketing strategy, you have to focus on the benefit of word-of-mouth referrals. Managers, especially C-level decision makers, usually aren't interested in theories or philosophies. Everyone loves customer testimonials and success stories and knows exactly how powerful they can be. *Pitch content marketing as the vehicle for maximizing word-of-mouth referrals.*

SARAH MITCHELL (@GLOBALCOPYWRITE)

Traditional advertising is the "pudding," and content marketing is the "proof in that pudding."

In other words, we use traditional advertising to make people aware of our brand and, in many ways, to demonstrate the heart of our brand. *It's the content marketing that can bring living proof of our brand to our customers* in the form of video demonstrations and interviews, educational webinars, case studies, white papers, blog insights and advice, and so much more.

This proof is what will keep them coming back to our website and encourage their loyalty to our brand.

LISA PETRILLI (@LISAPETRILLI)

Traditional advertising relies on the push—or outbound—mentality to get messages in front of a target audience. But today's business buyers are tired of being interrupted with one-size-fits-all messages. Fortunately for them, the Internet empowers buyers to search for and consume information that is valuable and relevant, enabling them to ignore the meaningless messages bombarding them at every turn. *By embracing the tenets of content marketing, companies can deliver the type of information that prospects are seeking—aligned with their interests, role, industry, and place in the buying cycle—and pull buyers to their sites.*

STEPHANIE TILTON (@STEPHANIETILTON)

Have you noticed how many of the *traditional advertising meth-ods you've relied on for connecting with customers aren't as effective as they used to be*? I have, and that's why I consider content marketing critical. But content marketing does not work against traditional marketing.

Content marketing works beautifully with established tradi-tional marketing tools. Even better, though, is that *content mar-keting adds relevance, meaning and dimension to traditional ap-proaches so you engage with potential customers. Content mar-keting helps your overall marketing work harder for you.*

More specifically, content marketing allows you to tell po-tential customers what you are about; it prequalifies customers. Imagine sharing in customer-relevant terms the story behind how you help customers. Visualize building trust and meaningful relationships with them before asking for the sale, before they realize they need you. The result is a richer, deeper, and more satisfying business relationship.

Isn't that worth bringing into your organization?

CB WHITTEMORE (@CBWHITTEMORE)

The takeaway? There are a lot of ways to explain the difference between traditional and content marketing, so think about what your management team cares about the most. Here's how content marketing compares with traditional marketing:

- It is about the customer, not you.
- It pulls customers in with relevant content instead of one-size-fits-all blasts.
- It is two-way conversation instead of a monologue. (You're talking to your customers instead of shouting at them.)
- It is more dynamic and easier to change.
- It involves less risk.
- It has a much longer shelf-life.
- It provides the proof that marketing is working and is easier to measure.
- It maximizes one of your most important assets: word-of-mouth referrals.
- It happens before and after a sale.

FOUR HIDDEN BENEFITS TO CONTENT MARKETING

Joe Chernov, Vice President, Content Marketing, Kinvey
(and 2012 Content Marketer of the Year)

CONTENT CAN GIVE YOU A RECRUITING EDGE

In a competitive industry, recruiting top-caliber talent is a priority of the highest order. In fact, according to venture capitalist (and content marketer extraordinaire) Fred Wilson, recruiting top talent is one of only three priorities for every CEO. Yet despite the importance of recruiting, it would be easy to overlook the impact an engaging content marketing program can have on this business-critical priority.

Here's the takeaway: *partner with your HR department.* When your company on-boards staff, have your recruiter ask new hires to share the reasons why they joined, and share this information with your internal teams. The ability to prove your content efforts have impacted recruiting will help make you—and your content efforts—indispensable to your organization.

CONTENT CAN HELP BOOST COMPANY MORALE

Back when I worked at a PR firm, I recall challenging a client who wanted us to help his company secure coverage in a publication that didn't necessarily influence its buyers. When I pushed back on the priority, the CEO told me, "The article isn't for our customers. It's for our staff. The place lights up when we get covered in the press . . . and I know a lot of our workers read this magazine." I've never forgotten that lesson, and content marketing can help accomplish this very same goal.

When you publish a popular asset, the cheering it receives on the social web can validate the efforts of the entire company. Your victory lap is *everyone's* victory lap, so make sure you "market" the popularity of your content to your colleagues—not to boast personally, but rather to remind them that as crowded as the social web is, your company managed to stand out.

CONTENT OPENS UP LINES OF COMMUNICATION

Remarkable content doesn't just get customers and prospects talking; it also gets your internal clients buzzing. It gives colleagues something to share with one another, something to debate, or something to challenge. It opens doors, rings phones, and makes heads gopher over cubicle walls. It also provides you with an opportunity to recruit advocates and participants.

When your colleagues engage with your content, it creates an opportunity to invite them to contribute to future programs. Because content marketing sits between so many different organizational functions, it is a surprisingly political role. Be sure to marshal your supporters when you have their attention.

CONTENT FOSTERS TRUST

In a recent *Fast Company* article, marketing leader Don Peppers convincingly argues that the key to competitive advantage is "being proactively trustworthy." *Creating content that is so valuable that people would pay for it, yet you give it away for free, is a reliable way to earn the public's trust.* This is precisely why the value transfer in content marketing should be from institution to individual, which is an upside-down model for traditional marketers. In other words, when trust is the goal, companies should strive to *sell by not selling.*

None of this is to suggest that content marketers shouldn't aspire to be measured—of course we should. But we also need to find ways to highlight the value we provide—especially if there's no key performance indicator (KPI) attached to it.

TWO FOOLPROOF METHODS FOR BUY-IN

Throughout my years in content marketing, I've seen two methods work the best when it comes to getting buy-in for new content marketing projects or additional budget.

THE PILOT

As most people know, before a television show is signed on by a network, a pilot is produced. A pilot is a sampling of what's to come, which gives the network executives enough consumer feedback to know whether more episodes should be produced.

If you present your content marketing plan as a pilot, you'll immediately see the key decision makers let their guard down. It's not as much of a commitment as a full-blown content marketing strategy. But as you sell the content marketing pilot, be sure to include the following:

- The length of the pilot; it should be at least six months.
- The overall goal of the pilot, or how the business will be different after the pilot.
- Agreed-upon metrics; if you hit them, you'll be able to move forward with "more episodes." This could be an increase in leads, more

subscriptions, shorter time to close business, and/or an increase in "quality" leads, to name just a few.

FEAR

When all else fails, fear can work as well or better than a rational argument. If you show how competitors are using content marketing to their advantage and to your disadvantage, you certainly ought to be able to get someone's attention.

For the "fear" plan to work, you have to do some research up front on your competition. Pick the leading content marketer in your field and determine:

- How many subscribers (e-mail, Facebook, Twitter, and so on) does it have to its content versus yours?
- How does it rank in key search terms versus your rankings?
- How does it compare in terms of social sharing?
- Do they have positive, online word of mouth (check Twitter for this one)?
- Are they actively recruiting online and landing the best talent?

These are just a few items. The key in this strategy is to determine what's of critical importance to the lead decision maker and then target that argument. Clearly show how the competitor is using certain content strategies that are leaving you (and your content) in the dust.

I've seen this work dozens of times to perfection when rational arguments are simply ignored. So if the pilot idea doesn't work, try the fear tactic.

EPIC THOUGHTS

- Traditional marketing has always been about getting products and services in front of the right audience. Content marketing is about meeting the informational needs of customers so they become interested in you.
- Don't go "all-in" on content marketing from the start. Begin with a pilot program, with specific measures. The proof will be in the pudding.

EPIC RESOURCES

- Don Peppers, "The Only Lasting Competitive Advantage Is Extreme Trust," *Fast Company*, January 19, 2012, http://www.fastcompany.com/1809038/the-only-lasting-competitive-advantage-trust.

CHAPTER 6

Tomorrow's Media Companies

If all you have is a hammer in the toolbox, everything looks like a nail.

BERNARD BARUCH

If you've ever seen the movie *Jerry McGuire*, you remember the blue mission statement. This is the moment in the movie when Jerry McGuire (played by Tom Cruise) wakes up in a cold sweat and writes what he believes is the future direction for his sports agency: one with fewer clients, more customer service, and more individual attention on the athletes.

Jonathan Mildenhall, vice president of global advertising strategy for Coca-Cola, had a similar vision—except that instead of being fired as Jerry McGuire was in the movie, he's leading Coca-Cola into the content marketing revolution. Mildenhall's "blue mission statement" is called Coca-Cola Content 2020 (see Figure 6.1).

Coca-Cola Content 2020 is made up of two videos (about 17 minutes long between the two) and outlines Coke's content strategy for the next decade. (If you haven't already viewed the videos, please take the time to review them at http://bitly.com/epic-cm2020.)

During the video Mildenhall states:

> All advertisers need a lot more content so that they can keep the engagement with consumers fresh and relevant, because of the

Source: youtube.com

Figure 6.1 Coca-Cola's Content 2020 project was at first an internal strategy piece for Coke's marketing department. Today it's used by organizations around the world as an example of content marketing strategy.

24/7 connectivity. If you're going to be successful around the world, you have to have fat and fertile ideas at the core.

WHY IS CONTENT 2020 SO IMPORTANT?

Content 2020 was originally created as an internal marketing video prepared especially for Coca-Cola's marketing group, executive team, and partner agencies, laying out the company's strategic vision for the future. Overall, it's the strategy that Coca-Cola's marketing future rests on the ideals of content marketing—what they call "liquid storytelling." The following are Content 2020's key points:

- Coca-Cola needs to move from *creative excellence to content excellence.*

- The company needs to develop content that *makes a commitment to making the world a better place and to develop value and significance in people's lives*, while at the same time driving business objectives for Coca-Cola.
- Through the stories Coca-Cola tells, to provoke conversations and *earn a disproportionate share of popular culture*.

In the beginning of the videos, the claim is made that Coca-Cola must create the world's most compelling content. Toward the end, the comment is made that Coca-Cola can no longer rely on being 30-second TV-centric. The fact that Coke spends billions of dollars on advertising each year makes this a very profound statement in the mostly paid media universe. Coke realizes that advertising isn't enough anymore, and that stories, not interruption, win the hearts and minds of customers.

A CONTENT 2020 INTERVIEW*

When I first came across the Content 2020 project, I was immediately struck by the business goal it presents at the very outset: "We intend to double the size of our business," Mildenhall says in the video. And, as he points out, they plan to do this while realizing that "consumer-generated stories outnumber their stories on most of their brands."

Have you told your boss that you want to double the size of your business? And that you're going to use brand storytelling [content marketing] as a primary driver to get there? So, yeah, I became a fan right then.

Robert Rose: Tell us about the birth of the Content 2020 idea.

Jonathan Mildenhall: First of all, as a company, the Coca-Cola brand has constantly defined its own benchmarks in marketing. We were the first brand to do sampling. We were the first brand to do coupons. We were the first to depict women in the workplace. Coca-Cola is a history of firsts. And, we found ourselves facing such massive change in terms of both the distribution of technology and the distribution of creativity.

We are lucky enough that millions of consumers now want to produce content and be a driving part of our conversation. This gave us the opportunity to take time out and really think about

*This interview was between Content Marketing Institute chief strategist Robert Rose and Jonathan Mildenhall (reprinted with permission).

how to articulate our evolved creative agenda for our key global and local brands.

Rose: So how did you actually create the initiative?

Mildenhall: We pulled 40 people from around the company—all of whom worked in the Creative Excellence group. We gave ourselves a five-day period where we would collectively write a content manifesto. We broke it down into subjects and allocated one subject area per minigroup. Executives would then present their thinking, and the rest of the room would rip the points of view apart and put them back together again. Monday through Thursday, my role was simply to be disruptive and ask questions.

Then, on Thursday night of that week, I took what we'd come up with and I stayed up all night and basically wrote the words to the manifesto you see in the video.

The next morning, I came in and presented this to the room, and when we were done, everybody put their signatures on it.

We knew immediately that we had created something significant.

Rose: How did you decide to "give it away"—that is, give away a core piece of your marketing strategy?

Mildenhall: The answer is very simple. Coca-Cola is the biggest purchaser of marketing services in the world. There is no way we can have a quiet conversation about this. I told my CMO that in order to put this into place, I could spend the next two years briefing every agency that we deal with on how to do this, or we can simply give it away and I can get straight to work.

We chose the latter, and it's been extraordinarily successful. We've been blogged about and talked about in innumerable publications across the globe. And, most importantly, the advertising industry has really responded. The Coca-Cola Company is enjoying our most successful year ever in terms of volume and creative awards this year.

Rose: How do you envision Content 2020 being integrated into traditional marketing and advertising? Is it infused into, additive to, or does it ultimately replace what you're doing from a traditional advertising and promotions perspective?

Mildenhall: It's additive for sure. We fully understand that we are still going to have to do promotions, price messaging, shopper bundles, traditional advertising, etcetera.—that isn't going away. But content is the way consumers understand the role and relevance of the Coca-Cola Company brands. We have to make sure that those "immediate stories" are part of the larger brand stories.

But, for the more financially minded of the organization I say this: if I can fill up the emotional level of the brand, then *I have to trade on it less and less.* Believe it or not, we're still engaging with new consumers that don't have their emotional well filled. New consumers enter the middle classes all over the world every day. So from a global perspective, we must deliver solutions for the first-time consumers—and of course keep those who know and love our brands wanting to come back for more.

Rose: I love the idea in the Content 2020 piece where you talk about different models requiring different processes under the same principles. This was music to my ears. It's often a struggle that I find that larger organizations I work with are trying to manage. They struggle with one process across multiple silos (brand marketing, product marketing, PR, and so on) and one source of content (for example, should we outsource or internalize it?). How have you desiloed (or have you?) the political battles among product marketing, brand marketing, PR, and other teams so that everyone speaks with one voice?

Mildenhall: We have a number of disciplines of course—and they each have their own mandates. That said, we have horizontal strategies from creative development, idea development, and production. So everyone's remit is to be horizontal or integrated in thinking. We're as siloed as any large organization. But in the end, you may be heading up social or PR or production, but your solutions, your team solutions, must work horizontally across every function in the marketing world.

Rose: In the video you talk about the 70/20/10 investment model. You say 70 percent of the budget goes to the content that you "must produce," 20 percent goes to content that is slightly out of the box, and 10 percent goes to "high-risk" creative content. Do you find you spend an outsize amount on the high-risk, super-cool content?

Mildenhall: Actually it's quite the opposite. It's actually much cheaper to produce the 10 percent. But it takes much more creative time to actually come up with. This is where I, admittedly, have a bit of an advantage. The Coca-Cola brand is one that any number of other brands has a desire to align themselves with—from other consumer brands to technology providers who want to innovate and explore new frontiers.

We are increasingly open to these ideas. If you think about it, Coca-Cola can be viewed as a huge media brand with amazing reach and frequency. If there are pitches out there from people who want to provide content and experiences, we are open to hearing from them. The question we ask ourselves is, "Can we use our assets as content, and can we create content out of our assets?"

Rose: Where do you see the future of content and marketing?

Mildenhall: Well, the big Holy Grail right now is how we get into real-time marketing. I've got to make sure that I'm taking content, news, and everything that's going on around the world and transforming it into marketing communications. I really do believe that technology and consumer engagement are creating the opportunity for real-time marketing. But things like usage rights, IP rights, and so on, are getting in the way right now. I could literally be producing fresh content every single day of the week. However, with a real-time agenda you get a lot of legal challenges.

I also think we're going to see a big move to brand curation, where brands can help to leverage each other; for example, our Super Bowl commercial where we had the polar bears commenting on other ads. This, again, is a real trend, but most large organizations will have to get over the nervousness of the legal challenges of this.

But that's really our goal. We want to give the audience the most compelling content—and earn that disproportionate share of popular culture. That's the power of content.

CONTENT 2020 IN ACTION

In 2006, Mildenhall hired the agency Starlight Runner to work on Coke's Happiness Factory campaign. Although most of the campaign involved paid advertising, Starlight Runner was hired specifically to write the

Source: youtube.com

Figure 6.2 For Coca-Cola's Happiness Factory project, a complete world was developed in the "Happiness Factory Bible," which included a backstory on all characters used in the campaign.

"Happiness Factory Bible" (see Figure 6.2), which became the backbone for the entire program.

According to *Forbes*, the Happiness Factory Bible was "a book that describes the entire world inside the vending machine, from geographic regions to the names and motivations of individual characters." Basically, Coca-Cola developed an entire script, or content marketing playbook, to help tell the Happiness Factory story online, in print, in social media, in video games, and on television.

What originally seemed like an odd experiment led to a 4 percent rise in global sales, something Coca-Cola attributes to the program.

COCA-COLA JOURNEY

In November 2012, Coca-Cola unveiled Coca-Cola Journey (see Figure 6.3). Instead having a typical website, Coke transformed its home page into

Source: coca-cola.com

Figure 6.3 Coca-Cola launched the Journey project with 4 full-time writers and 40 freelancers.

an online publishing machine. The new publication features company-specific content across nine categories, including all beverage brands owned by the Coca-Cola Company (such as Sprite).

According to the *New York Times*:

> Four full-time employees are devoted to the corporate Web site . . . and content is also being created by 40 freelance writers and photographers, as well as people throughout the Coke system, in marketing and public relations.

Coca-Cola has set up Journey as a hub for stories it believes will interest its customers, from business to sports to sustainability. The results aren't in yet for Journey's impact on Coke's bottom line, but it is

clear that Coke's marketing direction has changed … and business owners and marketers should be paying attention.

A NEW MEDIA COMPANY: RED BULL?

The Austrian energy drink brand cemented itself as the Coke
of the shareable content era, willing to spend freely to produce
content so good that it is indistinguishable from non-marketing
content. Red Bull truly is a media company that happens to sell
soft drinks.

BRIAN MORRISSEY, DIGIDAY

During discussions, when people ask me what is the best example in
the world of someone doing content marketing, I simply tell them "Red
Bull." At the center of Red Bull's storytelling universe is a group called
Red Bull Media House (named to *Fast Company*'s Most Innovative
Companies List for 2012). Through a variety of content efforts, Red Bull
has secured one of the most loyal audiences on the planet. Red Bull
Media House is the engine that makes this happen. It does this through
a number of initiatives:

- **Red Bull content pool.** The company licenses out over 50,000 photos and 5,000 videos to media companies. Yes, you heard that right:
  media companies pay Red Bull to license and purchase the rights to
  show Red Bull–branded content.
- **Red Bull records.** With offices in Los Angeles and London, Red Bull
  Records signs performers to record deals that align with Red Bull's
  "Give You Wings" mentality. In addition, Red Bull Music Publishing
  backs aspiring composers and songwriters. Additionally, Red Bull
  syndicates those songs as part of its content pool and in other Red
  Bull programs.
- **The *Red Bulletin*.** A monthly print and digital magazine the *Red
  Bulletin* is delivered to 4.8 million subscribers around the world and
  published in 11 countries and in four languages.

And that is just the start. Red Bull Media House encompasses dozens of other brands in television, radio, film, and special events such as
Red Bull Stratos. (Stratos was Felix Baumgartner's jump from the edge
of space, which was conveniently sponsored by Red Bull. The jump was
documented by Red Bull in the form of countless images, as well as 15
videos viewed over 350 million times on YouTube alone.)

According to *Fast Company*, Red Bull enjoys a 44 percent market share in the competitive field of energy drinks, with double-digit revenue growth. Today, Red Bull funds the majority of its content efforts through product (energy drink) sales, but in the future, Red Bull expects to profit directly from the stories and content it creates.

JYSKE BANK: MEDIA COMPANY AND A BANK

How many banks in the world also produce award-winning television and video shows on a daily basis? Probably none, except for one: Jyske (pronounced *You-ska*) Bank.

Jyske Bank has one of the most high-tech, in-house television production studios in Denmark. It proclaims itself as both a media company and a bank. Jyskebank.tv covers both amazing financial programming as well as compelling stories it believes are relevant for its core audience of younger consumers and small enterprises.

Its content program is made up of two key values: (1) holding true to the vision of the organization (called "the Foundation") and (2) telling good stories. To do this, it has a network of correspondents around the world made up of Jyske employees and freelance writers.

Every piece of content it shares is embeddable or shareable on other sites. Because of this "sharing" philosophy, *80 percent of its content is seen, not on its website or owned channels, but from outside sources.* This type of content sharing opens up revolutionary opportunities for any company, let alone a bank. Instead of paying for many traditional sponsorships as most banks and corporate brands do, Jyske is approached with media partnerships. This means that instead of Jyske outlaying cash, organizations partner with the company because of its credibility and reach (it is treated like a media company). Both the Mobile World Congress and the Cannes Lions Festival approached Jyske to do just that, offering Jyske access to logo placements and exclusive interviews previously reserved for media companies. With reach and a loyal audience comes great opportunity.

And this type of sharing doesn't stop with outside customers. Every Friday morning, Jyske holds a live, full-access television program available to every employee. This type of internal training shepherds the company's core vision of being open and honest with all people.

Jyske doesn't have to buy media attention; it is the first media company of its kind that just happens to be a bank as well.

OPENVIEW VENTURE PARTNERS: A SMALL COMPANY CASE STUDY

Perhaps you're thinking: *Coca-Cola, Red Bull, and even Jyske Bank can dominate because they have multimillion-dollar marketing and publishing budgets.*

Well, not so fast.

Scott Maxwell, CEO of OpenView Venture Partners of Boston, called me in the fall of 2008 with a problem. After reading *Get Content Get Customers*, Scott fully believed that content marketing was the future for his company, but he didn't know how to get started.

OpenView Venture Partners is a venture capital firm focused on helping entrepreneurs expand their companies. Generally, OpenView looks at companies between $2 and $20 million that want to raise between $5 and $15 million to fund growth initiatives. OpenView's mission has always been as a value-added venture capital firm—in other words, in addition to funding it does all the little things to add value, such as education, training, guidance, and mentoring.

Typically, OpenView would find new prospects through referrals from advisors, employees, and the executive team. Scott quickly found that this was not the best way to grow an organization.

He realized that the stories and content assets of the organization were in his 20 or so employees. For example, a portfolio CEO calls OpenView to get advice on an operational issue. The CEO is put in touch with an OpenView advisor, who works with the CEO to determine a helpful solution. Yes, the initial problem is solved, but that information was gold. What if OpenView could harness that one-on-one content, making the story available on the web for anyone to access?

Unlike the massive programs from Coca-Cola and Red Bull, OpenView's efforts began with a simple employee blog. In September 2009, OpenView launched its own blog, and since then the business has never been the same. Under Scott's direction and motivation, employees started to share key insights about marketing, operations, finance, and topics that entrepreneurs were actively searching for.

The results are simply amazing. In just three years, over 18,000 subscribers have signed up for OpenView's e-newsletter. Now, instead of going through an old-school referral process, OpenView gets thousands of entrepreneurs to its site every month by answering those people's key questions, not only in one-on-one meetings but also online, available to the world. OpenView's content is found easily through search engine results and shared via social media channels such as Twitter and LinkedIn. OpenView's sales cycle has essentially been cut in half, all because OpenView doesn't have to go out searching for prospects. The prospects come to them. OpenView now has the much easier job of working through the leads and then choosing who it wants to be its portfolio customers.

Today, the OpenView Labs site, a content platform for aspiring entrepreneurs, contains thousands of articles, blog posts, podcasts, and videos all aimed at helping OpenView prospects become more successful (see Figure 6.4). OpenView has become a worldwide trusted advisor, taking the initial one-to-one consultation to a whole new level.

Source: labs.openviewpartners.com

Figure 6.4 OpenView Labs, the content platform for OpenView Venture Partners, is one of the leading educational resources for technology entrepreneurs looking for funding.

RIVER POOLS AND SPAS

In late 2009, River Pools and Spas, a 20-employee installer of fiberglass pools in the Virginia and Maryland area, was in trouble. Homeowners were not running out and buying fiberglass pools during the "Great Recession." Worse yet, customers who had actually planned on buying a pool were calling up River Pools to request their deposits back, which, in some cases, ran around $50,000 or more.

For multiple weeks, River Pools overdrew its checking account. Not only was it becoming difficult to pay employees, but the company was looking at possibly closing up shop for good.

Marcus Sheridan, CEO of River Pools and Spas, believed that the only way to survive was to steal market share from the competition, and that meant thinking differently about how the company went to market.

At the beginning of this process, River Pools did just over $4 million in annual revenues and spent approximately $250,000 a year on marketing. There were four competitors in the Virginia area that had greater market share than River.

Two years later in 2011, River Pools and Spas sold more fiberglass pools than *any* other fiberglass pools installer in North America (yes, you read that right). The company also *decreased* its marketing spend from $250,000 to around $40,000, while at the same time winning 15 percent more bids and cutting its sales cycle in half. The average pool builder lost 50 to 75 percent in sales during the time that River Pools increased sales to more than $5 million.

Needless to say, River Pools and Spas stayed open for business.

Its recipe for success was content marketing, so successful for Marcus that he now travels the world talking to business owners about his story and the power of content marketing.

How did he do it? Actually, it was a simple process. Marcus wrote down every conceivable customer question and answered it on his blog. It worked so well that if you type into a search engine, "What is the cost of a fiberglass pool?," whether you are in Cleveland or Fort Lauderdale (I tried), the number one result in both locations is a blog post from Marcus Sheridan.

We'll share more later about how Marcus accomplished this feat. Until then, I had the opportunity to interview Marcus one on one about his marketing strategy and his process.

THE MARCUS SHERIDAN INTERVIEW

Joe Pulizzi: I've heard you say marketers tend to overthink content marketing. Rather than make all sorts of complicated plans, they should just get started and figure it out as they go. Where does that kind of no-nonsense attitude come from?

Marcus: I'm blessed to have come from the blue-collar world of a swimming pool company. I didn't go to school to become a marketer. If one of my kids came to me and said, "I want to be a marketer, and I want to go to school for marketing," I would be scared to death it would ruin him or her.

I've written about the curse of knowledge more than any subject on my blog. The curse of knowledge is something I've thought a lot about, and I see so many people suffering from it—especially online. Some of these "leaders" online that are talking about marketing, you can tell they've been wrapped up in their world too long. I read blog posts and don't know what the heck the person just said because it was so nebulous and in the clouds, saying nothing concrete and having no application. That's not who I want to be.

JP: You talk about respect and courtesy on your blog. Do you see examples of disrespect in business publishing or blogging? What kind of advice do you give to bloggers about that issue?

Marcus: Frankly, I don't see enough opinions. The majority of businesses, especially B2Bs, live in this world of gray. They're so afraid to have any opinion at all that their blogs stink. They're looking to appease everyone, and so they don't get any traction.

People ask me all the time, "How did you take a subject that was not very sexy (that is, swimming pools) and get such a huge following?" First, it's written in a personal voice. I write like I talk. Second, my blog is opinionated. I don't live in the world of gray. I live in black and white. We have a dearth of thought leadership because everyone is afraid to take a stand.

Now, you have to be respectful. I don't come out and say, "This guy is such an idiot." I'll never do something like that. But I will say, "I'm looking at this product, service, or belief, and it doesn't make sense to me—and here's why."

If you're not causing people to raise eyebrows in your industry, I don't think you're going to make it big time. Not today.

There's too much content. I talk about something I call CSI, the Content Saturation Index. The CSI in every industry is growing daily by leaps and bounds. It comes down to quality. Quality initiates the social side of things.

JP: You discuss the pros and cons of different tech platforms on your blog, like Alexa rankings and Livefyre. Which apps and platforms do you think bloggers need to know about—if not use—to be successful?

Marcus: The one that I talk a ton about is HubSpot. HubSpot was the first company that was a true all-in-one (for example, blogging, analytics, e-mail marketing, lead nurturing, social media). HubSpot goes way deeper in terms of getting to know your leads' behavior than Google Analytics.

Here's the thing: if, as a blogger, you cannot say, "I know my blog made me at least 'this many' sales in the past year," there's a good chance you're not measuring stuff the right way. You need to do better than just Google Analytics. Google Analytics tracks traffic, but it doesn't track people and names. There's so much more power in being able to say, "Jeff visited my site today, and he filled out a form. And Jeff viewed these five pages of my website." (See Figure 6.5 for a sampling of River's website traffic.)

The reverse is that Google Analytics says, "Today I got 1,000 visitors on my site, and these are the pages they looked at, and

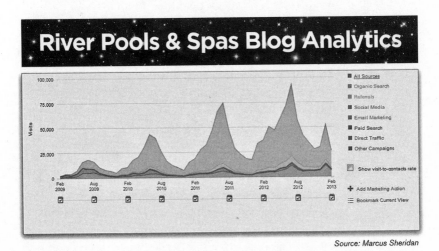

Source: Marcus Sheridan

Figure 6.5 After just a few years blogging, River Pools and Spas was able to attract almost 100,000 unique visitors to its blog site in just one month.

this is the bounce rate, and these are the places they clicked." Well, what the heck is that? As a salesperson, I want to know what Jeff did; I don't care about the other 999. I really, really want to know what Jeff did. That's why we need to be good inbound marketers, and we have to get people filling out forms on our website. We've got to be able to see true behavior, not have all these hypotheses based on what Google Analytics is telling us. Google Analytics is fine, but it's clearly not the depth you need from a sales perspective.

I wrote a blog post a while back, "My blog made over 2 million dollars in sales: How's that for ROI?" That was an eye-opening moment for a lot of people because they saw, "Wow, you can actually close the whole loop. You can say this is a keyword phrase the person typed, this is the article that they landed on, these are the pages they visited, and this is the form they filled out to become a lead." Once that person became a lead (we'll call him "John"), we started the sales process and began tracking him, not just based on the website but all our communications with John. When John eventually turns into a customer, we close him out in our analytics and track it back to that initial keyword and that initial article. At that point, you can say, "If I didn't write that blog article, John would never have visited the site and become a customer." Therefore that blog article is a direct reason for the sale. And that sale for that particular customer, John, was $75,000 for my company. That's a beautiful thing.

JP: You share a lot about yourself, your family, your faith—a lot more than the average business owner. Tell me why.

Marcus: I want you to start to develop a relationship with me early on. I want you to know, first of all, what I look like. That's important because you have to be able to put a face with content. Second, I want you to get a feel that I'm just like you, a real person with a real family, with real struggles, triumphs, tragedies, and so on. So when you read my stuff you can say, "I know who's talking to me." Even if I'm not a lot like you, you know that I'm a real person.

The number one need we have in life, in my opinion, is to feel understood. When I was just a "pool guy," I would knock on a customer's door and literally, the lady of the house would come out and give me a hug. She would address me like we'd known each other for years and talk about my kids. Sharing personal stories really tears down walls. This is deep. As marketers we talk about social media but yet we want to be antisocial; well, screw that. I'm all in, literally. All chips in the middle of the table. I'm here to be social, and this is who I am!

THE REST OF THIS BOOK

This first part of this book was designed to give you a solid foundation for what content marketing is and where the possibilities lie. The remainder of this book will focus on how you can find your story, how you can better understand the process of developing epic content, and how you can transform your organization into a content marketing factory that attracts and retains more of the right kind of customers.

Are you ready? Let's go!

EPIC THOUGHTS

- When Coca-Cola does anything, people listen. The fact that it is taking content marketing so seriously is important for all of us in marketing and business generation.
- Red Bull and Jyske Bank look more like media companies than an energy drink maker and a bank. Look for more of this trend in the future.
- Content marketing is not just for large companies. OpenView Venture Partners and River Pools and Spas have dominated through epic content creation. You can too.

EPIC RESOURCES

- *Jerry McGuire*, directed by Cameron Crowe (1996; Tristar Pictures/ Sony Pictures Entertainment).
- Joe Pulizzi, "Coca-Cola Bets the Farm on Content Marketing: Content 2020," ContentMarketingInstitute.com, January 4, 2012, http://contentmarketinginstitute.com/2012/01/coca-cola-content -marketing-20-20/.
- David M. Ewalt, "Once Upon a Soda," *Forbes*, January 25, 2013, http:// www.forbes.com/sites/davidewalt/2013/01/25/once-upon-a-soda/.
- Mark Sherbin, "Big Content Marketing Plays from Coke, Pepsi and Red Bull," ContentMarketingInstitute.com, November 18, 2012, http://contentmarketinginstitute.com/2012/11/content-marketing -plays-coke-pepsi-red-bull/.

- Stuart Elliott, "Coke Revamps Web Site to Tell Its Story," *New York Times*, November 11, 2012, http://www.nytimes.com/2012/11/12 /business/media/coke-revamps-web-site-to-tell-its-story.html.
- James O'Brien, "How Red Bull Takes Content Marketing to the Extreme," Mashable.com, December 19, 2012, http://mashable.com /2012/12/19/red-bull-content-marketing/.
- "The World's 50 Most Innovative Companies," Red Bull Media House, in FastCompany.com, 2012, http://www.fastcompany.com /most-innovative-companies/2012/red-bull-media-house.
- Brian Morrissey, "What Red Bull Can Teach Content Marketers," Digiday, October 15, 2012, http://www.digiday.com/brands/what-red -bull-can-teach-content-marketers/.
- Coca-Cola Journey, accessed March 5, 2013, http://www.coca-cola company.com/.
- Red Bull Media House, accessed on March 5, 2013, http://www.red bullmediahouse.com/.
- OpenView Labs, accessed on March 18, 2013, http://labs.openview partners.com.
- Jyske Bank Case Study, accessed on March 22, 2013, http://www .youtube.com/watch?v=-js2tMxBWH4.
- Jyske Bank Foundations, accessed on March 23, 2013, http://dok .jyskebank.dk/Unit/jyskebank/jyskebankinfo/Ourfoundations/.
- River Pools and Spas, accessed on March 28, 2013, http://www .riverpoolsandspas.com/.
- Mark Cohen, "A Revolutionary Marketing Strategy: Answer Customers' Questions," *New York Times*, February 27, 2003, http:// www.nytimes.com/2013/02/28/business/smallbusiness/increasing -sales-by-answering-customers-questions.html?_r=0.

PART II

Defining Your Content Niche and Strategy

CHAPTER 7

More Right or Less Right

Judge a man by his questions, not by his answers.

VOLTAIRE

In the Pulizzi household, it goes by just two words: the Disclaimer. Let me explain. Growing up, and on into the present, my mother is meticulous about how she chooses and buys gifts for members of our family. As I was presented with gifts for either my birthday or for Christmas, my mother would reach out to hand me the gift . . . and then pause. Before she handed me the gift, the words that came out of her mouth were what my sister, Lea, and I always called "the Disclaimer."

The Disclaimer was why I might not like the gift—why it might not be the perfect gift for me. It usually accompanied a gift receipt of some kind and sometimes a listing of other gifts that might suit me better. Frankly, I've always loved this about my mom. It always showed how much thought and caring went into purchasing any gift for any person.

So it is fitting that I cannot write a book on epic content marketing without my own version of the Disclaimer.

THE DISCLAIMER

Like many books, my hope is that this book is so valuable to you that it changes your life, career, and business in some way. But this book is no silver-bullet strategy. None exists.

I've been involved in literally hundreds of content marketing strategies from the biggest brands in the world to the one-person start-up. Every one of them (and I mean *every one*) has been different. Each one has worked in different ways for different reasons.

YOUR PERSONAL STATEMENT

In the 2012 James Bond movie *Skyfall*, Bond meets his new quartermaster (Q), who supplies him with his new weapon toward the beginning of the movie. Upon the exchange, Q states that the gun can only be activated with Bond's personal palm print, and that only he can shoot it, saying it is "less of a random killing machine, more of a personal statement."

Your content marketing strategy and plan also needs to be a personal statement that combines your own business objectives with the informational needs of your audience. Your content plan cannot be duplicated by any other company, but you can learn from other companies and take on the best of others into your own plan.

MORE RIGHT OR LESS RIGHT

My friend and colleague Jay Baer, author of *Youtility*, says there is no right or wrong when it comes to content marketing, only "more right" or "less right." So many marketers and business owners are looking for that silver-bullet methodology that will solve all their business problems. You can stop searching for this.

The best I can hope for you is that you start asking more of the right questions, which will lead you to plan for "more right" rather than "less right." The best business books I have read, from Seth Godin to David Meerman Scott, have always challenged me to ask better questions. Through the years, I've noticed that most marketing plans don't work because not enough questions are asked. Don't make this mistake.

WHERE ARE YOU? THE CONTENT MARKETING MATURITY MODEL

Robert Rose, CMI's chief strategist and my coauthor on *Managing Content Marketing*, has been working on a maturity model for content marketing. The purpose is to help businesses identify where they are with content marketing and where they need to be. He was kind enough to outline this model as follows.

Content marketing is an approach, a practice, to marketing that helps businesses deliver differentiated value to customers. As Jeff Ernst from Forrester says, "Consumers no longer buy our products and services; they buy into our approach to solving their problems." This is why companies like Zappos are so differentiated—because they have transformed the art of service and conversation into their marketing. This is why Red Bull is differentiated—because it understands it's not just about an energy drink, it's about building the aspirational story that comes along with that drink. And this is why Cisco Systems is differentiated—because it understands that it's not just about routers and cable, it's about demonstrating that real people can innovate communication given the right technology.

But this isn't an all-or-nothing proposition. Depending on what business you have, you may have varying needs for content development and sophistication. It's a scale—not of capability, but of approach. Understanding where you currently are in your content marketing journey (content aware, thought leader, or storyteller) is critical to getting started on the right path (see Figure 7.1).

CONTENT AWARE

At the base of this scale is what I call "content aware." This is simply using content to cut through the noise of interruption-based advertising and drive trusted awareness to your product or service. The classic example of this is inbound marketing (companies that use content to

Source: Content Marketing Institute/Robert Rose

Figure 7.1 Where are you in your content marketing journey?

"be found"). *It's a strategy that meets demand.* The strategy consists of generating lots of trustworthy and helpful content in order to be found, generate awareness, and engender trust with your target audiences.

Example: Tenon Tours. Tenon Tours uses HubSpot to generate lots of content on its blog about Irish culture, local events, and travel tips. It spends its time optimizing the posts for search ranking. As a result, it increased its site visitors by 54 percent. Key to success is focusing on which posts generate the best search engine rankings, which have the most social shares, and which ones drive the most visitors.

THOUGHT LEADER

After "content aware," the next stage is working to become a "thought leader," or "lead with engagement." This is where, as a brand, you create content that delivers value beyond the scope of your product or service. The business claims and earns leadership in the industry category by creating and facilitating content that not only meets demand but also creates trust in the brand beyond just how to use the product or service. At this stage, the business moves beyond creating content for its core buyer personas and moves into creating content for influencers. On the business-to-business side, this is creating a more efficient buying funnel (in essence, helping your buyers buy), because it is differentiating the business against its competitors by claiming and earning expertise. The business may create content that talks about the use of other products that complement its own. It may offer research or extended content that reaches (or is sourced by) industry influencers. The goal of this stage is to use content to elevate the brand into one that's trusted by the consumer, which therefore generates a differentiated approach to solving its problem, or simply put, whatever is getting in the way of your buyer's purchase decision.

Example: OpenView Venture Partners. OpenView takes a holistic approach to its content marketing strategy. The company has a complete blog, virtual events, physical events, videos, infographics, and social media channels that serve its core mission to communicate its belief that new forms of marketing can positively affect start-up companies. OpenView uses industry influencers as well as its own employees to tell its story. The company not only hosts influencers to help OpenView generate content, it has active outreach to influencers to generate content to them as well. The organization has truly established itself as a thought leader of entrepreneurial growth in the venture capital industry—one that cares deeply about its portfolio companies. This differentiates the organization from other venture capital firms. That subsequently elevates OpenView to be pitched by more creative and innovative entrepreneurs than it might otherwise be, given its size.

STORYTELLER

The final stage is the "storyteller" stage. At this stage, the brand integrates content into a larger brand narrative and aligns its content strategy completely around a customer engagement strategy. The business goes beyond becoming a thought leader in the industry by drawing prospects, customers, and influencers into an emotional relationship with the brand. The storyteller strategy educates, entertains, engages, and has impact on audiences because the content goes well beyond the scope of the product or service into why the organization exists at all. *It actually* creates *demand for products and services* the audiences may not know exist yet (or may never exist at all). It creates excitement and interest in those who aren't customers, makes evangelists out of existing customers, and focuses on drawing audiences in to engage with the brand in numerous ways. (This has traditionally been the role of the media company, such as the *New York Times* or NBC.) The goal of the storytelling strategy is to create better customers. It creates a global efficiency in marketing and sales because it enables the brand to differentiate to the point of being able to command a premium for its products and services or to have to discount them less.

Example: Coca-Cola. There are many of the storytelling strategy at work. Coca-Cola is probably the best one; it creates stories all which have the goal of "spreading happiness" (see Chapter 6). On the B2B side, Cisco Systems tells stories by creating documentaries that connect emotionally to consumers (even though they don't really sell to consumers any longer) so that there's an influence in the business to care about the Cisco brand. GE does this by talking about innovation and creating brand stories that engage consumers to care about the GE brand; that influences businesses that may buy GE products.

As you move through the rest of this book, it's important to think about where you want to be. Sometimes becoming content aware is sufficient to be able to meet demand, which is done through the creation of epic content. But the real revenue opportunities and growth are in the storyteller stage. It's something all businesses should strive to achieve. Regardless, this is a decision that you need to make as you mature in your practice of content marketing.

EPIC THOUGHTS

- There is no silver bullet when it comes to content marketing. Each business has to find its own way.
- Understanding where you are in the content maturity model is important. You need to know where you are currently before making a decision about where you want to be.

EPIC RESOURCES

- *Skyfall*, directed by Sam Mendes (2012; Eon Productions).
- Jay Baer, *Youtility*, Portfolio/Penguin, 2013.
- Jeff Ernst, "It's Time to Take a Stand . . . in Your Marketing," *Jeff Ernst's Blog*, Forrester.com, June 7, 2011, http://blogs.forrester.com /jeff_ernst/11-06-07-its_time_to_take_a_stand_in_your_marketing.
- Tenon Tours, accessed March 18, 2013, http://www.tenontours.com/.

CHAPTER 8

What Is Epic Content Marketing?

*The first problem for us all, men and women,
is not to learn, but to unlearn.*

GLORIA STEINEM

Before we dive into what makes content marketing work, let's look at why your current content may not work for or benefit the business.

It's all about you. Remember, customers don't care about you; they care about themselves and their problems. We often forget that point when we describe how wonderful our widget is (that no one cares about). The more you talk about yourself and your products, the less that content is spread and engaged in.

You are afraid to fail. Taking chances with your content and experimenting a bit reveals the possibilities for your content marketing and uncovers new and valuable customer stories.

You are setting the bar too low. Your content marketing should be the very best in your industry—better than all your competitors' and better than that of the media and publishers in your space. How can you be the trusted expert in your industry if it is not?

You are not sourcing correctly. The majority of brands outsource some portion of the content marketing process. Don't be afraid to find internal content champions and outside journalists, writers, and content agencies to help you tell your story.

You are communicating in silos. Are you telling different stories in PR, corporate communications, social media, e-mail marketing, and other media? Do all departments follow a consistent corporate storyline? Epic content marketing means that your company is telling a consistent story.

You don't seek out discomfort. Seth Godin states in his book *Linchpin* that if you don't consistently step out of your comfort area, you are doomed to the status quo. Do something completely unexpected with your content from time to time.

There is no call to action. Every piece of content should have a call to action. If it doesn't, at least recognize it as such and the real purpose behind why you developed the content.

You are too focused on one particular channel. Stop thinking in terms of just e-mail newsletters or Facebook. Think about the problem you are solving for your customers. Then tell that story in different ways everywhere your customers seek out authoritative information.

You create a backup plan. There is only try and reiterate. Forget a backup plan. A backup plan (for example, pay-per-click or sponsorship) is admitting to failure before you begin.

There is no content owner. Someone in your organization (possibly you) must take ownership of the content marketing plan.

There is no C-level buy-in. Organizations without C-Level buy-in are 300 percent more likely to fail at content marketing than are companies with executive buy-in (according to CMI research).

You are not immersed in your industry. Everywhere your customers are, you need to be (whether it be online, in print, or in person).

You are not serving a defined niche enough. You need to be the leading expert in the world in your niche. Pick a content area that is both meaningful to your business and attainable.

You are too slow. As much as I hate to say it, speed beats perfection in most cases. Figure out a streamlined process for your storytelling.

Distribution of content is inconsistent. Your content marketing is a promise to your customers. Think about the morning paper (if you receive it): when it doesn't come on time, how upset are you? You need to have the same mindset with your content marketing. Distribute content consistently and *on time*. Develop your content marketing editorial calendar (see Chapter 14).

There is not enough thinking with search in mind. Most likely, the largest portion of your website traffic comes from search engines. If you create pieces of your content with search in mind, you stay focused on the problem and how customers communicate that problem. You also get found!

THE SIX PRINCIPLES OF EPIC CONTENT MARKETING

Perhaps you now think that there no longer is a need for sales-related content. That's far from the truth. The problem is that customers only need sales-related content at a very particular moment in the sales process. If you are honest about the content you have, your organization has plenty of feature- and benefit-related content. What you need are stories that engage your customers . . . and that move them to take action.

Now, before the principles of epic content marketing are reviewed, remember that the goal with content is to "move" the customer in some way. We marketers need to positively affect them, engage them, and do whatever we must to help stay involved in their lives and their conversations. The following are the six principles of epic content marketing: follow them closely.

Fill a need. You content should answer some unmet need of or question for your customer. It needs to be useful in some way to the customer, over and above what you can offer as a product or service.

Be consistent. The great hallmark of a successful publisher is consistency. Whether you subscribe to a monthly magazine or daily e-mail newsletter, the content needs to be delivered always on time and as expected. This is where so many companies fall down. Whatever you commit to in your content marketing, you must consistently deliver.

Be human. The benefits of not being a journalistic entity is that you have nothing to hold you back from being, well, you. Find what your voice is, and share it. If your company's story is all about humor, share that. If it's a bit sarcastic, that's okay too.

Have a point of view. This is not encyclopedia content. You are not giving a history report. Don't be afraid to take sides on matters that can position you and your company as an expert.

Avoid "sales speak." When we at Content Marketing Institute create a piece of content that is solely about us rather than for an educational purpose, it only garners *25 percent of the regular amount of page views and social shares* (see Figure 8.1). The more you talk about yourself, the less people will value your content.

Source: Content Marketing Institute

Figure 8.1 We at CMI want to publicize the company's Content Marketing Awards but are very aware that promotional posts are only shared at a 25 percent rate of normal, instructional posts.

Be best of breed. Although you might not be able to reach it at the very beginning, the goal for your content ultimately is to be best of breed. This means that, for your content niche, what you are distributing is the very best of what is found and is available. If you expect your customers to spend time with your content, you must deliver them amazing value.

EPIC CONTENT MARKETING IN ACTION

Think about the content sources that you rely on every day. What makes them so special? Do they provide information that you can't find anywhere else? Are they consistently delivered around the same day and time? Is there a particular point of view that you appreciate? Do they help you live a better life or grow at your career?

There are a number of content sources that I have "subscribed" to that have become part of my life:

- *Inc.* magazine (a media company): I actually get excited when this print publication comes in the mail. Frequency: monthly.
- Novels by P. J. Tracy (an author). Frequency: annually.
- Seth Godin's blog posts (an author). Frequency: daily.
- Reports from Fisher Investments (an investment firm). Frequency: quarterly.
- Posts from Copyblogger Media (a software company). Frequency: daily.

As a business, your goal is to become part of the content fabric for your customers. If you do, selling to them becomes relatively easy. For example, I will usually try any software product that Copyblogger Media releases. I trust the organization that much.

THE PERFECT CONTENT PRODUCT

Jason Calacanis talks often about what he believes is the perfect content product: real-time, fact-driven, visual, efficient, and curated. Let's review:

Real-time content. Does your content take advantage of current trends and news stories? Oreo was incredibly successful with its now infamous Super Bowl tweet "You Can Still Dunk in the Dark," which was timed perfectly with the blackout during the Ravens-49ers game. The image was retweeted more than 10,000 times and received free press from nearly every media company on the planet. While Oreo might have caught lightning in a bottle, the point is clear: those that can create content off the back of popular culture or industry news have a competitive advantage.

Fact-driven content. Regardless of your point of view, the content you develop must be based on fact. Just as in high school, when all of us used to cite our sources, leveraging credible statistics and information has never been more important. Almost every media company on the planet employs a fact checker: someone whose sole responsibility is to make sure what the company is saying is 100 percent correct.

If just one piece of content you release is incorrect, the social web will be relentless on your brand. Your job is to set processes in place so that this never happens.

Visual content. In late 2011, Skyword, a content marketing platform, did an analysis of all its customers' content. It found that blog posts and articles with images performed 91 percent better than those without them. Why does this happen? In a separate study sponsored by 3M, 90 percent of information transmitted through the brain is visual in nature, and visual content is processed 60,000 times faster than the written word.

So even with textual content, visual design is critical and should be a part of every piece of your content marketing.

Efficient content. When we at CMI first started our daily blog posts, it was just two people doing it: Michele Linn and myself. We did the best we could with the resources we had. Now almost four years later, Michele leads the strategy, Jodi Harris manages the daily content, Lisa Higgs proofs and checks the content, Tracy Gold reviews all our titles, and Mike Murray edits our meta tags for search engine optimization.

Over the years, we've been able to refine the process, bringing in experts in key areas, so that we are as efficient with our resources as possible.

Curated content. Pawan Deshpande, CEO of Curata, defines *content curation* as "the practice of finding, organizing, and sharing the best and most relevant content on a specific topic, rather than solely creating all their content themselves." Even the smartest media companies on the planet, such as the *Huffington Post*, the *Wall Street Journal*, and *Mashable*, originate stories leveraging other people's content. Your job, like the job of a museum curator, is to unearth the best content on the planet in your niche so that your museum doesn't close for lack of attendance.

THE EPIC CONTENT MARKETING PROCESS

Now that you understand what truly epic content is made of, it's your job to develop an organizational process for content marketing. As you'll see in the next few chapters, this process starts with the following:

- The goal or objective
- Defining the audience
- Understanding how the audience buys
- Choosing your content niche
- Developing your content marketing mission statement

This may seem like a lot for just a part of your marketing program (actually, it's not), but this is exactly what leading media companies do when they launch a magazine, newsletter, or television show. Since you are a publisher too, you need these steps as well. So many small and large companies start to develop content without a clear plan in place. I'm hoping this doesn't happen to you.

EPIC THOUGHTS

- If you want to be successful in content marketing, your goal should be to develop and distribute the absolute best information in your industry. If not, why should your customers care?
- What are the informational sources on which you rely? Why do you engage in them? What makes them special? Can you be on that list for your customers?

EPIC RESOURCES

- "Oreo's Super Bowl Tweet: 'You Can Still Dunk in the Dark,'" *Huffington Post*, February 4, 2013, http://www.huffingtonpost.com /2013/02/04/oreos-super-bowl-tweet-dunk-dark_n_2615333.html.
- Caleb Gonsalves, "Skyword Study: Add Images to Improve Content Performance," Skyword.com, October 11, 2011, http:// www.skyword.com/post/skyword-study-add-images-to-improve -content-performance/.
- Mike Parkinson, "The Power of Visual Communication," BillionDollarGraphics.com, accessed July 9, 2013, http://www .billiondollargraphics.com/infographics.html.
- Pawan Deshpande, "4 Content Curation Tips You Can Take from Brand Success Stories," ContentMarketingInstitute.com,

February 27, 2013, http://contentmarketinginstitute.com/2013/02/content-curation-tips-from-brand-success-stories/.

- Seth Godin, accessed April 2, 2013, http://sethgodin.typepad.com/.
- P. J. Tracy, accessed on April 2, 2013, http://www.pjtracy.net/.
- Fisher Investments, accessed March 13, 2013, http://www.fisher investments.com/.
- Copyblogger Media, accessed April 13, 2013. http://copyblogger .com.

CHAPTER 9

The Goal of Subscription

See the ball. Hit the ball.

CLINT EASTWOOD IN *TROUBLE WITH THE CURVE*

My favorite Michael Jordan/Nike commercial came out toward the end of his career. It's a 30-second spot of Jordan getting out of his car, walking past photographers, and going out a door. There's no flash and no game winning shot. It's just Michael . . . and then you hear his voice.

> I've missed more than 9,000 shots in my career. I've lost almost 300 games. Twenty-six times, I've been trusted to take the game winning shot and missed. I've failed over and over and over again in my life. And that is why I succeed.

The one thing that most people take from this commercial is that you have to try in order to succeed. But I think the meaning is so much deeper than that when applied to marketing and content goals.

ON SETTING GOALS

Success is easier to define for athletes (sorry, athletes). *There is usually a very distinct goal that an athlete is shooting for*: a championship, a gold medal, a specific time goal, or simply a game win. Michael Jordan always stated that his goal was to be the best basketball player to ever play the game. He measured that goal by winning the National Basketball

Association championship six times, including countless scoring titles and Most Valuable Player awards.

For us mere mortals, business owners and marketing managers, this is where we must start: we must have at least one tangible goal.

Michael Jordan knows when he's failed because he knows what his goal is. If a person doesn't have a goal, there cannot be failure. I believe that is why so many people don't set goals—they don't want to set themselves up for any failure in life. In some cases, the same is true for marketers.

Finding content goals that ultimately drive your business can be an excruciating process. *It takes passion, determination, and some soul searching to truly determine what kind of content you need to create that will have an immediate impact on your customer.*

But is there a goal for us marketers and business owners that we can identify that is the *Moneyball* of content marketing? (Note: In the 2003 book *Moneyball* by Michael Lewis, and subsequent movie with Brad Pitt, the success of the Oakland Athletics baseball team was reliant on one number. That number, which determined the overall value of a baseball player, was the on-base percentage.) Is there one overarching number, measure, or goal, like the number of championships won, that can drive our business?

THE BUSINESS GOALS OF CONTENT MARKETING

With content marketing, there are a number of possible business goals you can have. The following paragraphs show some of them, which make up key goals behind the content marketing buying funnel (see Figure 9.1).

BRAND AWARENESS OR REINFORCEMENT

Almost always the first thing that is thought of when you look at content marketing is brand awareness. The goal may be that you are just trying to find a more effective way than advertising to create awareness for your product or service. This is the long-tail strategy. Content marketing is a great vehicle for that, as it's organic, authentic, and a great way for you to start driving engagement with your brand.

LEAD CONVERSION AND NURTURING

How you define a lead will vary, but from a content marketing perspective lead conversion is where you have encouraged others, through the exchange of engaging content, to give up enough information about

The Content Marketing Funnel

Visitors
Leads
Opportunities
Sales

Customers   Customers

Satisfaction
Retention
Upsell
Evangelism

Source: Managing Content Marketing

Figure 9.1   The content marketing funnel takes into account the buying process before, during, and after the life cycle of a customer.

themselves that you now have permission to "market" to them. This information exchange can include signing up for a "demo," registering for an event, subscribing to your e-newsletter, or gaining access to your resource center. Once you have the prospect's permission, you can use content to help move him or her through the buying cycle.

CUSTOMER CONVERSION

In many cases, you already have a lot of content for customer conversion. We marketers have traditionally focused on this area—the "proof points" to the sale. Examples include case studies you send to your prospects that illustrate how you've solved the problem before, or a "testimonials" section on your client page. Ultimately, this is the content you've created as a marketer to illustrate to the hot prospect why your solution is better or will uniquely meet his or her needs.

CUSTOMER SERVICE

Content marketing can really earn its "subscribe" stripes with customer service. How well are you using content to create value or reinforce the customer's decision *after* the sale? This endeavor goes well beyond having a user manual, a documented process for success, and a "frequently asked questions" (FAQs) section on your website. These are the best practices for how to use your product or service. How can customers get the *most* out of your product or service? What are the successful, innovative ways that you've seen your product or service get extended into other solutions?

CUSTOMER LOYALTY AND RETENTION

Just as you have a planned lead nurturing process to turn prospects into customers, you also need a planned customer retention strategy. If your ultimate goal is to turn customers into passionate subscribers who share your stories, this area needs major attention. Options may be a customer e-newsletter or printed newsletter, a print or tablet magazine, or possibly a user event or webinar series.

CUSTOMER UPSELL

Marketing doesn't stop at the "checkout" button any longer. If you're particularly good at using content to service the customer in a subscribe model, you also have the opportunity to be effective at creating ongoing engagement for the other products and services you offer. Why stop communicating with prospects once they become customers? Instead, communicate with them more frequently (certainly not in a creepy way), and engage them with additional value. Customer upsell and customer retention goals can work hand in hand.

PASSIONATE SUBSCRIBERS

If you can successfully move customers to this stage, you have really accomplished something. Content—and especially content generated by satisfied customers—can be one of the most powerful ways to reach any business goal. This is when content marketing starts to work for you exponentially. CMI has over 40,000 active e-mail subscribers to our daily or weekly content. Those people have "opted in" to our content and have given us the permission to market to them. The majority of our revenue sources comes from that subscriber base. The business really started to take off once we started focusing on subscription as a key content marketing goal.

So which of these goals makes sense for your content marketing? Maybe it's only an inbound marketing initiative and you're just trying to help drive more leads into the sales and marketing process. Maybe you're trying to create a program that increases awareness, drives down the cost of organic traffic to your website, and increases your position with search engines. Maybe you are working to improve your customer retention rate. Take a moment now to get your mental juices flowing. Write down your content marketing goal, and put it up somewhere so that you see it every day.

SUBSCRIPTION

Great ideas often receive violent opposition from mediocre minds.
ALBERT EINSTEIN

Brian Clark and his software business Copyblogger Media have approximately 200,000 people signed up to get his regular content updates.

Kraft Foods has over one million people that request and pay to receive the company's print magazine, *Kraft Food & Family.*

OpenView Venture Partners has approximately 20,000 business owners and CEOs who request to receive the organization's weekly e-newsletter.

Two individuals known as Smosh started developing and distributing videos on YouTube back in 2005. Eight years later, Smosh runs the most popular YouTube channel with eight million subscribers.

Copyblogger sells software to bloggers. Kraft is one of the largest food companies in the world. OpenView is a venture capital company. Smosh is a comedy network. Even though the businesses couldn't be any more different from one another, subscription is key.

CONTENT AS AN ASSET

Do most marketing professionals view content marketing as an asset?

The answer is no—almost across the board. Marketers view spending on content marketing as an expense. *This has to change.*

First, a question: what is an asset?

According to *Investopedia*, an asset is "a resource with economic value that . . . [a] corporation . . . owns or controls with the expectation that it will provide future benefit." An asset, like a house or a stock investment, is a purchase that can increase in value over time.

Traditionally, marketing spend has been viewed as an expense. Take advertising: advertisers create the ad and distribute it over a fixed time, and then it's over. Hopefully, that expense has transferred into some brand value or direct sales exchange, but the event itself is over.

Content marketing is different; it needs to be viewed and treated differently.

ACQUIRING THE ASSET OF CONTENT

Whatever your goals—whether direct sales, lead generation, search engine optimization, or social media presence—you are spending money on content acquisition and distribution. For that reason alone, you need to think differently about acquiring content assets.

You are not acquiring content expenses. You are acquiring an asset!

THINKING LIKE A PUBLISHER

We are all publishers, and that means thinking differently about content and its importance to your organization.

When you invest in a video, a podcast, or a white paper, those pieces of content create value in a couple of significant ways.

One, *the finished content is used over a long period of time; it has shelf life.* The content you create has value long after the investment is paid off (fitting the definition of an asset; see Figure 9.2). An example is content created for search engine optimization. One blog post can deliver returns for years after production.

Two, *content can be and should be reimagined and repurposed.* You may start by investing in a video, but at the end of the year, that one video may result in 10 videos, 5 blog posts, 2 podcasts, and 30 sales tools fit for different levels of the buying cycle.

When you think like a publisher, everything you develop for publishing purposes is an asset. Having that mentality means that you need to think about all the resources that create and distribute that content differently. It's not about a marketing campaign; it's about creating long-term engagement with customers through epic content.

HOW DOES THINKING ABOUT CONTENT AS AN ASSET HELP?

Thinking in these terms will help you in a couple of ways.

If you treat content as an asset, people in your organization will *stop treating content as that "soft, fluffy thing" that they can take or leave.* In

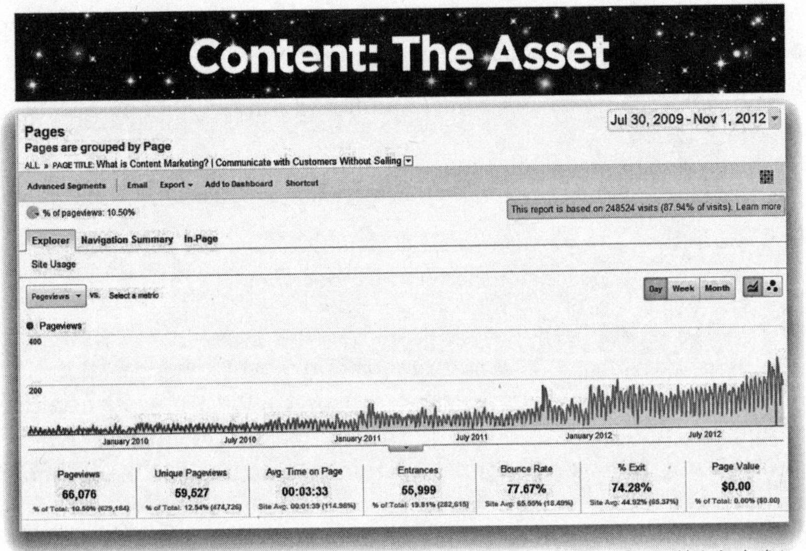

Source: Content Marketing Institute

Figure 9.2 CMI's "What Is Content Marketing?" blog post has consistently seen traffic for years (and averages over 200 visitors a day . . . just to that one post). This is the reason why we at CMI love to create "evergreen content" that can be relevant for years after creation.

every meeting or conversation you have, use the word *asset*. Live it. That effort will start to rub off, and content will gain importance in the company.

By thinking this way, you will more actively *market the asset*. I heard a story recently about a company that invested $30,000 in a white paper and received one download. That's a marketing problem, not a content problem. Would you plan to sell your house but not tell anyone about it? A lot of organizations do just that with their content: they produce the content but then don't let customers and prospects know it's available through basic paid and organic marketing (see Part IV of this book for more on marketing your stories). Make sure you don't make that mistake.

We need to elevate the practice of content marketing.

BEGIN WITH THE END IN MIND

In 2008, the Content Marketing Institute was just a year old. We had around 3,000 subscribers to our weekly e-newsletter, which was sent out each Friday. As we were becoming more sophisticated with our marketing, we decided to do an analysis of our subscribers. What we found about the average CMI subscriber both surprised and delighted us:

- The subscriber was more likely to attend our events and purchase our products.
- The subscriber was more likely to share our content with his or her network.
- Once in the sales process (for our consulting service), the subscriber closed three times faster than a nonsubscriber.

We at CMI had the goals of brand awareness, lead generation, and thought leadership, just as your organization most likely does. But what we didn't realize until this analysis was that we could accomplish a number of marketing goals through the one, unified goal of subscription.

We found that by developing epic content marketing on a consistent basis, we were creating better customers for our business as well as accomplishing a number of marketing goals.

Our understanding of the value of our subscribers turned our little business from something that was just surviving into a brand that was thriving and growing. It's that important.

THE DIGITAL FOOTPRINT

In 2009, I had the pleasure of hearing a speech by Dan McCarthy, then CEO of Network Communications and now a partner with DeSilva & Phillips, a leading media investment bank. Dan spoke about the changing mentality of his media company and how it had expanded its definition of *subscription*.

Subscription, for most media companies, is better known as *circulation*. The circulation of a magazine or newsletter is what you can sell against. For example, CMI's magazine, *Chief Content Officer*, is delivered to 22,000 marketing executives every quarter. This 22,000 (the number of executives reached) is the figure on which we base the amount we charge our sponsors (generally around $7,000 per full-page advertisement). If we only had an audience of 10,000, we would have to charge much less for a full page of advertising.

Dan said that his media company was evolving away from this mentality and focusing on subscription where customers were hanging out—in other words, the "digital footprint."

Owned subscription sources (for example, print and e-mail) are still primary, because content originators (a.k.a. publishers) can actually own the data from those channels. Secondary subscription sources, such as

Twitter followers or YouTube subscribers, are important as well, but since that data is owned by other companies (and not by the originators of the content), you can't place as high an emphasis on those.

You are your own media company. As a media company, you need to focus on your subscription channels in order to deliver on your marketing goals. And the only thing that keeps those subscription channels growing and vibrant is consistent amounts of epic content.

Here are some tips to drive subscription:

- **Make content-for-content offers.** As readers are engaging in your content, be sure you have a clear offer that takes your content to the next level. This means offering a valued e-book, research report, or white paper in exchange for subscribing to your e-mail list.
- **Pop-ups work.** As much as I loathe pop-ups or pop-overs as a reader, I *love* them as a content marketer. At CMI, we use Pippity as our pop-over service, where we offer an e-book on *100 Content Marketing Examples.* Over 50 percent of our daily sign-ups come from Pippity. (Pippity also integrates nicely with WordPress, our content management system.)
- **Focus.** So many companies want to throw 100 offers in front of their readers. Don't confuse the issue. If your goal is subscription, that should be your main (and only) call to action.

Once you focus on subscription as your goal, *make it a priority to find out what makes a subscriber different to your business than a non-subscriber.* Once you find that thing that makes a subscriber truly unique, everything will start coming together for your content marketing program.

EPIC THOUGHTS

- As a content marketer, don't create content for content's sake; do it because you want your business to grow. Focusing on your objectives is key.
- Stop thinking about your marketing as an expense. Invest in assets that will continually grow the business over the long term. If you look at marketing more like renewable energy, it makes all the difference in your planning.

EPIC RESOURCES

- Michael Jordan "Failure" Nike Commercial, YouTube.com, uploaded August 26, 2006, http://www.youtube.com/watch?v=45mMioJ5szc.

- Kraft Food & Family Magazine Archive, accessed June 11, 2013, http://www.kraftrecipes.com/foodfamilyarchive/magarchive /magazine_archive.aspx.
- SMOSH, accessed March 22, 2013, http://www.smosh.com/.
- Joe Pulizzi, "The 7 Business Goals of Content Marketing: Inbound Marketing Isn't Enough," ContentMarketingInstitute.com, November 11, 2011, http://contentmarketinginstitute.com/2011/11 /content-marketing-inbound-marketing/.
- Pippity.com, accessed April 2, 2013.

CHAPTER 10

The Audience Persona

The true delight is in the finding out rather than in the knowing.

ISAAC ASIMOV

Repeat this sentence: I am not the target for my content. This thought is critical as you go through this chapter. Business owners and marketers tend to bend their content to their thinking. Don't fall into this trap.

If you are thinking and acting like a media company and publisher, everything you do with your content marketing will begin and end with your audience. If you do not understand the wants and needs of your audience, there is no way you can be successful with your content.

Most of the time, marketers think that their content audiences are the same as their buying audiences. For example, John Deere distributes the *Furrow* magazine to farmers. These farmers are the same people that buy John Deere equipment. But, for your situation, your direct buying audience may not be the same as the audience for your content.

Let's use a university as an example. It has many audiences: some are buyers, some are influencers, and some are stakeholders. The first, most likely audience, are the students. But there are also parents, who help support and fund the students. And there are alumni. Don't forget the teachers. What about local, state, and federal government? Depending on the goal of your content program, you could target dozens of different audiences.

So before you start any content program, you need to have a clear understanding of who the audience is and ultimately what you want them to do.

WHY ARE AUDIENCE PERSONAS IMPORTANT?

An audience persona is a helpful tool to use as part of your content marketing plan. It's the "who" you are talking to and with.

When content is developed for your content marketing program, it is the persona that gives context. At any one time, you may have employees, freelance writers, agencies, and even outside bloggers creating content for you. *The persona keeps everyone on the same page with who is being talked to and why the communication matters for the business.*

MULTIPLE PERSONAS

You're going to need one persona for every group for whom you create content. In other words, if one person goes through a different buying process than another, you need a different persona for each one. Is that process different for a man than a woman? That depends: if you are selling jewelry, the answer is yes; if you are selling marketing automation software, the answer is no.

But don't get overwhelmed. If you are just getting started with content marketing, you may start with just one or two personas. For example, if you are selling air-conditioning servicing and equipment, you may start with one main audience persona: the woman of the household (who makes most of the decisions about heating, ventilating, and air-conditioning). Once you are comfortable with that person and with creating content for her, you can move on to the next audience.

PUT YOUR JOURNALIST HAT ON

What do you need to know about your persona? The easiest way to find out is by asking the following questions.

1. Who is he or she? How does this person live the average day?
2. What's the person's need? This is not "Why does (s)he need our product or service?" but "What are his or her informational needs and pain points as it relates to the stories we will tell?"

3. Why does this person care about us? Remember, the persona most likely doesn't care about your products or services, so it's the information provided to him or her that will make that person care or garner attention.

Your audience persona doesn't have to be perfect, but it needs to be detailed enough so that your content creators have a clear understanding of whom they are engaging.

A SAMPLE PERSONA FOR A CONSUMER FINANCIAL SERVICES COMPANY: ELITE EDDIE (WEALTHY PERSONA FOR FINANCIAL COMPANY)

Eddie is 42 years old, has been married for 17 years, and has two teenage daughters (Dar, 16, and Mary, 14). Eddie, now an executive vice president with a large international firm, has amassed quite a nest egg.

Eddie travels the world as part of his job (accruing 200,000 travel miles last year), and he also enjoys as much as possible traveling to the islands off Croatia on holidays. Wherever Eddie goes, his BlackBerry keeps him up to date with the office, although for the past few months he's been thinking about switching to an iPhone or Samsung Galaxy. Golf is Eddie's definition of living.

Over the past few weeks, Eddie has been working to consolidate his finances with one provider; he has made steps in that direction by recently developing a trust for his family. Eddie is consistently concerned that he makes the right decision so that over the long term his family is taken care of.

COMMON MISTAKES WHEN CREATING PERSONAS

Adele Revella, founder of the Buyer Persona Institute, is perhaps the leading expert on the creation and implementation of personas. In her e-book *The Buyer Persona Manifesto* she defines the persona as "a composite picture of the real people who buy, or might buy, products like the ones you market, based on what you've learned in direct interviews with real buyers."

The following are Adele's four key persona mistakes and how to fix each one.

MISTAKE NUMBER 1: MAKING UP STUFF ABOUT BUYERS

Marketers typically gather facts about buyers by talking to a sales representative, meeting with a product expert, or conducting online research.

It shouldn't be surprising that these sources don't have the information that marketers really need. Sales reps will readily admit that buyers mislead or even lie about how they compare and choose one solution over another. Moreover, even product experts are unlikely to be buyer experts, since they interact mostly with current customers as well as a select few big prospects. And mining online data leads to personas that are little more than job descriptions with high-level pain points.

If content marketing is going to benefit from persona development, it needs to uncover specific insights unknown to your competitors or anyone inside your company. This information is so valuable that you would never post it on your website. However, it will tell you, with surprising accuracy, exactly what you need to do to deliver content that persuades buyers to choose you.

How to fix this mistake. The only way to gather clear, unexpected insights about how your buyers make decisions is *to have a conversation with them.* Make it a goal to spend a few hours a month interviewing recent buyers, including those who chose you and those who did not. Ask buyers to walk you through their decision, starting with the moment they decided to solve this problem. Each in-depth conversation should take 20 or 30 minutes, but the time it will save you in planning, writing, and revising content will be immeasurable.

MISTAKE NUMBER 2: GETTING SIDETRACKED BY IRRELEVANT TRIVIA

Marketers sometimes make the mistake of gathering buyer information that doesn't really help them deliver more effective content or campaigns. If your marketing team is debating whether your buyer persona is a man or a woman, or if you are bogged down finding just the right stock image of your persona, then you are focusing on the wrong things. Unless you're a business-to-consumer (B2C) marketer, the buyer's gender, marital status, and hobbies are rarely relevant.

How to fix this mistake. You may decide to include other data in your buyer personas, but content marketers really need only five insights:

1. **Priority initiatives.** What are the three to five problems to which your buyer persona dedicates time, budget, and political capital?
2. **Success factors.** What are the tangible or intangible metrics or rewards that the buyer associates with success, such as "grow revenue by X" or a promotion?
3. **Perceived barriers.** What factors can prompt the buyer to question whether your company and its solution can help with achieving his or her success factors? This is when you begin to uncover unseen factors, such as competing interests, politics, or prior experiences with your company or a similar company.
4. **Buying process.** What process does this persona follow in exploring and selecting a solution that can overcome the perceived barriers and achieve his or her success factors?
5. **Decision criteria.** What aspects of each product will the buyer assess in evaluating the alternative solutions available? To be useful, the decision criteria should include insights from both a buyer who chose a competitor and one who decided not to buy a solution at all.

These "Five Rings of Insight," when gathered directly from buyer interviews, will tell you how to reach undecided buyers with content that addresses their key decision-making process points. Using the Buyer Persona Profile and Five Rings of Buying Insight (go to EpicContentMarketing.com's bonus resources page to access this template) will help you organize your findings from your calls so that everyone on your team has access to these critical insights.

MISTAKE NUMBER 3: DEVELOPING TOO MANY BUYER PERSONAS

This mistake happens when marketers layer buyer personas onto their existing market segments, frequently defined by demographics such as industry or company size. Many people think they should create a new buyer persona for each of the relevant job titles in each of these segments. Not so.

One company I worked with initially planned to build 24 different buyer personas. Ambitious? Yes. Necessary? No. When they started interviewing their buyers, they were able to pare that list down to 11. Because their marketers are continually conducting new buyer interviews and gaining new insights, they expect to consolidate that list even further.

How to fix this mistake. When you have captured the Five Rings of Insight about buyers, you will see that differences in job titles, company size, and industry do not necessarily relate to differences in your insights. For content marketing and most other marketing decisions, you only need a separate persona when there is a significant difference on several of those findings. For example, you may find that buyers of your RFID (radio-frequency identification) technology in both the hospitality and consumer products industries have nearly identical priority initiatives (a mandate to be more competitive) and perceived barriers (an incremental approach is needed). If you have a strong story to communicate on each of these points, one persona may be the best way to ensure effective messaging and content marketing.

MISTAKE NUMBER 4:
CONDUCTING SCRIPTED QUESTION-AND-ANSWER INTERVIEWS WITH BUYERS

Using a telephone script or online survey to learn about your buyers won't reveal anything you don't already know—inevitably, your buyer's first answer to any question is something obvious, high level, and not particularly useful. The structure imposed by surveys and scripts leads to nice charts, but it fails to reveal the new insights that you need.

How to fix this mistake. It takes a bit of practice, but you can learn how to have the unscripted, agenda-driven conversations that will lead recent buyers to tell you, in incredible detail, exactly how they weighed their options and compared your solutions with your competitors' offerings.

The key to success is asking probing questions based on your buyers' answers. For example, if buyers tell you they chose you because your solution is easy to use, you might ask follow-up questions to understand why the solution needed to be so. Or you might ask about what training the buyers expect to attend before the solution is considered to be "easy" in their minds. Another follow-up question might seek perspectives on the resources the buyers will consult, or steps they will take, to compare your solution's ease of use to their other options.

When you avoid these four mistakes, your buyers' needs will be the focus of your marketing strategies and tactics. You'll become so attuned to your buyers' perspective that you will consistently impress them, confidently delivering content that answers their questions and persuades them to choose you.

SETTING UP LISTENING POSTS

I started in the publishing industry in February 2000 at Penton Media. I learned what great storytelling was all about from my mentor, Jim McDermott. Jim constantly talked about the importance of "listening posts." Listening posts are all about getting as much feedback from a variety of sources as possible so you can find the truth.

Setting up listening posts is critical for all editors, journalists, reporters, and storytellers to make sure they truly know what is going on in the industry. For you, listening posts are critical so that you have accurate audience personas and truly understand the "pain" they are going through on a daily basis. All of us need listening posts to truly discover our customers' needs. The following are all means of getting feedback from customers—in effect, functioning as listening posts.

1. **One-on-one conversations.** As in Adele Revellas's key point, nothing can replace talking to your customers or audience directly.
2. **Search of keywords.** Using tools such as Google Trends and Google Alerts to track what customers are searching for and where they are hanging out on the web.
3. **Web analytics.** Whether you use Google Analytics or another provider such as Omniture, diving into your web analytics is key. Finding out what content your customers are engaging in (and what they aren't) can make all the difference to your success.
4. **Social media listening**. Whether through LinkedIn groups or Twitter hashtags and keywords, you can easily find out what your customers are sharing, talking about, and struggling with in their lives and jobs.
5. **Customer surveys.** Survey tools like SurveyMonkey can easily be deployed to gather key insights into your customers' informational needs.

SAMPLES OF AUDIENCE PERSONAS

We at the Content Marketing Institute (CMI) have six different personas that we target with our content programs. I have included the summaries here for helpful reference. Note: CCO stands for *Chief Content Officer* magazine; CMW stands for Content Marketing World (our event) attendee.

CMI PERSONA SUMMARY

20-Something Susan: Marketing Associate
- *CMI relationship*: CMI/CCO reader, CMW attendee, potential blogger for CMI

30-Something Ben: Marketing Manager
- *CMI relationship*: CMI/CCO reader, CMW attendee

30-Something Jim: Marketing VP
- *CMI relationship*: Influencer promoting CMI, CMI/CCO contributor and reader, CMW speaker.

40-Something Lisa: Marketing Director
- *CMI relationship*: Influencer promoting CMI, CMI/CCO contributor and reader, CMW speaker

40-Something Robert: Marketing Consultant
- *CMI relationship*: Influencer promoting CMI, CMI/CCO contributor and reader, CMW speaker

50-Something Brian: Chief Marketing Officer
- *CMI relationship*: Influencer promoting CMI, CMI/CCO contributor and reader, CMW attendee

ONLINE-ONLY BONUS SECTION: For a complete breakout of each of these buyer personas, go to EpicContentMarketing.com's bonus resources section to download the details.

HELPFUL TOOL

MLT Creative and Ardath Albee have built a helpful persona creation tool at upcloseAndPersona.com. It's free and can help guide you through the persona-building process.

EPIC THOUGHTS

- As you grow as a content marketer, you'll have many, perhaps dozens or more on your team creating content. Audience personas get all contributors on the same page.

- Almost certainly, you have multiple personas that purchase your products or services. It can get complicated. Start with the most important persona for your content plan.

EPIC RESOURCES

- Adele Revella, "Developing a Buyer Persona? Avoid These 4 Common Mistakes," ContentMarketingInstitute.com, August 23, 2012, http://contentmarketinginstitute.com/2012/08/4-common-persona-mistakes-to-avoid/.
- Buyer Persona Institute, accessed March 22, 2013, http://www.buyerpersona.com.
- Up Close and Persona, accessed March 22, 2013, http://www.upcloseandpersona.com.

CHAPTER 11

Defining the Engagement Cycle

They say that time changes things,
but you actually have to change them yourself.

ANDY WARHOL

Creating an engagement cycle for your content is incredibly difficult. Most smaller businesses never even try to tackle it at all. But it's important ... very important.

DOES ANYONE CARE ABOUT YOUR SALES PROCESS?

Simply put, the engagement cycle is a combination of your internal sales process and how you have defined the customer's buying cycle. If your goal is to (try to) deliver the right content at the right time for your customers and subscribers, you need to understand how both work together in harmony. Without a defined engagement cycle, you are just creating lots of content and hoping for the best.

Just as in real life when you meet someone, determining what you want to say to a persona is a combination of two things: content (which is a function of your point of view) and context (you have to determine the correct time and place to start the right conversation).

The traditional way of advertising is to take your point of view and blast out the message to (it is hoped) a target group for your product or service. The theory goes that if you blast loud enough, long enough, and in the general direction of our personas, eventually you will reach some of them. While advertising still works, there is always a lot of waste—it may not be done at the right time, in the right place, with the right content, and so on. The buying process has changed. The consumers now control the engagement with you; they control when and if they want to receive your message. It's up to you to have a relevant conversation with them from the very first time you meet.

But the reality is you can't be prepared to have *every* conversation about your product or service at any time. No matter how many resources your organization may have, it's almost impossible to prepare for every scenario where you will be talking with a customer or prospect.

Additionally, when consumers have access to information at every moment, the customer buying process can be chaotic and nonlinear. In the past, when there were very few sources for consumers to get buying information, a business could predict, with some certainty, how a customer learned about the need for a product. That gave businesses a lot of control over how they marketed their products.

This is why, historically, marketers developed a sales process (or funnel) so that we might put some order to this chaos and have common language in our business for the categories of sales opportunities. Depending on your business, you may categorize your consumers as "visitors," "leads," "prospects," or "readers"—and, ultimately, "customers" or "members."

If your organization is like most, even if you don't have a formal sales process, to some degree you try to deliver a relevant message to the customer during the sales process. For example, if you're selling widgets online, you may always try to cross-sell and upsell *after* the users have put items into their shopping carts. If you're selling big-ticket items, your salespeople probably have a well-defined funnel through which pass leads (leads, prospects, qualified, and so on), and they give out case studies and testimonials after they've become "qualified."

But today businesses are trying not only to create a "customer" but also to create subscribers who actually want to engage in the companies' content. And while it's important for you to internally map your content to your sales process, you must remember that whether it's your shopping cart experience, a traditional lead-nurturing sales funnel, or conversion of customers into evangelists that love to talk about your company, this sales process is an internal and artificial process that you superimpose on the customers' buying experience.

Your buyers don't care one bit about your sales process. The sales funnel does not capture the emotional and realistic decision points that the buyers go through during their "buying process." And in fact, the goal or call to action may *not* be to have the "customers" purchase anything at all. Instead, it may be to have them "refer a new customer" or "share their story."

THE ENGAGEMENT CYCLE

To deliver the best content at the right time, you need a better, more granular process. You need to combine your internal sales process with your customer's "buying" process and develop something new . . . something I call the "engagement cycle."

An engagement cycle is a defined process that your audiences go through as you help them increasingly engage with your brand. The engagement cycle is not perfect, but it can help with the development of compelling content at certain stages of the buying process that either aids the prospect in buying or assists the customer in spreading your content. In short, you need to be working hard to deliver the right conversations at the right time.

Let's look at each of the processes separately before we layer them together.

MAP YOUR AUDIENCE PERSONAS TO YOUR SALES PROCESS

The sales process is how you watch the consumer proceed through your sales and marketing efforts. Your funnel might be very well organized— as in the case of enterprise B2B marketing or considered purchases in B2C sales (for example, a car or house). In these cases there are very defined and tight conversion layers where each stage is defined by the consumer behavior (lead, prospect, qualified, and so on).

However, if you run an online retail or brick-and-mortar shop, you might have looser or more generalized sales processes. One process might involve the following progression: visitor, browser, shopper, to buyer; interestingly, these stages might happen within seconds. Or, if you're a publisher, the funnel might be visitor to subscriber. Many publishers just have a goal of creating a subscriber, whom they then use to monetize through advertising or upselling. Regardless of the time involved or the name for it, the sales cycle is how we content marketers identify those customers who:

- Know nothing about us
- Then know something about us
- Then are interested in what we have to offer
- Then compare us to other solutions
- Then do what we want them to do

For example, if you are a small business software company targeting IT decision makers, you have a fairly simple sales funnel process, which involves the following:

- **Contacts.** These are people whom you've contacted or with whom you have some level of introduction.
- **Leads.** These are people you've identified who have an active interest in your solution.
- **Qualified opportunities.** You have qualified leads having interest and a budget and from whom a purchase of some kind is likely.
- **Finalists.** These are qualified opportunities with people who have pared down their list to one or two options and who have your company in the mix.
- **Verbal agreement.** You are the chosen solution and in the negotiation process.

Your sales funnel may be more (or less) complex than that, or it may be completely different. But regardless of its complexity, you should have *some* kind of funnel for your business that tries to make sense of buying patterns.

THE CONTENT SEGMENTATION GRID

Simply put, the content segmentation grid is a mash-up of your sales process and the content you have that moves customers through that process. Why is this grid so important?

I'm sure you've seen companies, possibly competitors, create lots of content and throw it anywhere they possibly can. While this can and has worked in the past, it's not much different from "spray-and-pray" advertising. Developing a content segmentation grid minimizes the possibility that your content doesn't work and also provides you with clear opportunities to capture feedback and make improvements.

Now to build the content segmentation grid. You'll do this along two axes. The first axis is the personas and the second is the sales funnel.

Once you have your grid, start filling in the cells with your existing or new content items (you can choose from among the types in Chapter 16). Going back to the software example, your content segmentation grid might look something like Figure 11.1.

Content Segmentation Grid

		SALES	CONTACTS	LEADS		QUALIFIED		FINALIST	VERBAL
PERSONAS	Ben Marketing Manager	White Paper 1 White Paper 2	Blog Subscription			Online Assessment	Webinar	Case Study 1 Case Study 2	
	Haley CMO	White Paper 3		Magazine		Online Assessment			

Figure 11.1   **The content segmentation grid in action.**

One thing you may notice in this example is that most of the content marketing is focused at the top of the funnel. This is almost universally common, so don't worry if this is true for you as well. A content marketing strategy always starts by focusing on awareness and education, which is almost inevitably at the top of the funnel.

One benefit of this exercise is that it often reveals that the content marketing is either very light or very heavy on one stage or one persona. The middle of the content segmentation grid, often called the "messy middle," is usually where one needs to develop fresh content to fill in the gaps.

Once you are armed with your content segmentation grid, you are ready to take the next step, which is to layer in each audience persona's buying process.

MAP YOUR PERSONAS TO THEIR BUYING CYCLE

The buying process is how your customers buy from you or, once they've bought, what you want them to do next. What's their process? For your product or service it might vary by product—or by persona—but what you want to do is map out how your customers buy from you. Figure 11.2 shows the customer's buying cycle for the IT software example.

The buying cycle is represented as an orbit because it's usually not a linear process. In fact, during the buying process consumers often jump in and out of orbits as they move closer in. But as consumers move closer to the center of gravity, the focus on what they want becomes more pronounced and what they're looking at becomes more limited as they go through each phase. So, for example with the IT software solution, each phase looks as follows:

- **Awareness.** The consumers are trying to figure out what options exist.
- **Information search.** Now the consumers are searching for information and finding solutions for their problems; this may be the first time you get a phone call.

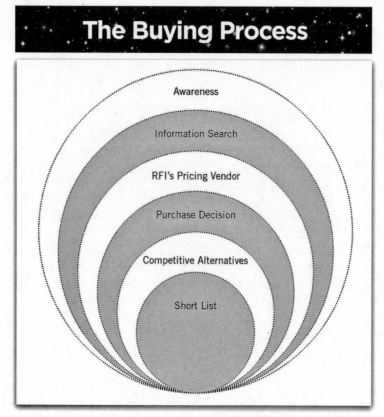

Figure 11.2 The buying process orbit.

- **Request for pricing/vendor information.** You have been identified. Ask yourself: "What makes us better? What is our pricing for this solution?"
- **Purchase decision.** This is not always the last step. People often go through researching a solution to their needs and then decide to *not* make a purchase. But those who do decide to make purchase will go back to vendors and do a final comparison.
- **Competitive alternatives.** The online searches begin. Have you ever gotten a call from consumers who seem to be late in their process? This is where they are. This is the feature comparison stage. In many cases, consumers may be surprised by what's missing (or what's there) and may go all the way back out to the awareness stage.
- **Short list.** At this stage the solutions are looked at very closely and then a contract for the sale is presented.

Again, this is not perfect, but mapping this out is an invaluable exercise.

CREATE THE CUSTOMER/CONTENT SEGMENTATION GRID

Now the sales process has been outlined and laid out side by side with the buying process, you can better understand the engagement cycle by mashing these together with your content assets.

As you see in Figure 11.3, the sales funnel is mapped with contacts turning into leads, then being qualified, and then going to finalist (or short list). But then, under that, the buying process, awareness/education, and so forth are mapped.

Notice: there's overlap with the sales funnel and the buying process. There are actually a lot more conversion layers—or decision points— through the buying process than in the sales funnel. But this gives you a way to start to get a common vocabulary and a common way to map out a content marketing strategy.

You may find, for example, a lot of content developed for leads that are in the "Awareness/Education" stage but not a lot of content for leads that are in the "Information Search" stage. This tells you that you may want to spend additional time developing content that not only educates the audience to the benefits of your type of solution but also positions your company as a provider of it.

Don't get overwhelmed with this process; it's not a requirement to go to this extent. And you certainly don't have to develop content segmentation grids for every product, process, or audience persona. You may only do it for the process to which your new content marketing initiative is directed. Or perhaps you only need to do it to help move customers to evangelists that love you and will actively share everything about you and your company.

Content Segmentation Grid with Buying Cycle

	SALES	CONTACTS	LEADS		QUALIFIED		FINALIST	VERBAL
	Buying Cycle	Awareness & Education	Information Search Vendor	RFI Vendor Information	Make the Purchase Decision	Alternative Searches	Short List of Vendors	Agreement
PERSONAS Ben Marketing Manager		White Paper 1 White Paper 2	Blog Subscription		Online Assessment	Webinar	Case Study 1 Case Study 2	
Haley CMO		White Paper 3		Magazine		Online Assessment		

Figure 11.3   The content segmentation grid combined with the buying process.

In the end, creating an engagement cycle and mapping that with your personas to create a complete content segmentation grid is a powerful way to see where there are gaps in your story.

EPIC THOUGHTS

- Your sales process (internal) has nothing to do with how your customers buy (external).
- The easiest course is to populate your content grid with lots of content at the top of the funnel. This is a completely natural impulse, but the opportunities may lie in the "messy middle," where customers need a little push to get close to that buying decision.
- Don't get stuck on this part of the process. If you feel you aren't ready, move on to Chapters 12 and 13, which deal with the content niche and the content marketing mission. Honestly, most companies don't map their content to the buying process (which is why there is such an opportunity here).

EPIC RESOURCES

- Robert Rose and Joe Pulizzi, *Managing Content Marketing*, Cleveland: CMI Books, 2011.

CHAPTER 12

Defining Your Content Niche

If you want to make an apple pie from scratch, you must first create the universe.

DR. CARL SAGAN, ASTRONOMER

As part of CMI's content marketing workshops for small businesses, I normally ask the following question:

On what topic can you be the leading informational expert in the world?

Brands don't take their content seriously enough. Sure, they create content in dozens of channels for multiple marketing objectives. But is your organization's *mindset* focused on being the leading provider of information for your customers? If not, why isn't that your priority?

Your customers and prospects can get their information from anywhere to make buying decisions. Why shouldn't that information come from you? Shouldn't that at least be the goal?

GETTING UNCOMFORTABLE WITH YOUR NICHE

One of my favorite parts of *The 10x Rule* by Grand Cardone is on *setting uncomfortable goals:* "Those who succeed were—at one point or another in their lives—willing to put themselves in situations that were uncomfortable, whereas the unsuccessful seek comfort from all their decisions."

The same goes for your content marketing goals. Your ultimate objectives . . . those big hairy audacious goals (BHAGs), should make you cringe at least a little bit.

I *completely disagree* with marketing experts and consultants who say it's not necessary to be the leading information provider for your industry.

Yes, it is a bit audacious to go out on a limb and clearly state that your content marketing should be an irreplaceable resource for your customers . . . that you are indeed driving where the market is going from an information standpoint (like a media company). That said, be audacious!

If you are not striving to be the go-to number one resource for your industry niche, *you are settling for the comfortable*, whatever that means to you in goal-setting terms.

WHAT IF YOUR CONTENT WAS GONE?

Let's say someone rounded up all your marketing and placed it in a box, as if it never existed. *Would anyone miss it? Would you leave a gap in the marketplace?*

If the answer to this is no, *then you've got a problem.*

You should have customers and prospects needing—no, *longing for—* your content. It ought to become part of their lives and their jobs.

Makes you a bit uncomfortable, right? Darn straight.

What will you and your content marketing team have to do to reach that goal? What unique, audacious content creation, distribution, and syndication will you have to get involved in to truly be the leading resource?

This is your turf. Don't stand there and let your informational competitors steal time away from your customers.

THE TRUSTED EXPERT

If you truly have a product or story that is worthy of being talked about (if you don't, you have bigger problems than content marketing), then *becoming the trusted expert in your industry is central to you selling more on a consistent basis.*

Today, it's harder and harder to buy attention. You have to earn it. Earn it today, tomorrow, and five years from now by delivering the most impactful information your customers could ever ask for. Set the uncomfortable goals that will take your business to the next level.

THINKING BIG, GOING SMALL

Let's say you run a small pet supplies store in the local community. You think your content niche is pet supplies. You're wrong!

Think about this for a second: is it possible to be the leading expert in the niche area of pet supplies? Probably not. Companies such as Petco and PetSmart put millions behind that concept.

That means even though you want to think big with your goals, your actual content niche needs to be small. How small? As small as possible.

Let's go back to the pet store example. By looking at the key audience personas, you've noticed that the most questions, as well as your highest margin products, are around aging pet owners who like to travel with their pets. Bingo! While you can't be the leading expert in just pet supplies, you can be the leading expert in pet supplies for elderly pet owners that travel around the country with their pets.

But let's break this down even more by using Google Trends. The trending for "traveling with pets" has been steadily going down over the past eight years. This means that fewer people are searching for that exact topic. Now if you click on the "Rising" tab to see search terms that are performing ahead of the pack, you'll find that flying with pets, traveling with cats, and traveling with dogs are all breakout terms (see Figure 12.1).

While not an exact science, you can use search trends to identify content opportunities for your niche area.

HOW WE CHOSE CONTENT MARKETING AS OUR CONTENT NICHE?

I launched what is now the Content Marketing Institute in April 2007. Even though I've used the term "content marketing" on and off for the previous six years, back then it was still a very young term.

The dominant industry term used to be "custom publishing." From my conversations with senior marketing executives (one of CMI's target audiences), I could tell that that term was not something that resonated with them. But was there an opportunity for content marketing?

I started to tinker with the Google Trends tool in looking at a variety of phrase variations. Here is what I found.

"Custom publishing." If this was a stock phrase, we at CMI definitely wouldn't want to own it. Every year people searched for this term less

Figure 12.1 Hunting for "breakout terms" in Google Trends can give some insight into what the hot topics are for your customer base.

often. In addition, many of the articles referred not to our idea of brands creating content, but to customized print books. This confusion was a problem.

"Custom content." This was a rising term, but again we found some confusing results. We found "custom content" used as a description for a software bundle in the popular *SimCity* game. This was a big warning if we were trying to cut through the clutter and bumping into irrelevant searches.

"Content marketing." The term didn't even register on Google Trends. I began to think that if enough of the right content was created, a movement around the term could be started. With confusion around the other terms, it was likely that the industry needed a new term around which to rally key thought leaders together. In addition, without a clear leader in the "content marketing" group, we at CMI could move quickly and gain search market share if we did it correctly. As you can see in Figure 12.2, this strategy paid off.

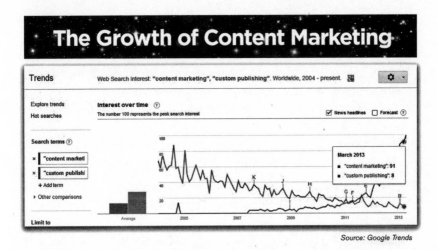

Figure 12.2 Which stock would you like to own: content marketing or custom publishing?

So, a combination of talking to our audience, as well as using free tools like Google Trends, helped colleagues and I at CMI to define our content niche.

FRACTAL MARKETING

Your content niche can actually target an audience of one. Andrew Davis, author of the book *Brandscaping*, defines a concept called "fractal marketing" as repeatedly splitting your customer into a more specific niche. In this way, he develops a more defined content niche to a smaller population of valuable customers. Andrew has used this technique to perfection over the years. Here are two examples.

Early in his career, Drew wanted to work at the Jim Henson Company. There were two problems: Drew had limited experience, and he had no connections at the Jim Henson Company. The solution? Drew wrote a letter every month for three years until the company finally yielded and hired him full-time.

More recently, Drew has been on a crusade to help fix the newspaper industry. He believes that there is one person on the face of the earth who can help with his effort, the one and only billionaire philanthropist Warren Buffett.

On his "Letters 2 Warren" Tumblr page reads the following: "My goal: sit down with Warren Buffett and Terry Kroeger to revitalize the newspaper industry. My method: A hand-written letter a week."

Drew's original note on December 17, 2012, reads:

Mr. Buffett,

I do hope you're having a wonderful holiday season! As I embark on my quest to revolutionize the Newspaper industry, I can't help but believe that the most under-utilized resource at newspapers today is the power of the individual journalist to build an audience and drive demand for the content they create. Let's change the way brands build an audience!

—Andrew Davis

On March 12, 2013, Drew updated his page with a following note to his readers:

I'm pleased to let you all know that I've received confirmation that Mr. Buffett is receiving and reading my letters.

Last night, Carol Loomis, the author of *Tap Dancing To Work* (which I referred to in last week's letters), called me to clarify her working arrangement with Fortune, Time Warner and her publisher.

Carol explained that Warren had mailed her a copy of my letter and she wanted to reach out to help me understand how her book deal benefited Fortune (as it pertains to the licensing of the previously published articles in her book).

I couldn't be more thrilled to know that Mr. Buffett is taking the time each week to consider new ways to drive revenue for the Newspaper business.

Next step: a meeting with Warren Buffett.

Drew shows us that the smaller you go with your content niche, the higher the payoff in the long run. While you may never target an audience of one, the more you can narrow your audience persona, and thus your content niche covering that audience, the more successful you will be.

THE BEST PLACE TO START

Ardath Albee, the author of *eMarketing Strategies for the Complex Sale*, states that sometimes focusing on your best customers is the place to start with your content strategy. When she launched the company Einsoft, she didn't have the resources to target multiple buyers with multiple niches. So, she decided to group her 10 best customers and look at the similarities among those customers. That become the audience persona, and the content niche was created focusing on that group (of just 10).

There is no silver bullet, but starting with a smaller, profitable group of customers is the best method for deciding which content niche you should explore as a business. Once you perfect a content strategy for that group, you can move on to other content niches targeting different audiences.

EPIC THOUGHTS

- The natural inclination is to go big with your content niche, to try to cover more of your market. Avoid this urge. Go big with content marketing by going small with your niche.
- Focus your niche on the most valuable portion of your audience . . . and maybe, even the few best customers you have.

EPIC RESOURCES

- Grant Cardone, *The 10x Rule*, Wiley, 2011.
- "Traveling with Pets," Google Trends, accessed April 6, 2013, http://www.google.com/trends/explore#q=traveling%20with%20pets.
- "'Content Marketing' [versus] 'Custom Publishing,'" Google Trends, accessed April 6, 2013, http://www.google.com/trends/explore#q=%22custom%20publishing%22%2C%20%22content%20marketing%22&cmpt=q.
- Andrew Davis, *Brandscaping*, CMI Books, 2012.
- Andrew Davis, *Letters 2 Warren*, Tumblr.com, accessed July 9, 2013, http://letters2warren.tumblr.com/.
- Ardath Albee, *eMarketing Strategies for the Complex Sale*, McGraw-Hill, 2009.

CHAPTER 13

The Content Marketing Mission Statement

I cannot give you the formula for success,
but I can give you the formula for failure, which is:
Try to please everybody.

HERBERT B. SWOPE, AMERICAN JOURNALIST

In the dining room of our house, there is a mission statement on the wall. I refer to it often. So do my two boys, now ages 10 and 12.

The mission statement is our family purpose. It's what we strive to be today and into the future. I believe that mission statement has been crucial to our family's success and happiness.

Here is what it says.

THE PULIZZI MISSION

As Pulizzis, we hold true the following with ongoing purpose and action:

- We *thank God* every day for our blessings, even on days when we are challenged or face hardships.

119

- We *always share* what we have with others, and help out whenever we can to whoever is in need.
- We *praise each other*, as we are each blessed by God with unique talents.
- We *always finish* what we start, *always try* even though we may be afraid, and *always give* the activity of the moment our full attention.

Short Version:

- Thank God. Always Share. Say Nice Things. Give Our Best.

To be honest, I initially thought this was just a nice idea and a motto for our family to live by. Now a dozen years in the making, our mission statement has played a critical role in our lives. Why? Because there is never any gray area for our family goals. When the kids have questions about what they should and shouldn't do, my wife and I refer to the mission statement. Now, after years of this, my kids refer to the mission statement themselves—sometimes reluctantly.

And the best part? When visitors come into our house, the mission statement is noticed right away and almost always commented upon. It's one of those little things that make a difference.

THE CONTENT MARKETING MISSION STATEMENT

A mission statement is a company's reason for existence. It's why the organization does what it does. For example, Southwest Airlines' mission statement has always been to democratize the travel experience. The mission statement for CVS is to be the easiest pharmacy retailer for customers to use. So, in simple terms, the mission statement must answer the question, "Why do we exist?"

In almost every one of my keynote presentations, I cover the content marketing mission statement. It's critical to set the tone for the idea of content marketing . . . or any marketing, for that matter. Marketing professionals from small and large businesses get so fixated on channels such as blogs, Facebook, or Pinterest that they really have no clue of the underlying reason why they should use that channel in the first place. So the *why* must come before the *what*. This seems obvious, but most marketers have no mission statement or core strategy behind the content they develop. Epic content marketing is impossible without a clear and formidable *why*.

Think of it this way: What if you were the leading trade magazine for your niche area? What if your goal was not to first sell products and services but to impact your readers with amazing information that changes their lives and careers?

WHY *INC.* SUCCEEDS

Inc. magazine (see Figure 13.1) has its mission statement in the first line of its About Us page.

> Welcome to Inc.com, the place where entrepreneurs and business owners can find useful information, advice, insights, resources and inspiration for running and growing their businesses.

Source: Inc.com

Figure 13.1 What if we all started thinking about our websites like publishers do?

Let's dissect this a bit. *Inc.*'s mission statement includes:

- **The core audience target:** Entrepreneurs and business owners
- **What material will be delivered to the audience:** Useful information, advice, insights, resources, and inspiration
- **The outcome for the audience:** Growing their businesses

Inc.'s mission statement is incredibly simple and includes no words that can be misunderstood. Simplicity is key for how you will use your content marketing mission statement.

CONTENT MARKETING MISSION STATEMENTS IN ACTION

P&G (Procter & Gamble) has produced HomeMadeSimple.com for more than a decade now (see Figure 13.2). Millions of consumers have signed

Source: HomeMadeSimple.com

Figure 13.2 HomeMadeSimple.com, one of P&G's many content marketing platforms.

up at Home Made Simple to receive regular updates and tips to help them be more efficient in the home.

This is the content marketing mission statement for HomeMade Simple.com:

> Whether it's a delicious recipe, an inspiring décor idea or a refreshing approach to organizing, we strive to help you [a mom] create a home that's truly your own. Everything we do here is designed to empower and inspire you to make your home even better, and most importantly, a place you love to be.

Home Made Simple's mission includes:

- **The core audience target:** On-the-go moms (P&G doesn't explicitly say this on its site for obvious reasons, but this is its audience.)
- **What will be delivered to the audience:** Recipes, inspiring ideas, and new approaches to organization
- **The outcome for the audience:** Improvements to your home life

So, for P&G, if the story idea doesn't fit into these three tenets, it's a nonstarter.

Why is the content marketing mission statement so critical for businesses and their content? Your team needs to come up with great content ideas all the time—for the blog, for your Facebook page, for your newsletter. The way that you know whether or not story ideas are appropriate or not is to check each one against your content marketing mission statement.

If someone from P&G has a great idea targeted to dads and wants to put it on Home Made Simple, it won't get accepted; it's the wrong target audience. What if the story is about how to fix a tire? Nope, it doesn't fit with the promise of what you'll consistently deliver.

Here are other mission statements worth checking out:

- **American Express OPEN Forum.** "OPEN Forum is an online community to exchange insights, get advice from experts, and build connections to help you power your small business success."
- **Content Marketing Institute.** "Deliver real-world how-to advice about content marketing in all channels (online, print, and in-person) to help enterprise marketing professionals become less reliant on outside media channels."
- **Parametric Technology (PTC) Product Lifecycle blogs.** "Deliver non-product-specific, general interest news stories that relate, directly or indirectly, to the topic of product development and how it relates

to design engineers. The goal is for design engineers to think differently about innovation and product development."

- **Kraft Foods.** "Create delicious meal solutions that inspire amazing food stories which spread to drive sales and create value for Kraft Foods."
- **Williams-Sonoma.** "Be the leader in cooking and entertaining by delivering great products, world-class service and *engaging content*" (emphasis mine).

AUTHORITY TO PUBLISH

Julie Fleischer, director, media and consumer engagement for Kraft Foods, makes the case that brands should create content programs only out of authoritative topics. "At Kraft, it makes sense to our customers to talk about food, recipes and the like," states Fleischer. "Kraft can be authoritative about those topics, and it works for our customer and in turn our marketing goals. But we are not authoritative about financial issues or home repair. If you are a brand and you are getting into content marketing, you'd better understand what topics you have the authority to communicate on."

AMEX doesn't talk about food. John Deere doesn't talk about energy drinks. IBM doesn't talk about horses.

Have you ever seen an image on a company Facebook page or an article on a corporate blog that just doesn't fit? We all have. Companies that do this most likely don't have a content marketing mission statement as a filter.

As you develop your content marketing mission statement, be sure that the content around which you create stories is an area in which you truly have expertise. If you don't, then what's the point?

CM MISSION BEST PRACTICES

Remember, content marketing is not about "what you sell," it's about "what you stand for." The informational needs of your customers and prospects come first. *Although there must be clear marketing objectives behind the mission statement, they don't need to be outlined here.* The *Inc.* mission statement doesn't say anything about selling more advertising or paid event registrations. The P&G mission statement doesn't say anything about selling more Swiffer pads. To work, your mission statement has to be all about the pain points (in other words, "what keeps your customers up at night?") of your readers and followers. If it isn't, it simply won't work.

WHAT DO YOU DO WITH IT?

Not only does the content marketing mission statement provide the basis for your content strategy moving forward, it's also instrumental to your entire content creation process. Here's what you need to do with your content marketing mission statement.

- **Post it.** Display the mission statement where it can be found easily by your audience. The best place to put it is anywhere you develop non-product-oriented content for your customers, such as your blog site, a Facebook page, or main content site (such as an American Express OPEN Forum).
- **Spread it.** Make sure everyone involved in your content marketing process has the mission statement. Encourage others to print it out and pin it up on the wall. Give it to employees involved in the content creation process as well as any agency partners or freelancers you may be using. So often, content creators in a company are not aware of the overall content mission. Make sure you don't let that happen.
- **The litmus test.** Use the mission statement to decide what content you will and won't create. Often, a bad judgment in content creation can be fixed by running the content by the mission statement.

MATCHING WITH THE BUSINESS OBJECTIVE

Ultimately, it's all about marketing. It's about selling more products and services. If you are not changing behavior for the good of the business in some way, you are just producing content, not content marketing.

Let's reexamine the four company examples mentioned previously in terms of how their business objective should coincide with their mission statements:

- **American Express OPEN Forum.** OPEN Forum positions American Express as the trusted expert to small business owners. OPEN Forum, in order to be truly valuable, must include content other than just financial or credit issues, so it includes operations advice, marketing insights, and consumer research. OPEN Forum now delivers as many inbound leads as any other initiative from American Express.
- **Content Marketing Institute.** CMI gives away most of its educational content for free through daily updates. When subscribers want

to take that education to the next level in the form of an in-person "paid" event, they sign up, which almost always happens after they have been receiving the content as a subscriber for months.

- **Parametric Technology (PTC) Product Lifecycle blogs.** The blogs cover real insight into the challenge of product development. The results have been twofold. First, current customers become more loyal, and second, prospects are more likely to choose PTC because they rely on the blog content as a true industry resource.
- **Kraft Foods.** Not only can Kraft show that its content programs deliver, the company actually has over 1 million customers that pay to receive Kraft content on a regular basis.

Sometimes your content marketing mission statement is fully aligned with what you sell (as is the case with the Content Marketing Institute). Other times, the content you develop may be broader than what you actually have products and services for (as is the case with American Express). The important thing is to be aware of your mission statement and know what kind of products or services need to be sold at the end of the day. Knowing is half the battle, and if your audience isn't showing the right kind of behaviors in the long run, that may mean the content alignment and what you sell are just too far from each other.

THE SWEET SPOT

Once you decide on your content marketing mission, take some time and really think about your "sweet spot." Your sweet spot is the intersection between your customers' pain points and where you have the most authority with your stories.

This takes us back to one of the original questions: where can you be the leading expert in the world? But this time, let's add a short statement at the end: where can you be the leading expert in the *world that truly matters to your customers and your business?*

EPIC THOUGHTS

- For your content marketing mission statement to work, you need to clearly define three things specific to your content creation: (1) the core audience target, (2) what you will deliver to the audience, and (3) the major audience takeaway.
- Once your mission statement is created, distribute it to every content creator on your team (both inside and outside the company).

- Epic content marketing, in most cases, means telling a different story each time, not the same story repeatedly, but incrementally better each time. Is your mission statement innovative or just a retread of someone else's story?

EPIC RESOURCES

- *Mission statement* definition, accessed April 2, 2013, http://en.wikipedia.org/wiki/Mission_statement.
- About *Inc.com*, accessed April 2, 2013, http://www.inc.com/about.
- A listing of company mission statements, accessed April 2, 2013, http://missionstatements.com.
- Home Made Simple, accessed April 2, 2013, http://homemadesimple.com.
- American Express OPEN Forum, accessed April 2, 2013, http://openforum.com.
- Content Marketing Institute, http://contentmarketinginstitute.com.
- PTC Product Lifecycle Blogs, accessed April 2, 2013, http://blogs.ptc.com/.
- Kraft Foods, accessed April 3, 2013, http://www.kraftrecipes.com/home.aspx.
- Simon Sinek, *Start with Why: How Great Leaders Inspire Everyone to Take Action,* Portfolio Trade, 2011.

PART III

Managing the Content Process

CHAPTER 14

Building Your Editorial Calendar

Not doing more than the average is what keeps the average down.
WILLIAM LYON PHELPS, AMERICAN AUTHOR

Over the past 13 years of my publishing career, I've noticed a few things about editorial calendars.

First, they are utterly critical for any content marketing program to be successful.

Second, most businesses don't use them.

New social media platforms are sexy. So are new marketing ideas. Calendars, for most of us are ... not so sexy.

Let's be honest, even though content marketing has existed in various forms for hundreds of years, most marketers are short-term, campaign-driven types—similar to the people you might see on *Mad Men*—who tend to shower their campaigns with the latest social media tools.

But that's not content marketing. Content marketing is not a short-term campaign; it's a long-term strategy to attract, convert, and retain customers.

You can't have a long-term content strategy without the tools to manage it. And one of the most effective tools you can use is the editorial calendar.

So let's take a look at how this works.

THE THREE COMPONENTS OF AN EDITORIAL CALENDAR

Traditional marketing departments used to gear up around the latest product push. But more and more marketing resources are starting to look like publishing operations, similar to what you'd see from *Inc.* magazine or *Entertainment Weekly*.

Because content marketing is a long-term strategy and often involves multiple content producers, customers, and outside influencers, keeping track of all the stories and formats (online or offline) can be tricky. . . . and problematic.

Note: Though I've use the terms *spreadsheet* and *document* below, there are many online tools that can work as your customized editorial calendar. Start with simple tools such as Google Drive (formerly Google Docs) combined with the WordPress Editorial Calendar plug-in. (If WordPress is your content management system, this is available for you to use.) As your business progresses, consider moving up to a paid software-as-a-service offering such as Kapost, Central Desktop, HubSpot, Contently, Compendium, Zerys, and Skyword (to name just a few).

COMPONENT 1: UNDERSTANDING WHAT AN EDITORIAL CALENDAR IS AND IS NOT

The editorial calendar is much more than just a calendar with content assigned to dates. A good editorial calendar maps content production to the audience personas (whom we want to sell to), the engagement cycle (delivering appropriate content based on where the prospect is in the buying process), and the various media channels.

Beyond dates and headlines, your editorial calendar should include the following things.

- **A prioritized list of what you are publishing based on the content strategy you've developed.** This may contain existing content that will be redesigned or repackaged, content that will come from partners, or content yet to be developed. It's your inventory.
- **Assigned content producer(s) and/or editors responsible for the content.** Here you name the people responsible for producing the content. If you have multiple editors, identify them as well.
- **The channel(s) for the content.** A listing of formats and channels targeted for the content. For example, you may have a blog post that is part of an e-book series that you are publishing on SlideShare. In this case, you may want to also deliver pieces through multiple dis-

tribution outlets such as your e-mail newsletter or social sites like Twitter or Google+.

- **Metadata.** These are "tags" you assign to keep track of what you're working on and what role it plays in your content strategy. The number of tags you want to include is really up to you. You'll probably want to include tags for important aspects of the content such as "target persona" or "engagement cycle" so that you can make sure you're balancing your editorial content to your overall goals. You may also want to include columns (or tags) for things like content type (for example, white paper, video, or e-mail) or even SEO keywords.
- **Dates for both creation and publishing.** These include the dates that the content is due to the editor, along with target dates for publishing. As you become more sophisticated, you may want to include the refresh date (a triggered date to update the content when needed).
- **Workflow steps.** If you work for a larger organization, you may want to add workflow steps including legal, fact checking, proofreading, or other elements that will affect your content creation and management process.

As you begin to assemble the elements in your editorial calendar, remember that the calendar is a management tool.

Include only the elements you need to manage your process. For example, if you write one blog post a week and two e-mail messages a month to support your small business, there's no reason to overcomplicate your editorial calendar. Keep it as simple as you can. Figure 14.1 shows what a basic editorial calendar looks like.

COMPONENT 2: ORGANIZING THE CALENDAR

Set your calendar document up in the way that works best for you.

For the sake of simplicity, let's assume that you'll have one spreadsheet for the year—and that each tab will be one month. Across the columns you might have:

- Content headline
- Content type
- The audience persona you're writing this piece for
- The person who will write or create the content
- Date due
- The person who will edit the content
- Channels—where does this get published?
- "Metadata" tags
- Publish date

Sample Editorial Calendar

	Author	Topic	Status	Call to Action	Main Keyword	Category	Next Update
Week of May 21							
Monday, May 21							
Tuesday, May 22							
Wednesday, May 23							
Thursday, May 24							
Friday, May 25							
Week of May 28							
Monday, May 28							
Tuesday, May 29							
Wednesday, May 30							
Thursday, May 31							
Friday, June 1							
Week of June 4							
Monday, June 4							
Tuesday, June 5							
Wednesday, June 6							
Thursday, June 7							
Friday, June 8							
Week of June 11							
Monday, June 11							
Tuesday, June 12							
Wednesday, June 13							
Thursday, June 14							
Friday, June 15							
Week of June 18							
Monday, June 18							
Tuesday, June 19							
Wednesday, June 20							
Thursday, June 21							
Friday, June 22							

Figure 14.1   A basic look for an editorial calendar.

- Status (perhaps indicated by green, yellow, or red)
- Any notes
- Key metrics (for example, comments posted, pageviews, and downloads) (I recommend keeping your key metrics on a separate sheet, however.)
- Call to action (the primary action or behavior you've asked for)

Sometimes a visual calendar can help make better sense of the content types you are using as part of your content strategy. Figure 14.2 shows a sample from Velocity Partners, a content agency in the United Kingdom.

Finally, as separate documents—or even tabs within your editorial calendar—you may want to include "brainstorming" elements (for example, ideas that are under consideration or new stories that come up during the process). If you are using a tool like Kapost, it will keep a log of all your ongoing ideas as well as your active content assets.

In the end, your editorial calendar will become the most frequently used tool in your process. And whether it's a combination of documents,

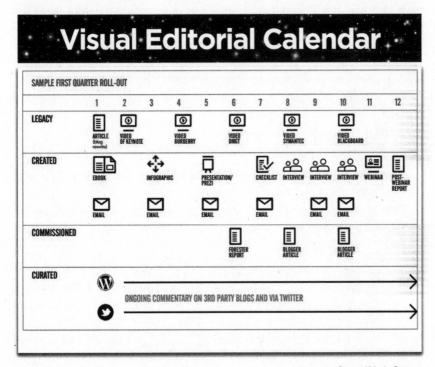

Source: Velocity Partners

Figure 14.2 This visual editorial calendar from Velocity can help staffers make sense of your content plan.

a single spreadsheet, an online production tool, or just a monthly e-mail that you send to your team, the key is that it works for you. In the end, whatever helps smooth out your process and keep you and your content team on track is the best editorial calendar format.

COMPONENT 3: DEVELOPING THE EDITORIAL STYLE GUIDE

Obviously, when any of us talks about a "calendar," the first thing that person thinks of is a guide for planning what content gets created and when.

But your "calendar" has another important function. It's the basis for developing an editorial style guide as a tool for your content creators, editors, and producers. (Yes, even if those people are all you.)

This style guide can also develop into a social conversation style guide (in other words, a social media policy), providing guidelines for how people respond and converse.

As more people start "telling the story" of your brand, be sure that they have the right tools and training to properly communicate your brand's voice. You also need to police or monitor them to make sure they are keeping to that voice.

And even if you're flying solo right now, keeping your editorial voice consistent will keep your content more professional and trustworthy. And it makes it *much* easier if you ever need to bring other writers in.

As with the continuing story, it's easy to let the tone, quality, and style slip bit by bit until the story is way off track. This is where your editorial style guide comes into play.

Here are some key things to include:

- **The overall tone and voice of your content marketing.** Who are you? What do you convey in your content?
- The average (or minimum/maximum) length of pieces developed.
- **Branding guidelines.** How to refer to the company, product lines, individuals, and so on.

For grammar, style, and word usage, you can also choose to conform to guides such as the *Associated Press Stylebook* and *The Chicago Manual of Style* (published by the University of Chicago). In addition, many content marketing strategists—especially those focused on the web—are using the *Yahoo! Style Guide*. Bonus: For a complete sample of CMI's style guide, go to EpicContentMarketing.com.

EPIC THOUGHTS

- Ultimately, your editorial calendar is your most powerful tool as a content marketer. If you don't plan for epic content, it doesn't happen.
- There are many technology tools out there, but use what's easiest for you.

EPIC RESOURCES

- Plugin Directory, WordPress.org, accessed July 9, 2013, http:// wordpress.org/extend/plugins/editorial-calendar/.
- *The Associated Press Stylebook 2013*, Basic Books, 2013.
- *The Yahoo! Style Guide*, St. Martin's Griffin, 2010.
- "Content Marketing Strategy Checklist," Velocity Partners, June 2012, http://www.velocitypartners.co.uk/wp-content/uploads/2012/06 /Content-Marketing-Strategy-Checklist-Velocity-Partners.pdf.

CHAPTER 15

Managing the Content Creation Process

There is nothing so useless as doing efficiently that which should not be done at all.

PETER DRUCKER

Let's face it, *content marketing is a new muscle for most organizations.*

Most brands have been doing things the same way for so long that thinking like a publisher is, well, quite taxing. Worse yet, these brands aren't set up for publishing; they are set up for traditional marketing practices organized in the usual silos. That means they might not have an awareness of the types of roles needed to succeed with managing the content marketing process.

In order to do content marketing successfully, you need to have the following four things:

- People to do it
- Roles and responsibilities for those people to fill
- A schedule by which the tasks are fulfilled (See Figures 14.1 and 14.2 for sample editorial calendars.)
- Rules and guidelines

The most difficult of these may be finding the roles within the company to drive the process. If that's the case for you, the paragraphs that follow tell you how to do so.

ASSEMBLING A TEAM WITH SPECIFIC ROLES AND RESPONSIBILITIES

Given the size of your organization, you may have one person—or many—responsible for your content marketing initiative; in general, however, no matter how many people actually take responsibility for the function, the following roles are needed.

Note: The following are roles within the organization, not necessarily position titles (although they could be).

THE MANAGER OR CHIEF CONTENT OFFICER (CCO)

At least one person in your organization should own the content initiative. More recently, organizations call this a chief content officer or CCO (There is now a dedicated magazine for this position. See Figure 15.1.) Kodak calls this role "vice president of content strategy"; Monetate, a small B2B software company, calls this a "content marketing director." (In a small business, the owner or partner or even a general marketing person may be the one performing this function.)

This is the "chief storyteller" role for your content effort; the person performing this role is responsible for executing the goals that you set out to accomplish. *When content marketing fails, it's usually not because of a lack of high-quality content; it's because of a drop in execution.* That is why this manager may be your most important asset, even though this person may not be creating *any* of the content. The CCO must ensure excellence in every content marketing tactic, including:

- Content/editorial
- Design/art/photography
- Web resources for content
- Integration of marketing and the content, including social media
- Project budgeting
- Contract negotiation with freelancers
- Audience development
- Research and measurement

In organizations where there is no budget for a dedicated CCO, this role may be filled by the director or vice president of marketing. Many brands, such as UPS, have a manager inside the company who oversees

Source: Content Marketing Institute

Figure 15.1 *Chief Content Officer* magazine, specifically designed for the CCO role, is produced bimonthly by the Content Marketing Institute.

internal content production as well as the production of content by an outside agency. Although brands can outsource a wide variety of content production through outsourced vendors, *it's important to keep the CCO inside the organization.*

To access a complete job description for the chief content officer position, go to EpicContentMarketing.com and select *bonus resources.*

MANAGING EDITOR(S)

The editors have a critical role in the content marketing process, and are probably the most sought after by brands today. As more brands develop content, employees are being asked to blog and write on behalf of their companies. Unfortunately, the writing style of employees who have never created content before often leaves much to be desired. That's where the managing editor comes in. This role, sometimes outsourced and sometimes part of the CCO's responsibility, manages the editorial functions of the content marketing effort. These are your day-to-day content execution people. They help internal employees develop and write content, and they assist external people in aligning their writing with the company's organizational goals.

The managing editor works with the employees on the following:

- Content production
- Content scheduling
- Keyword selection for search engine optimization (SEO)
- Search engine optimization of posts
- Style corrections
- Tagging and images

Sometimes the managing editors are there to teach so the employees can do more on their own. They also may act as coaches, encouraging the managers, executive team, or even external writers to produce content against the schedule. OpenView Venture Partners has a managing editor who oversees all the content on the OpenView blog, but the editor only creates a small portion of it. Nearly every employee is responsible for developing original blog posts, so the managing editor works with content from the entire enterprise.

CONTENT CREATORS

Content creators produce the content that will ultimately help to tell the story. This role typically overlaps with the managing editors who are also producing content, but it also may simply be performed by a subject matter expert within the organization. For example, typical content producers include anyone in the C-suite, the head of research and development, the product manager, the customer service director, or a hired consultant. In many cases this role is outsourced when there is a lack, or gap, in resources to produce the content. It's important to note that this person does not need to be a writer (although it's really helpful if she or he is). In general, this person is there to be the "face" or "voice" of the authentic organization. The content creator may be interviewed for content, or he or she may produce a long, rambling e-mail that is transformed into a cogent blog post.

CONTENT PRODUCERS

Content producers format or create the ultimate package in which the content is presented (that is, they make the content "pretty"). Chances are this role already exists in your organization to some degree; it is either handled in-house or by an agency. It might be a web agency if the end product is a blog or a website.

CHIEF LISTENING OFFICER

The role of the chief listening officer (CLO) is to function like an air-traffic controller for social media and your other content channels. CLOs are there to listen to the groups, maintain the conversation, and to route to (and/or notify) the appropriate team members who can engage in conversation (customer service, sales, marketing, and so on). For the content marketing process, this function serves as the centerpiece of your "listening posts." You establish listening posts so you can continue to get a "feed" of information; you can then always be ready to react and adapt as your subscribers react and change.

So often today companies have CLOs for social media response purposes but don't leverage these roles for purposes of content marketing feedback. Hopefully, your content creates a number of reactions in the community. The CLO can then route important feedback to the CCO, so that the chief storyteller can modify the plan on an ongoing basis.

CHIEF CONTENT OFFICER JOB DESCRIPTION

NOTE: This job description is more than you'll ever need for the role of the CCO. I have purposely included all possible aspects of the job to be the most helpful for you. For your particular case, use what you need to build a job description that makes sense for your organization.

- Job description: chief content officer
- Reports to: chief executive officer/chief operating officer (smaller enterprise) or chief marketing officer/VP of marketing (larger enterprise)

POSITION SUMMARY

The chief content officer (CCO) oversees all marketing content initiatives, both internal and external, across multiple platforms and formats to drive sales, engagement, retention, leads, and positive customer behavior.

This individual is an expert in all things related to content and channel optimization, brand consistency, segmentation and localization, analytics, and meaningful measurement.

The position collaborates with the departments of public relations, communications, marketing, customer service, information technologies, and human resources to help define both the brand story and the story as interpreted by the customer.

RESPONSIBILITIES

Ultimately, the job of the CCO is to think like a publisher/journalist, leading the development of content initiatives in all forms to drive new and current business. This includes:

- Ensuring that all content is on brand, consistent in terms of style, quality, and tone of voice, and optimized for search and user experience for all channels of content, including online, social media, e-mail, point of purchase, mobile, video, print, and in person. This is to be done for each buyer persona within the enterprise.
- Mapping out a content strategy that supports and extends marketing initiatives, both short and long term, and determining which methods work for the brand and why. Continuous evolvement of strategy is a must.
- Developing a functional content calendar throughout the enterprise verticals and defining the owners in each vertical to particular persona groups.
- Supervising writers, editors, and content strategists; being an arbiter of best practices in grammar, messaging, writing, and style.
- Integrating content activities within traditional marketing campaigns.
- Conducting ongoing usability tests to gauge content effectiveness; gathering data, handling analytics (or supervising those who do), and making recommendations based on those results; working with owners of particular content to revise and measure particular content and marketing goals.
- Developing standards, systems, and best practices (both human and technological) for content creation, distribution, maintenance, content retrieval, and content repurposing, including the real-time implementation of content strategies.
- Leveraging market data to develop content themes/topics and execute a plan to develop the assets that support a point of view and educate customers in a way that leads to critical behavioral metrics.

- Establishing work flow for requesting, creating, editing, publishing, and retiring content; working with technical team to implement appropriate content management system.
- Conducting periodic competitive audits.
- Supervising the maintenance of content inventories and matrices.
- Ensuring consistent global experience, and implementing appropriate localization/translation strategies.
- Participating in the hiring and supervising of content/story leaders in all content verticals.
- Creating a strategy for developing Short Message Service (SMS)/ Multimedia Messaging Service (MMS) outreach and advertising, apps, and so on, as needed.
- Work closely with company's chief design officer on all creative and branding initiatives to ensure a consistent message across channels.

SUCCESS CRITERIA

The CCO is measured on the continual improvement of customer nurturing and retention through storytelling, as well as the increase in new prospects into the enterprise through the consistent development and deployment of content to each persona group. Success criteria include the following:

- Positive brand recognition and consistency across chosen published channels
- An increase in defined customer engagement metrics (measured by users taking the desired action, for example, conversions, subscription, and purchase)
- Website and social media traffic growth
- Conversion metrics definition and growth
- Social media positive sentiment metrics
- Customer feedback and survey data
- Increases in key search engine keyword rankings
- A decrease in sales/buying cycles
- A clear definition of content distribution during particular stages of the buying cycle (lead nurturing)
- Identification of upsell and cross-sell opportunities through content analysis, and deploying content assets for higher conversion rates.

Primary criteria for success are customer and employee affinity. Success is measured around lifetime customer value, customer satisfaction, and employee advocacy.

EXPERIENCE AND EDUCATION REQUIRED

- Bachelor's degree in English, Journalism, Public Relations, or related communications field. An MBA in marketing a plus.
- Five to ten years of experience as a respected leader in multichannel content creation (publishing, journalism, and so on).
- Experience with creating compelling messages for different target demographics. Crisis communications experience a plus.
- Expertise in major business software applications a plus (Adobe Creative Suite, Microsoft Office, and so on).
- HR-related experience, including hiring, managing, performance reviews, and compensation packages, required.
- Multilingual abilities (specifically Spanish and Chinese) a major plus.
- Audience development and subscription strategies experience a plus.

SKILLS REQUIRED

The CCO requires a combination marketing and publishing mindset, with the most important aspect being to think "customer first." In essence, the CCO is the corporate storyteller that must be empathetic toward the pain points of the customer. Specific skills required include:

- Proven editorial skills; outstanding command of the English (or primary customer) language.
- Training as a print or broadcast journalist; having a "nose" for the story. Training in how to tell a story using words, images, or audio, and an understanding of how to create content that draws an audience. (It is critical that the CCO retain an "outsider's perspective" much like that of a journalist.)
- The ability to lead and inspire large teams of creative personnel and content creators to achieve the company's stated goals.
- Skill at both long-form content creation and real-time (immediate) content creation and distribution strategies and tactics.
- The ability to think like an educator, intuitively understanding what the audience needs to know and how they want to consume it.
- A passion for new technology tools (that is, using the tools you preach about) and use of those tools within your own blogs and social media outreach. Social DNA is a plus!
- Clear articulation of the business goal behind the creation of a piece (or a series) of content.
- Leadership skills required to define and manage a set of goals involving diverse contributors and content types.

- Project management skills to manage editorial schedules and deadlines within corporate and ongoing campaigns. Ability to work in a 24-hour project cycle utilizing teams or contractors in other countries.
- Familiarity with principles of marketing (and the ability to adapt or ignore them as dictated by data).
- Excellent negotiating and mediating skills.
- Incredible people skills.
- Basic technical understanding of HTML, XHTML, CSS, Java, web publishing, Flash, and so on.
- Fluency in web analytics tools (Adobe Omniture, Google Analytics), social media marketing applications (HootSuite, Tweetdeck, and so on).
- A willingness to embrace change and to adapt strategies on the fly.
- Great powers of persuasion and presentation (Visio, PowerPoint).
- Experience creating a resource or library of content organized around search engine optimization, translations, and version control.
- Knowledge of the latest platforms, technology tools, and marketing solutions through partnerships (The CCO needs to continually be learning this.)
- Ability to screen out sales pitches and look for the relevant brand and customer story.
- Comfort with acting as the company's spokesperson and advocate via media appearances, interviews, sales calls, trade shows, and so on.

ATTRIBUTION

Thanks to all of those people who enabled the creation of this chief content officer job description, including Katie McCaskey, Peggy Dorf, Don Hoffman, Wendy Boyce, Sarah Mitchell, Pam Kozelka, Kim Kleeman, Reinier Willems, Joe Pulizzi, DJ Francis, Josh Healan, Christina Pappas, CC Holland, Stallar Lufrano, Lisa Gerber, Kim Gusta, Cindy Lavoie, Jill Nagle, and Ann Handley.

Final description prepared by Joe Pulizzi, Content Marketing Institute.

WHAT TO LOOK FOR IN FREELANCE WRITERS

Whether you represent an experienced digital publishing machine or a novice brand looking for the benefits of content marketing, you most likely need the help of freelance writers to help tell your story. You may find that you need help developing ongoing content—or that you need additional content producers to keep up with the velocity.

How do you go about finding good external content contributors (sometimes called "stringers")? Should you look for a good writer and teach him or her your business? Or should you hire someone who knows your industry and teach him or her to write? The following are a few tips to consider.

Expertise is helpful, but not a deal killer. Given the choice between a good writer with a personality that closely matches your organization (but who is short on industry expertise) and an industry veteran who knows how to write but with whom you can't stand to be in the same room—*go with the personality.* Chemistry and personality are things that are entirely hard to change; research is a skill that can be taught—passion isn't. If you and your freelance content producer don't have good chemistry together, the relationship will go nowhere fast. And while it might be a strategic advantage to bring in an industry "rock star" to get your content some attention (and there are great reasons to do this occasionally), unless there's a great personality fit, be very careful that you don't wrap your story into the star's and get lost in the middle.

Hire right—copywriters, journalists, technical writers, oh my! Because you've spent so much time on your strategy and your process, you should be very aware of what kind of writer you're looking for. Understand that copywriters work very differently and have very different sensibilities than journalists do. If you're looking for someone to write blog posts for you, a copywriter is probably not your best bet. On the other hand, if you're looking for someone to beef up your persuasive call to action for all the great white papers you're putting together, then a great copywriter may be exactly what you need.

Develop the right business relationship. Understand the elements of your business relationship, and make them clear. For example, will there be one content item per week—and your writer will be paid a monthly fee? If so, how will you handle months that have 4½ weeks? Will there be an extra post that week? Spell out the invoicing and payment terms. Given the size of your organization, you need to make clear the invoicing and payment terms—or understand what the writer needs. Also be clear on expectations. At this point, you should know your velocity and how long and how detailed the content needs to be. There should be no surprises such as blog posts suddenly becoming 300 words, when they're supposed to be 500 . . . or content themes going wildly off topic.

Here are some of the things you'll need to communicate to your freelance writers:

- What content they will produce, and where it falls on the editorial calendar (Be very specific when drafts are due.)
- The goals for their specific contributions (especially if it's a custom-branded piece versus a piece for your publication)
- What expertise or other third-party information they will need access to (Will they be interviewing internal people, bringing in external information, or reworking your existing material?)
- Your budget (per piece, hourly, retainer, or barter)
- The number of revisions for each piece

Over the past 12 to 18 months, new models of performance have taken shape in the digital content world. Many publishers are adopting the pay-for-performance model, where a smaller base fee is paid for the raw content but the writer is paid a bonus for content performance (based on both sharing metrics and search engine placement). New tools like Skyword now make this possible. Writers, who in the past were not open to this, are now very aware of this type of model and are more open to it than ever before, but setting clear expectations is a critical first step.

BUDGETING FACTORS

In the near publishing past, freelancers used to get paid $1 per word. This still remains true for high-quality and unique content, like that for research reports and white papers. For article content, some services, such as Zerys, can price your content as low as 5 cents per word, if you'd like.

Word of warning: you usually get what you pay for. At CMI, we've found the most success in the retainer model—that is, working with a freelancer on a number of content assets over a period of time and then paying a monthly fee for the work. This arrangement is usually appreciated by both sides. The business can budget easier with a set number, and the freelancer doesn't have to count words. After all, a piece of content should only be as long as it needs to be, so why set a limit? (A range should be just fine.)

BEFORE DIVING IN, TEST

With the amount of writer supply in the workforce, there is no need to start a long-term relationship at first. Test out a few stories, and see how they work. Ask yourself: Is the person's writing style to your expectations? Does he or she deliver on time? Is the person actively sharing the content via his or her own social network? (This is very important.)

Once the writer has met your expectations in these areas, then set out on a long-term deal. I've seen too many marketers and publishers get their "rock star" freelancers, only to kill the deal a few months later with neither party happy. Test it out first so you don't waste your time.

A CODE OF ETHICS

Wherever there is talk of content marketing, there is talk of transparency, ethics, and the credibility of branded content. One content network and publishing platform, Contently, has been doing some excellent work in this area.

I asked Shane Snow, Contently's CEO, about the "Code of Ethics" he developed. Here's a bit of background from Shane:

> We started Contently because we wanted to help talented, professional journalists survive as freelancers and build careers doing what they loved. As our business grew into providing tools and talent for content marketers, we saw the need to educate our clients and journalists on the ethical expectations they should have as they do business together.
>
> Brands don't have decades of publishing experience, and thus they often aren't familiar with the accepted standards of ethical publishing. Journalists can be uneasy about taking on clients who don't understand those standards. We talked to editors at major newspapers like *The New York Times* and ethicists from the Society of Professional Journalists in order to understand whether editors would hire journalists who'd previously worked for brands (the answer is yes, so long as they're transparent about it), and to establish the different responsibilities that we felt should go along with creating content for brands versus traditional, constitutionally-protected media publishers.

And thus, the Content Marketing Code of Ethics was born. Here it is, in its entirety, reprinted with permission.

CONTENT MARKETING'S CODE OF ETHICS

Content marketing should seek to adhere to stricter standards of reporting than traditional journalism, due to its different legal position and increased commercial motivations. Content marketers should take care to disclose the sponsorship and intent of their work while abiding by the following practices:

- Adhere to journalism's core values of honesty, integrity, accountability, and responsibility.
- Acknowledge facts that may compromise the integrity of a story or opinion.
- Minimize potential harm to sources or subjects of stories.
- Expose truth as fully as possible.
- Always credit sources of content or ideas, never plagiarizing or repurposing stories or prose, whether one's own or another's, whether written content, photography, or other media, whether the original source is known or not.
- Fulfill promises made to contributors and sources in the course of reporting.
- Ensure that the reader understands the source, sponsor, and intent of the content
- Disclose all potential conflicts of interest or appearance of conflict.

MANAGING INFORMATION LIKE A PRODUCT

Although each brand we've worked with at CMI executes the content marketing process differently, there seems to be one key differentiator between those organizations that are successfully changing behavior through content and those that aren't: *information as a product.*

Whether you sell products or services, the new rules of marketing require that, along with everything else you sell, the process of delivering consistently valuable information must be considered throughout the organization as, yes, a product.

What do I mean by that? When people from an organization look at its content marketing as a product, they inherently create a number of initiatives and processes around that product, including:

- Up-front business planning
- Product testing
- Research and development
- Product success measures (marketing return on investment)
- Customer feedback channels
- Quality control
- Product evolution planning

Successful companies such as Procter & Gamble, IBM, and SAS have all approached their content in a similar fashion.

WHY APPROACH INFORMATION AS A PRODUCT?

The answer to that question is simple: organizations today have no choice but to place that kind of importance and processes behind their content initiatives. Customers today are in complete control; they filter out any message that does not benefit them in some way. Since that is the case, organizations must first build a solid relationship with customers through the use of valuable, relevant information—then, and only then, will organizations be able to sell the other products and services that grow the top line.

THIS IS HAPPENING NOW

This trend is happening now, as more businesses morph themselves into media companies. You are seeing appointments of titles such as "chief content officers" (Petco recently created this position) and businesses that are starting to hire full-time journalists. *Traditional* businesses either are starting to purchase media companies themselves (such as Google's purchases of Zagat and Frommer's in the travel industry) or are building out media empires like Red Bull is doing.

WHAT YOU NEED TO DO

Any company serious about growing top-line revenues while at the same time being concerned about how to market in the future needs to make the "information as a product" concept a priority.

Small organizations with limited budgets should start seeking out expert journalists and storytellers to begin overseeing their content program. Midsize to large organizations may want to look into hiring an agency that understands that storytelling, and not paid media channels, are the key to future growth.

In order to be successful, you need a marketing culture that includes both a strong marketing *and* publishing core, and a keen understanding of how consistent editorial content can maintain or change customer behavior. Here are three things you should always keep in mind when establishing and maintaining a content marketing culture.

THREE TAKEAWAYS

Start to think about your content packages as a series (like a television show). Set up the pilot as a test, and then, if it's successful, roll ahead with the series. Eloqua has done a fantastic job of this with its Grande Guide series.

Train all product managers in the basics of content marketing. The power of story revolves not in the product; instead, it depends on the true needs and pain points of the target audience. The product manager must have a thorough awareness of this. Most product managers never think about this aspect, and the opportunities are wasted.

Establish a pilot team. Content marketing is not a difficult concept, but it means thinking differently about how to communicate with both customers and employees. A full marketing makeover takes time, especially in a larger brand. Find the storytellers in your marketing department, and set up a "skunk works" operation (that is, one that functions independently from the company's main R&D operation) as your testing ground (as with the pilot programs discussed in Chapter 5). Focus on achieving an objective or two instead of getting them all—in effect, hitting a single or two instead of a home run. Once you have reached some objectives with this group and success is clear, then you can push it through the entire organization.

ON WORKING WITH CONTENT MARKETING AGENCIES

Content marketing agencies seem to be popping up everywhere nowadays, but this trend has been happening for years now. In the search for "content gold," providers of marketing services have been "heading west," as more brands continue their move toward creating owned media programs and establishing content marketing dominance.

THE FIGHT FOR CONTENT

The battle royale to establish or increase budgets for content development and distribution is being fought by both the usual suspects and the uninitiated in the content marketing industry, including:

- Pure content marketing agencies, formerly known as custom publishers
- Advertising agencies that have a newfound appreciation for branded storytelling outside of media placement
- Traditional media companies that have either editorial teams or full content divisions dedicated to working on editorial and branded content projects

- Public relations organizations that are starting to focus less on placement and more on owned channels
- Direct marketing agencies that are moving from "offer-focused" to "engagement-focused" content
- Search engine optimization companies that are shelving the SEO business in response to Google Panda and Penguin updates (These are frequent algorithm updates from Google that have changed search rankings to focus on quality content creation from credible websites.)
- Social media agencies that are realizing that it's not the channel but what goes into the channel that counts
- Web content and user experience agencies that are moving away from solely technical website production, audits, and analysis to advise on multichannel content
- Digital agencies that are pairing interactive services with consistent content production
- Research organizations showcasing industry experts and thought leaders for strategic content and consulting assignments

These agencies and more are battling for content marketing dollars from brands. Some have legitimate budgets, and others are working with a pile of Monopoly money trying to figure out the secret to social media success.

Whatever your feeling is on who owns the rightful mantle of "content marketing agency" really doesn't matter. The truth is that thousands of agencies formerly touting any one or a number of the aforementioned banners are now trying to "ride the wave" to content marketing salvation.

REALITY BITES

If you do not provide marketing services for other companies, you have a tough time of it. At the Content Marketing Institute we receive multiple calls, e-mails, and inquiries each day asking for content help, from strategy to blog posts, visual content, content distribution, integration, hiring, research, and everything else under the sun. Here's what we've learned: *there is good help out there, but it's hard to tell the partners from the posers.*

In the following paragraphs you'll find some truths about content marketing agencies, and how smart brands should view the outsourced marketing services provider of the present.

A lot of people in our industry haven't had very diverse experiences. So they don't have enough dots to connect, and they end up with very linear solutions without a broad perspective on the problem. The broader one's understanding of the human experience, the better design we will have.

STEVE JOBS

Most content marketing agencies don't market with content. I hear it all the time: the "shoemaker's shoes" conundrum, that is, most content agencies rarely make time to practice epic content marketing, saving it all, apparently, for their customers. Agencies of all kinds have a long history of producing advertising and marketing programs for clients, while forgetting to market themselves. No clearer examples of this exist than with content marketing.

Marketing services organizations are notorious for focusing on sales-led marketing programs, where cold calls and sales relationships rule. Whether a lack of resources or a lack of patience is cited as the reason, agencies that offer content marketing services very rarely produce epic content that attracts and helps to retain their own customer base.

The lesson for brands: Before you hire any content marketing agency, ask to see the work it has performed—on its own behalf. Take a deep dive into all of its content. Is the content truly great, or is it "me-too" blog content that you can find anywhere?

Most search engine optimization agencies don't know Jack about content marketing. Search engine optimization is an incredibly important tactic. As search engines gets smarter, it's almost impossible to game the system. Today, getting found through search engines has more to do with amazing online storytelling than most anything else.

I had a conversation with an SEO executive team, and team members were seriously contemplating taking the entire company in a new direction—to content marketing. Why? Their reasoning was (besides the fact that pure SEO budgets were drying up) that the value they used to provide to customers (which used to be immense) simply wasn't there anymore.

Hundreds, if not thousands, of SEO agencies are in the same position. I've seen a few—such as TopRank Online Marketing and Vertical Measures—make this transition incredibly well. Others have simply put the "content marketing" moniker on their SEO content production service and called it "content marketing." Yes, they've added such services as infographics creation, video production, and blog content creation, but content production is only one small part of the content marketing process. Strategic planning aspects of mission statement creation, audience persona gathering, internal content integration, and measurement outside of content consumption metrics are often absent.

The lesson for brands: A holistic content marketing strategy includes up-front planning and multiple goals, which in turn must bring in nondigital channels (such as print and in-person vehicles). SEO is just one very small part that covers a few marketing objectives. Make sure your content marketing strategy goes beyond top-of-the-funnel considerations.

Most agencies are less concerned about strategy than they are about execution. Want to hear a dirty little secret that content agencies subscribe to?

Give away the strategy to get the execution.

I was guilty of this many times while I was at Penton Media. I would give away whatever strategic insight I needed to in order to win the content project. It was the ultimate "value add." Why? Planning lasts just a short time, while execution can last forever. The thinking was that giving up the planning guidance for free could result in a content project contract (such as producing a serial blog, custom magazine, or video series) that may last for years or more.

Like it or not, strategy and planning usually have been viewed not as a useful service to customers but as a closing strategy to get the execution business. This also has meant that the majority of internal talent has gone to execution, not strategy.

And today? This is exactly the reason why so many businesses are struggling to find solid strategic partners for content planning, while content execution increasingly is becoming a commodity.

And the worst part? I've never seen a content planning document from an agency that recommended *less* content or (God forbid) stopping the content program altogether (which is sometimes the correct remedy).

The lesson for brands: Regardless of whether you hired agencies to just do content execution, you must ask them for a sample of an executable content marketing strategy as well. You at least need to see if they understand the strategic argument for—and more importantly, against—content creation. There may be a time for producing less content, but without strategic guidance, the answer will always be more (and this is just shortsighted).

Most agencies still see content marketing as a campaign. As you've learned throughout this book, content marketing is not a campaign—it's an approach, a philosophy, and a business strategy.

Similarly, a viral video—and its resultant success or failure—is *not* content marketing. A campaign is *not* content marketing. A campaign can be the *result* of a content marketing approach, but in and of itself, it is not content marketing. In other words, releasing the long form of a 30-second advertisement is *not* a content marketing approach—it's just a clever form of advertising.

Most agencies aren't built for consistent, long-form content creation and distribution. They're built for speed, for great creative that makes an immediate impact (one hopes). Compare this to what it takes to create content marketing efforts such as Procter & Gamble's Home Made Simple or American Express's OPEN Forum: day-in, day-out content planning, production, and evolution over a long period of time, with the goal of attracting and/or retaining customers.

The lesson for brands: Be wary of any agency pitching you a "campaign" over a "program." There is one thing that's certain with any campaign: it has an end date. Not so with content marketing.

A REVIEW

Even though content marketing is more than 100 years old, we are in the middle of a revolution. Total consumer control, combined with an absence of technology barriers for brands, has resulted in a content marketing renaissance. At the same time, it has forced marketing service providers to alter their business models, and their sales speak, to include editorial-based content creation.

While, overall, this is good for the industry, it has created a confusion of what true content marketing is—and what the practice of content marketing can look like for both agencies and brands.

If you feel you need to work with an outside partner to help you manage your content marketing process (which is completely fine), make sure you heed the warning mentioned previously and choose a content marketing agency that will truly help you attract and retain customers through epic content creation and distribution.

EPIC THOUGHTS

- No matter what you call it, your company's story—your content strategy—has to be tended by someone in your organization. If you don't assign someone to do this, be prepared for duplication and confusion.
- Start looking to add to your organization marketers who understand how to tell a story. Those with journalism backgrounds should be a priority.

EPIC RESOURCES

- "Contently's Code of Ethics for Journalism and Content Marketing," Contently.com, accessed July 9, 2013, http://contently.com/blog /2012/08/01/ethics/.
- *Chief Content Officer* magazine: http://contentmarketinginstitute .com/chief-content-officer/.
- Skyword, accessed April 3, 2013, http://skyword.com.
- Eloqua's Grande Guides, accessed April 15, 2013, http://www.eloqua .com/resources/grande-guides.html.

CHAPTER 16

Content Types

Individuals and organizations that are good
react quickly to change. Individuals and
organizations that are great create change.

ROBERT KRIEGEL, *SACRED COWS MAKE THE BEST BURGERS*

This chapter is all about content, or media, types.* These are not channels (such as LinkedIn or your website), although some, like blogs, can mean both a content type and a channel. Regardless, as you run through these content types, think of the types of content that will make the most sense based on your marketing objectives.

BLOGS

WHAT A BLOG IS

Shorthand for "weblog," the blog offers an easy way to present brief chunks of frequently refreshed web content. Backed with easy-to-use technologies for syndication (for example, RSS) and commenting, blogs are often the centers of social media solar systems that can incorporate sophisticated SEO strategies and community-building campaigns. In Chapter 19, we'll review leveraging a blog as your main content platform.

---

*Generally, the more popular content types appear first, and some other, lesser used content types are found toward the end of this list. Special thanks to Jonathan Kranz, author of *Writing for Dummies*, who helped put together this section.

THREE KEY PLAY POINTS

1. Encourage conversations: even "bad" comments can be an opportunity for developing good customer relations.
2. Be a good "netizen": participate on other blogs as well as your own. Develop a Top 15 hit list where you need to be "hanging out" (more on this in Chapter 22).
3. Loosen up. Authenticity trumps perfection when connecting with readers.

QUESTIONS TO ASK BEFORE YOU BLOG

One of the most frequent questions I receive while traveling is about blogging. The questions revolve around *how to get started, what to talk about,* and even *what software to use.*

My questions back to them usually startle people, because so many of them start thinking about what *they want to say* rather than how they can impact the reader. Here are a few questions I ask:

- *Who* will be primary reader (subscriber) of your blog?
- *What* do you want to tell him or her? (What's your story?)
- Do you understand the key informational needs of that person? *What are his or her pain points?*
- *Are you hanging out online where your customers are?* Do you or can you make a target hit list of blogs or sites that your customers frequent online?
- Are you leaving comments that *add to the online conversation* on the blogs you cover?
- Do you have a firm grasp on the types of *keywords* to focus on that your customers are searching for? (See Google's Keyword Tool.)
- Do you *follow those keywords* using Google Alerts or watch their usage on Twitter? (Do so to find the influencers in your market.)
- Can you *commit* to blogging at least two times per week? (Content consistency is key.)
- *What is your ultimate goal in starting a blog?* One year after you start blogging, how will the business be different?
- How will the execution *process* work within your company and how will you *market the blog*?
- How will you *integrate the blog* with the rest of your marketing? How can the blog make everything else you are doing better?

These are the general starter questions for both businesses and individuals. It might be a bit overwhelming for first-timers, but knowing the answers is necessary.

The majority of blogs out there don't make it. The worst thing you can do as a business is start a consistent dialogue with your customers and then stop. It's better not to do anything at all than to stop cold turkey. According to IBM research, 85 percent of corporate blogs have five posts or less. That means we (brands) are really good at starting content projects but not really good at continuing the process.

Remember, blogging is just a tool. That said, it can be a very powerful tool to consistently communicate valuable, compelling content on a consistent basis. If you are ready to get started, here are six steps to successful blogging.

BLOG EXAMPLES

Deloitte Debates. * Remember "Point/Counterpoint" on *60 Minutes*? Deloitte's taken a lesson from one of network television's most successful "news magazine" programs by posting weekly debates, pro and con, on hot business and finance issues. Instead of the same old, same old, *Deloitte Debates* provides lively and thoughtful discussions (see Figure 16.1).

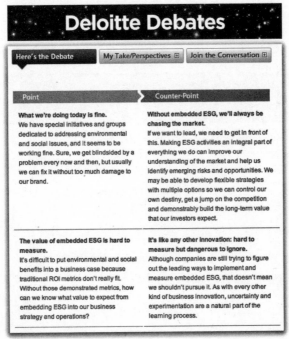

Source: deloitte.com

Figure 16.1 *Deloitte Debates.*

*Thanks to Erica Dipyatic, Deloitte, for input on this section.

PK Wadsworth *Home Comfort* Blog. Who says that service contractors don't blog? PK Wadsworth, from Solon, Ohio, rejects all that hot air. Its *Home Comfort* blog has become central to the company's online strategy. PK Wadsworth focuses on solving problems that its customers have with their heating and air-conditioning, attracting customers and prospects through search engines and social media tools such as Twitter and Facebook. PK Wadsworth has been blogging two times per week for three years now, and has steadily grown a larger audience over that time (see Figure 16.2).

10 BLOGGING TIPS TO REMEMBER

1. Use killer titles. Your blog title is like the cover of a magazine. There is one purpose for a magazine cover: *to get you to open the magazine.* The same holds true for a blog post. The greatest blog post in the world might not be read unless you have a compelling title.

In an analysis of our top content marketing posts, we at CMI found that the most popular and most effective posts had some kind of number in them (for example, "The 10 Most Popular Posts for 2013"). Even better was putting in two numbers. Controversial is also good.

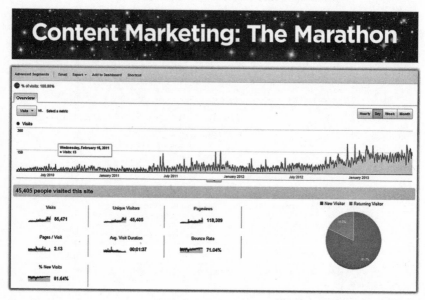

Source: PK Wadsworth

Figure 16.2 PK Wadsworth's blog traffic has steadily increased each year.

Headline Tips

- Think about the problem (see tip number 2).
- Focus on important keywords for your business (use Google's Keyword Tool for help with this).
- Numbers rule.

With titles, be *very* specific. For example, instead of saying "Ways to Increase Your Stock Return" say "10 Ways to Make More Money with Small-Cap Stocks."

2. Focus on the problem. This is where you always should start. *What are the pain points of your target reader? What keeps her or him up at night?*

If your blog focuses 100 percent of the time on what keeps your customers and prospects up at night, you most likely will be successful.

3. Less is more. Blogs are best when they are short, instructive, and to the point. Only on a rare occasion is there a need to ramble on about an issue.

Short Tips

- Keep sentences short.
- Use bullets.
- Short paragraphs
- Get rid of unnecessary words.
- Edit, edit, edit.

One of my most popular posts ever, "A Blog Is Like a Miniskirt," was only 23 words. If your blog draft ends up having 500 words, try to edit it down to 350. That cuts out the clutter.

4. Think first about the call to action. Each blog post should have some sort of call to action. Here are calls to action you can—and should—put on your website:*

- Download our white paper.
- Join us on Twitter (or Facebook, LinkedIn, YouTube, or whatever).
- Ask us a question.
- Download our e-book.
- Sign up for our free webinar.

*I am grateful to Debbie Weil for providing the list items.

- Request our toolkit.
- Sign up for our e-newsletter.
- Request a demo.

Remember, *much of your blog traffic will probably never come back.* Show your readers additional, relevant content offers, such as a valuable niche e-newsletter, so you can continue to communicate with them. Getting opt-in e-mail names should be one of your top blogging goals (to grow the database).

5. Think "content packages." This book started out as a series of blog posts. As I continued to develop blog posts, I started to think about how they could evolve into a book.

Continually think about how you can take blog posts and repackage them into something more substantial. Planning for this ahead of time instead of repackaging after the fact. It will save you immense amounts of time and resources by planning up front.

One blogging idea could be 10 pieces of content. Think about that for a second.

6. Spread the love: guest blogging. Target the top 15 blogs in your industry, and offer to do relevant guest posts on their blogs. Never turn down an opportunity for a guest post.

I've done guest blogs for more than 100 blogs, and it has been one of the most important keys to building CMI's social media and search engine presence.

7. Promote key influencers with lists. Everyone loves lists, especially the people on the list.

- Create a niche list.
- Be sure it's easily shareable (including a widget).
- Do a blog post about the list.
- Let those featured on the list know about it.
- Do a press release about the list.
- Repeat, repeat, repeat.

8. Measure, measure, measure. Here are a number of blog metrics you can measure as part of your blog (all of these metrics can be accessed through Google Analytics or another analytics program). Choose the ones that make the most sense with your overall content marketing and blogging goals. Make sure you and your team know what the goal of the blog is and that everyone sees the statistics. Measure the following:

- Visits and unique visitors
- Pageviews
- Time on site
- Signups to your e-newsletter
- Search rankings
- Inbound links to your blog

9. Do an influencer question-and-answer session. Most industry heavy hitters will do a podcast interview or question-and-answer session (Q&A), if you ask. They will probably also share it with their network when it's finished.

10. Outsource. According to CMI/MarketingProfs research, more than 50 percent of companies of all sizes outsource their content marketing.

Most businesses outsource a portion of their content marketing. Find a great writer to help you. Find a content agency or content team to take your blogging/strategy to the next level.

Some companies have a difficult time telling engaging stories. Enlist help; it's available.

E-NEWSLETTER

WHAT AN E-NEWSLETTER IS

An e-newsletter is a permission-based means of regular communication with current and future customers, usually distributed monthly or weekly. Available electronically via text-based or HTML pages, e-newsletters can include complete articles or brief descriptions with links to articles on your website.

THREE KEY PLAY POINTS

1. Don't spam your e-newsletter. Get permission and offer opt-out links at the bottom of every e-newsletter you send out.
2. It can be a good vehicle for promoting other content: webinars, e-books, white papers, live events, and so on.
3. A roundup of the blog content into your e-newsletter is a solid one-two punch. Try daily blogging and a weekly or monthly e-newsletter review.

E-NEWSLETTER EXAMPLE

Whidbey Camano Island Tours.* This group produces "premium" content—videos and infographics—tied to a monthly e-newsletter delivered by ExactTarget (owned by Salesforce.com). Since launch, this site has increased unique visits by 60,000 via these activities and doubled the size of the e-newsletter database. This work was governed by an editorial calendar, with the monthly e-newsletter as the major publishing date of focus.

10 WAYS TO OPTIMIZE YOUR
E-NEWSLETTER LANDING PAGE†

In our new social media world, e-mail assets are more important than ever. As content marketers, it is critical that we develop audiences and build channels, with a primary emphasis on e-mail in conjunction with social channels such as Facebook and Twitter. Why? Theoretically (and legally) the customer names that sign up to our social channels do not belong to us (they belong to Facebook and Twitter). *Your e-mail database, on the other hand, is a significant business asset.*

Here are 10 steps you can take now to optimize your e-newsletter landing page to get more customers and prospects to sign up for your content.

1. **Spell out the benefits.** On the landing page, clearly list why someone should sign up for your e-newsletter.
2. **Show them a picture.** Show readers a sample picture of what they will be receiving. (What does the e-mail newsletter look like?)
3. **Link to a sample.** Link to a sample e-newsletter, and have that sample open up in a "daughter window" (that is, don't take them away from the landing page).
4. **Bring the signup above the fold.** If prospects have to scroll down to get to your signup area, there is a problem. The signup needs to be above the fold.
5. **Have no more than five to seven fields.** The fewer fields, the more likely prospects will be to sign up. Only ask for the fields you truly need.
6. **Be sure to have a clear link to a privacy statement (below the fold).** Although very few (if any) people will ever click on it, be sure to have a privacy statement available that has been checked by your legal team.

*Thanks to Russell Sparkman, FusionSpark Media, for his input on this section.
†Thanks to Jeanne Jennings for her input on this section.

7. **Tell customers what you will and won't do with their information.** At the bottom of the page, be very clear about how you will use the customers' information they'll be giving to you.

8. **Include a button that says "subscribe" or "sign up" (not "submit").** Words like *submit* and phrases like "click here" don't accurately spell out the positive action you want prospects to take. Use "subscribe" or "sign up."

9. **Get rid of needless distractions.** The landing page for your e-newsletter has one goal: to get people to sign up for the e-newsletter. Get rid of all the distractions that may take them away from the signup page, such as the *general navigation, third-party advertising, house ads,* or other calls to action.

10. **Be sure to include testimonials and awards.** Put at least one good testimonial about what a user thinks about your e-newsletter. Get permission to use that person's name and title. Have you won any awards? List those as credibility points as well.

Remember, you want a simple form that shows at least as much value as the information they are giving you (you are trading your content for their name). Don't overcomplicate the process.

As always, *test your changes.* The behavior of buyers is not consistent across industries, so be sure to test what works for you and what doesn't.

WHITE PAPER

WHAT A WHITE PAPER IS
The "granddaddy" of content, white papers, are topical reports, typically 8 to 12 pages long, on issues that require a lot of explanation. Also known as conference papers, research reports, or technical briefs, they are perfect for demonstrating thought leadership on issues vital to your buyers.

THREE KEY PLAY POINTS
1. A white paper can generate leads.
2. It positions the company as a thought leader.
3. It's applicable to print, electronic PDF, or digital magazine formats.

WHITE PAPER EXAMPLE

IBM. Surprisingly, some of the best thought leadership on sustainability is coming from IBM. Check out Figure 16.3, which shows a cutting-edge

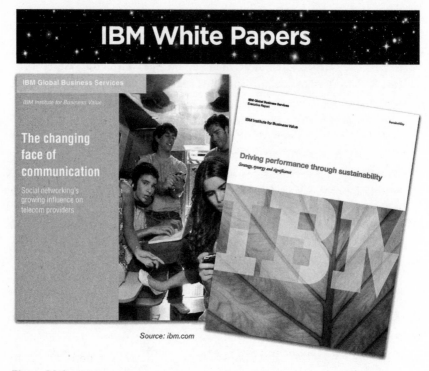

Source: ibm.com

Figure 16.3 IBM has led the way for years with its research-based white papers.

white paper on "Driving Performance Through Sustainability" and its IBM Institute for Business Value.

IBM asserts leadership within the telecom community through its provocative paper, "The Changing Face of Communications: Social Networking's Growing Influence on Telecom Providers."

ARTICLE

WHAT AN ARTICLE IS

A flexible medium, both in length and format, the article opens opportunities for companies to address issues, trends, concerns, and topics of immediate interest to their intended audiences. An ongoing article publishing campaign, complemented with a roster of speaking engagements, has been the traditional tool for establishing thought leadership in numerous industries.

THREE KEY PLAY POINTS

1. Once isn't enough; plan on a series of articles to create impact.
2. Look for opportunities to place your articles in print media *and* on the web, on your website as well as others in need of great content.
3. Always think from the editor's point of view; your article must conform to the publication's requirements (length and tone, for example) and be of immediate interest to its readers.

THE DIFFERENCE BETWEEN ARTICLES AND BLOGS?

Marketers always ask the difference between articles and blogs. Blogs have a clear point of view—a personality. Articles have no point of view but are informational treasure troves. Think of FAQ (frequently asked questions) articles or an informational series of articles on your website.

Tip: When customer service answers a key customer question via e-mail, think about putting it in your article repository.

E-BOOK

WHAT AN E-BOOK IS

Think of an e-book as a white paper on steroids: a report, generally 12 to 40 pages or more in length, that presents complex information in a visually attractive, reader-friendly format. The content is both informative and entertaining; the tone, collegial; the format, "chunky" rather than linear, to facilitate skimming and scanning.

THREE KEY PLAY POINTS

1. Develop your distribution strategy early: how will you get your e-book into readers' hands?
2. Think visually: make liberal use of bullets, callouts, sidebars, graphs, and so on.
3. Conclude with a solid call to action: what should readers do next? For that matter, include some call to action or link on every page. Why not?

E-BOOK EXAMPLE

ARX. Consisting of 12 business cases that illustrate the bottom-line value of digital signatures, ARX's e-book (see Figure 16.4) transforms signatures from an operational afterthought to an urgent business issue.

Figure 16.4   *Think Twice Before You Sign Anything Again* e-book from ARX.

CASE STUDY

WHAT A CASE STUDY IS

The case study is a document, typically one to two pages long, or video that combines the first-person authority of the testimonial with the narrative structure of a story. Based on real-life events, it leverages reader empathy with the featured client to build credibility and trust.

THREE KEY PLAY POINTS

1. Most case studies follow a simple, three-stage format: challenge, solution, and results.
2. Use direct client quotes to reinforce the story, especially when addressing the results.
3. Share case studies online, in direct mail, in press kits, as sales handouts, and so on.

CASE STUDY EXAMPLE

PTC. Mechanical design and automation company PTC featured customer College Park, which used PTC technology to develop a prosthetic foot. PTC put together both a textual case study and an amazing five-minute video featuring thrill seeker Reggie Showers doing things with College Park and PTC that he would never have been able to do (see Figure 16.5). For a text case study, go to http://bitly.com/epic-ptc-text; for video, go to http://bitly.com/epic-ptc-video.

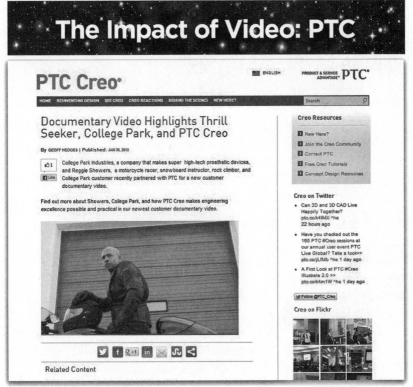

Source: ptc.com

Figure 16.5 PTC tells the story of two-time world motorcycle champion Reggie Showers in this video case study.

TESTIMONIALS

WHAT A TESTIMONIAL IS

A testimonial is, figuratively speaking, a quote from the horse's (that is, the customer's) mouth. Boasting is unseemly when we do it ourselves. But when praise comes from a trustworthy source—a client or customer—it acquires a credibility that helps overcome skepticism and purchasing hesitation.

THREE KEY PLAY POINTS

1. Create a process for consistently requesting testimonials from your customers. Many marketers are starting to leverage their LinkedIn pages for testimonials on products and services.
2. Good testimonials offer specifics: the what, why, and how of your work with or for the customer.
3. Don't bury testimonials on a separate "Testimonials" web page; spread them throughout the site.

WEBINAR/WEBCAST

WHAT A WEBINAR/WEBCAST IS

Take your presentation and put it online: that's the essence of the webinar (slides and audio) or webcast (slides, audio, and video). Visually, the content is delivered slide by slide in the online equivalent of a live presentation. The audio component can be delivered via telephone or computer. Remember, you can do this live or on demand.

THREE KEY PLAY POINTS

1. Webinars make an excellent call to action or follow-up offer to other forms of content, such as e-books, white papers, e-newsletters, and so on.
2. You benefit twice: first, from the live event; then from the people who download the archived event. In a six-month period, generally 80 percent of those people who register for a webinar will attend either the live or archived version.
3. A successful webinar requires an aggressive promotions strategy, typically via your website, blog, e-newsletter, and other media or social media channels.

WEBINAR EXAMPLE

Content Marketing Institute produces two webinars every month on an issue pertaining to content marketing. CMI recruits both an industry thought leader and a technology expert company for each webinar. Ninety-nine percent of the attendees come from two direct e-mail promotions to the CMI e-mail list. On average, about 750 people register for each webinar, and about 35 percent of those who register attend the live event. CMI leverages ON24 to run the technology for the webinars.

VIDEO

WHAT VIDEO IS

Sites such as YouTube and Vimeo have greatly simplified a once difficult web challenge: uploading and sharing videos. With these tools at your disposal, you can embed or link video code easily. And the video sites provide social media options for conversing and sharing that can help your content go viral.

THREE KEY PLAY POINTS

1. Think beyond the "talking head" approach. Inexpensive editing tools such as iMovie or Final Cut make it easy to assemble professional-looking video content.
2. Instead of taking a one-shot approach, consider a video series that builds interest, and an audience, over time.
3. Don't sweat "perfection": many of the most successful online videos have production values that would scandalize traditional media broadcasters. Actually, the most important part of the video is the audio, so focus your tools on the audio equipment first.

VIDEO EXAMPLE

Converse, the shoe company, built a music recording studio in Brooklyn, New York. There, it acts as a patron of the arts, inviting musicians and bands to come record in its state-of-the-art facility for free. Each week, Converse releases amazing video content highlighting a Track of the Week on YouTube (see Figure 16.6*); check it out at http://bitly.com/epic-converse.

*Kudos to Andrew Davis for the find.

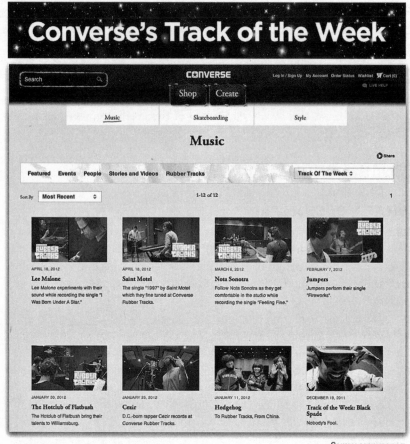

Source: converse.com

Figure 16.6   Converse's Track of the Week.

ONLINE NEWS RELEASE

WHAT AN ONLINE NEWS RELEASE IS

A press release is any written or recorded communication directed at the general news media. Services such as PR Newswire can post your press releases online for faster and more widespread distribution. The big news? As David Meerman Scott famously explained in *The New Rules of Marketing and PR*, press releases are no longer just for the press anymore. By using the release services effectively, you can appeal directly to your buyers.

THREE KEY PLAY POINTS

1. Don't wait for big news; find reasons to send releases all the time.
2. Include specific calls to action that compel customers to respond to your release in some way.
3. Try a new format. There is no reason why you have to send out the same old news releases. Tell a story with your news release, and feel free to change the feel of it. Don't worry: distribution companies will still send it out, no matter what you do.

CUSTOM PRINT MAGAZINE

WHAT A CUSTOM PRINT MAGAZINE IS

All brands are now publishers. The custom print magazine takes this approach quite literally, offering the familiar magazine format with a new twist: it's sponsored, produced, and issued by one company or brand.

THREE KEY PLAY POINTS

1. Be prepared to spend at least $40,000 USD for even a small initial distribution.
2. The most effective frequency is quarterly or more often.
3. It can be an excellent way to bypass gatekeepers.

PRINT NEWSLETTER

WHAT A PRINT NEWLETTER IS

Whether it's merely a double-sided sheet or a 16-page document, a print newsletter offers attention-grabbing content meant for rapid consumption. As a tactic, consider it for customer retention, and remember that the average length runs between 4 and 12 pages.

THREE KEY PLAY POINTS

1. Print newsletters are terrific for on-the-go audience, including business travelers and commuters. Also think about those audiences that haven't yet adapted to smartphones or iPads.
2. Production quality matters: the way your content is presented is as important as the content itself.
3. Make sure you know your audience's precise information needs before you commit to an editorial platform.

PRINT NEWSLETTER EXAMPLE

RSM McGladrey.* As part of an integrated content marketing program, RSM McGladrey's newsletter (see Figure 16.7) helped the consulting firm increase top-of-mind awareness among target CEOs and CFOs by nearly 60 percent.

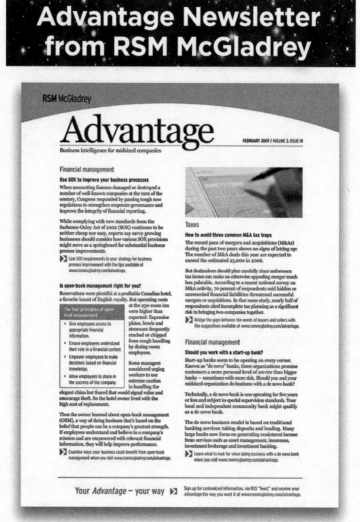

Source: Hanley Wood Marketing

Figure 16.7   RSM McGladrey Advantage newsletter.

*Thanks to Hanley Wood for input on this section.

THE OPPORTUNITIES IN PRINT

I was on the phone recently talking to a customer about different options in print. He was interested in the discussion because he felt his company needed to do more *nontraditional marketing*.

Just think about that for a second: print is *nontraditional* marketing. That's where we are today. Blogging, social media, web articles . . . that's all very traditional. Because of that, brands should be looking at print as an opportunity right now to get and keep attention

THE *NEWSWEEK* MOVE

Newsweek has ceased publication in the print format. *SmartMoney* recently made the same declaration.

When I have conversations with marketers and publishers about these kinds of moves, I always hear the notion that "print is dead." Well, I'm here to tell you that there has never been a bigger opportunity for brands in the printed channel than right now.

While I would not want to be in the broad-based, horizontal print game (as *USA Today* is), highly niche, highly targeted publications are flourishing as a marketing tool. For example, *ThinkMoney* magazine from TD Ameritrade (see Figure 16.8) has about 90 percent of its customers take direct action on a product it sells through the print magazine. The magazine is a true collision of amazing design and provocative information. It's the type of content that is anticipated by its trader audience. And better yet, since traders are in front of computers all day long, they look forward to the opportunity to disconnect and discover.

Even CMI's own *Chief Content Officer* magazine has a clear competitive advantage in the marketplace because it's in print. At a recent event (not CMI's), three marketing executives came up to me and told me how much they enjoy the magazine and can't wait until the next one arrives. (They didn't mention our daily digital content; they just mentioned print.)

PRINT IS NOT DECLINING ANYMORE

Many prognosticators say that by 2020 most printed media will be gone. I think anyone who makes those types of comments doesn't understand history. Just type into a search engine "The Death of TV" and you'll see hundreds of articles predicting the end of television. One could make the argument that right now is the golden age of television, with amazing shows such as *Boardwalk Empire, Mad Men,* and *Homeland* leading the way.

Source: T3 Publishing

Figure 16.8 *ThinkMoney* magazine produced by TD Ameritrade.

The evolution of the Internet doesn't kill off these channels; it makes us look at them differently *because they are used differently by consumers.*

Among the findings of CMI's 2013 Content Marketing Research, the usage of *every* channel, including print, is flat or up. After years of seeing the usage of print magazines on the downside, we saw no change year over year. Yes, marketers, for the most part, have stopped fleeing from the print channel.

Of course, content marketing strategy comes first, followed by channel strategy. But as a content marketer, it is our responsibility to look at all available channels to tell our stories.

SEVEN REASONS TO RETHINK PRINT

Here are a few reasons why there might be an amazing opportunity in the print channel.

1. **It grabs attention.** Have you noticed how many fewer magazines and print newsletters you are getting in the mail these days? I don't know about you, but I definitely pay more attention to my print mail. There's just less mail, so more attention is paid to each piece. Opportunity? The decisions that magazines like *Newsweek* are making leave a clear opportunity for content marketers to fill the gap.

2. **It focuses on customer retention.** Sixty-four percent of B2B marketers create original content for customer retention and loyalty goals. Historically, the reason custom print magazines and newsletters were developed by brands was for customer retention purposes. In a recent CMI webinar, Carlos Hidalgo, CEO of Annuitas Group, stated that one of the biggest problems marketers have with their content is that they forget to nurture customers *after* the purchase decision is made.

3. **There are no audience development costs.** Publishers expend huge amounts of time and money qualifying subscribers to send out their magazines. Many times, publishers need to invest multiple dollars per subscriber per year for auditing purposes. (They send direct mail, they call . . . they call again . . . so that the magazine can say that their subscribers have requested the magazine. This is true for controlled [free] trade magazines.)

    So let's say a traditional publisher's cost per subscriber per year is $2 and its distribution is 100,000. That's $200,000 per year for audience development.

    That's a cost that marketers don't have to worry about. If marketers want to distribute a magazine to their customers, they just use their customer mailing lists. That's a big advantage.

4. **What's old is new again.** Social media, online content, and iPad applications are all part of the marketing mix today. Still, what excites marketers and media buyers is what *is not* being done (think: *nontraditional*). They want to do something different and something new. It's hard to believe, but the print channel is new again and is seeing a rebirth. Could we possibly be seeing a golden age in print, as we are seeing in television?

5. **Customers still need to know what questions to ask.** I love the Internet because buyers can find answers to almost anything. But where does someone go to think about what *questions* he or she

should be asking? I talked to a publisher recently who said this: "The web is where we go to get answers, but print is where we go to ask questions."

The print vehicle is still the best medium on the planet for thinking outside the box and asking yourself tough questions based on what you read; it's "lean back" versus "lean forward." If you want to challenge your customers (as *Harvard Business Review* does), print is a viable option.

6. **Print still excites people.** I talked to a journalist recently who said it's harder and harder to get people to agree to an interview for an online story. But mention that it will be a printed feature and executives rearrange their schedule. The printed word is still perceived as more credible to many people than anything on the web. It goes to the old adage, "If someone invested enough to print and mail it, it must be important."

We at CMI have seen this firsthand with *Chief Content Officer* magazine. Contributors love being featured on the CMI website, but they crave having their article in the printed magazine. It's amazing how different the perception is of the print versus online channel when it comes to editorial contribution.

7. **Print lets people unplug.** More and more, people are actively choosing to unplug, or disconnect themselves from digital media. I'm finding myself turning off my phone and e-mail more to engage with printed material. A year ago I didn't see this coming. Today, I relish the opportunities when I can't be reached for comment.

For example, our entire family does "electronics-free Saturday." This means no computer, no iPhone, no Xbox, no e-mail, and no Facebook. We've been doing this since January 2012, and although it's been difficult, it's been an amazing experience for our family. I love when all four of us are sitting in the family room reading books and magazines. We've also done much more together as a family.

If I'm right, many of your customers, especially busy executives, are feeling the same way. Your print communication may be just what they need.

Online content marketing is definitely here to stay. So say yes to social media, apps, and the rest of it. But don't forget that print can still play an important role in your overall content marketing mix.

DIGITAL MAGAZINE

WHAT A DIGITAL MAGAZINE IS

A hybrid between the traditional magazine and a souped-up PDF, a digital magazine offers self-contained, visually compelling periodical content that doesn't require special software to open and read. Issues are generally distributed by e-mail via brand websites.

THREE KEY PLAY POINTS

1. If you don't like the confinement of a digital replica, consider repurposing print magazine content on your blog.
2. Digital magazines are great for integrating print content with a web presence.
3. Consider adding video and podcasts to your magazine content.

DIGITAL MAGAZINE EXAMPLE

ZN **Magazine.** Zappo's *ZN* magazine (see Figure 16.9) captures the look and feel of traditional print content while adding convenient features (like searching, printing, and shopping) unique to digital.

Source: zappos.com

Figure 16.9   Zappos *ZN* magazine.

E-LEARNING SERIES

WHAT AN E-LEARNING SERIES IS

A carefully planned curriculum of educational content that may be delivered through a variety of mediums, including audio podcasts, video, slide presentations, webinars, and more.

THREE KEY PLAY POINTS

1. Tailor the content to the different learning needs of different audiences: buyers doing research, prospects close to making a purchasing decision, current customers, and so on.
2. Use the mediums most popular with your constituencies.
3. Be generous with real-life examples and illustrations.

E-LEARNING SERIES EXAMPLE

Oracle Technology Network. Whether you are a database administrator or even an architect, Oracle has provided one place where their users can get all the answers (see Figure 16.10). This helpful site includes not only

Source: oracle.com

Figure 16.10   **Oracle Technology Network.**

wikis, helpful articles, and support issues but also ongoing educational webinars and reports.

MOBILE APPLICATION

WHAT A MOBILE APPLICATION IS

Known familiarly as "apps," mobile applications come in two broad flavors: as native apps developed for specific devices (such as the iPhone, Android, BlackBerry, iPad) or as web apps that can be distributed without depending on specific marketplaces (but you need an Internet connection at all times). These downloadable tools allow users to turn their PDAs into handy devices that meet their very specific, idiosyncratic needs.

THREE KEY PLAY POINTS

1. Effective applications must have a regular (daily or weekly) reason for use (think utility).
2. They should have easy interfaces with social networks such as Facebook or Twitter.
3. A survey function needs to be included to gauge satisfaction and collect intelligence for the next release (iPhone Apps solicit feedback that affects the volume of downloads).

MOBILE APP EXAMPLE

SitOrSquat by Charmin. Ever concerned about finding a clean public bathroom? Well, worry no more. Charmin's SitOrSquat is a real-time mobile application that tells you where the cleanest bathrooms are closest to your location (see Figure 16.11). Well over 1 million people have downloaded the app.

TELESEMINAR

WHAT A TELESEMINAR IS

Hello, content calling! The teleseminar is a virtual presentation stripped to the bare essentials: the only technology required is a phone. Depending on the nature of the content, participants may have an outline, agenda, or presentation slide deck sent in advance of the phone call.

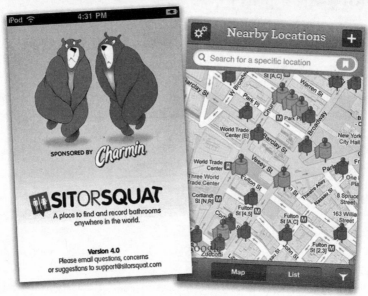

Figure 16.11 Charmin's SitOrSquat mobile application.

THREE KEY PLAY POINTS

1. For many small to midsized firms, the teleseminar is an ideal way for multiple employees to attend a presentation.
2. Record the teleseminar; now you have a podcast, too.
3. Schedule your teleseminar for maximum convenience across multiple time zones.

PODCAST

WHAT A PODCAST IS

A podcast is simply an audio file you can listen to on a computer or MP3-type player, often distributed via RSS or iTunes. Podcasts are generally 5 to 30 minutes long, but longer podcast downloads are becoming popular.

THREE KEY PLAY POINTS

1. Define a podcast theme, and stick to it.
2. Establish a release schedule listeners can expect: weekly, biweekly, monthly, and so on. Be consistent.
3. Integrate podcast content with your blog to gain listener insights.

PODCAST EXAMPLE

Entrepreneur on Fire. John Lee Dumas developed a daily podcast featuring amazing entrepreneurs from just about every industry on the planet (like Seth Godin and Barbara Corcoran of the television show *Shark Tank*). The interviews last about 30 minutes, and they have helped John grow an amazing business and following because of his consistent interviews. Now, thousands tune in every day to listen. I've had the honor of being interviewed by John; to listen, go to http://bitly.com/epic-eonfire.

EXECUTIVE ROUNDTABLE

WHAT AN EXECUTIVE ROUNDTABLE IS

An executive roundtable is a gathering of industry executives who are experts in their field and who have enough drawing power to pull in your prospects. Through brief presentations and interactions among roundtable participants, you have the opportunity once again to position yourself as a thought leader.

THREE KEY PLAY POINTS

1. Look for executives whose personalities are as appealing as their ideas.
2. Consider asking the roundtable executives for guest blog posts that complement their live topic ideas.
3. Turn the resulting discussion into a summary report you can offer as a white paper or e-book. Leverage video, audio, and transcripts to keep the content flowing long after the actual roundtable has taken place.

ROUNDTABLE EXAMPLE

McKinsey. McKinsey regularly hosts executive roundtables around key, complex topics, and it shares the resulting content afterward for maximum distribution (see Figure 16.12).

Source: mckinsey.com

Figure 16.12   McKinsey's Executive Roundtable series.

INDUSTRY RANKING SYSTEM

WHAT AN INDUSTRY RANKING SYSTEM IS

People love lists. (Remember Moses and his two tablets?) An industry ranking system gives readers a preassembled "best-of" list that ranks available options in a given topic area—and subsequently ranks high with search engines. A list, whatever its contents, positions its assemblers as industry experts and gives their prospects a helpful reference tool.

THREE KEY PLAY POINTS

1. Rankings can be determined by some objective and measurable means or by subjective criteria.
2. Make liberal use of links to the listed resources.
3. Announce updates to the ranking system via blogs, Twitter, press releases, and so on.

PRINTED BOOK

WHAT A PRINTED BOOK IS

Even in the revolutionary age of Web 2.0, a full-length book still carries an aura of authority. Whether self-published or created via a traditional publishing house, the book is the "big" content piece that often leads to press exposure, speaking invitations, and a privileged status as *the* expert.

THREE KEY PLAY POINTS

1. Books are a major investment of time, so plan carefully! If you have a blog, think about how your blog posts can serve as chapters for your book.
2. Get your PR people on board fast to leverage the media potential.
3. Consider developing a microsite or Facebook fan page to create communities around your book.

WHY YOUR BRAND SHOULD WRITE A BOOK

Frankly, if you are going to position yourself and/or your company as the leading expert in your niche, you need a book. No, not an e-book distributed solely online. You need a "makes-a-big-thud-when-dropped-on-a-desk" book that is produced from dead trees.

I'm astonished and saddened that more organizations aren't looking seriously at developing a book. But yet, here are some amazing examples of brands that understand the power of a book.

***Revenue Disruption* from Marketo.** Penned by Phil Fernandez (cofounder of Marketo), this baby is a Marketo product (see Figure 16.13). I received a signed copy in the mail as part of a very smart promotional effort by Marketo, and have also seen the book in multiple airport bookstores. The book title, *Revenue Disruption*, is a perfect description of Marketo's mantra and purpose about automating the marketing process focused on revenue growth.

***Precision Marketing* from Ricoh InfoPrint.** From authors Sandra Zoratti and Lee Gallagher, the concepts in *Precision Marketing* (see Figure 16.14) play perfectly into the core of what Ricoh provides for customers: highly targeted and personalized content solutions. The book makes a

Source: amazon.com

Figure 16.13 Marketo's *Revenue Disruption* by Phil Hernandez.

slew of comparisons using real numbers about how precision marketing pays off more than traditional marketing.

***Engagement Marketing* from Constant Contact.** From Constant Contact CEO Gail Goodman, *Engagement Marketing* (see Figure 16.15) provides a great road map for small businesses for how they can communicate more effectively with customers. Constant Contact, like Marketo, used a signed copy as part of its direct mail program. Honestly, it's a helpful book and provides some great Constant Contact case studies.

Why have these companies developed a book? First, there is no better way to show true thought leadership than a printed book. A close second is this: it may be the best customer giveaway ever created (as was the case with Marketo and Constant Contact). And third, once the book has been developed, you have an amazing resource from which to develop ancillary content, such as blog posts (excerpts), e-books, SlideShare packages, white papers, and much, much more.

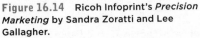

Figure 16.14   Ricoh Infoprint's *Precision Marketing* by Sandra Zoratti and Lee Gallagher.

Figure 16.15   Constant Contact's *Engagement Marketing* by Gail Goodman.

EIGHT TIPS FOR MAKING YOUR BOOK HAPPEN

Creating a book that makes an impact on your industry and business is anything but easy. That said, here are some tips I've picked up along the way that can make a difference in getting the book off the ground.

1. **The deep dive content audit.** You may already have a treasure trove of material that can be repurposed, or at the very least you have content that can be collected to form the initial workings of some key chapters. Be sure you do the work up front to see what you have to start with.

2. **Mine the blog.** For both of my books, *Get Content Get Customers* and *Managing Content Marketing*, much of the material came from existing blog posts, just reworked. If you have been blogging for at least six months, you might already have half a book.

3. **Co-creation**. Do you have key, noncompetitive partners that target the same prospects and customers as you? If so, consider reaching out to them about partnering on the book concept. Also, once you start promoting, you have two different networks to reach out to.

4. **Get it funded.** *Get Content Get Customers* was self-published before McGraw-Hill purchased the rights. Much of the up-front investment

came from selling bulk shipments to partner companies. If you don't like that route, find a sponsor that really wants to get your message out there and have that person or organization support it through either distribution or monetary funding.

5. **The mission.** Be very clear what you want your readers to get out of the book. Write your thoughts down, and keep that information posted to your wall as you work on the book. So many companies focus on what they are trying to say instead of pinpointing the focus on the pain points of the reader.

6. **Include the influencers.** If possible, include key examples from industry influencers, as well as partners, as long as it's good content. The more people you can include into your stories, the more opportunities for outside sharing.

7. **Consider a ghostwriter.** Believe it or not, many of the books from the authors you love have been written by someone else. It's hard to believe, isn't it? But it's true. The best ghostwriters out there start at about $50,000 and then go up from there. If you simply can't make the internal time or don't have the resources to get the writing done, consider using one.

8. **Stop somewhere and realize that perfection is unattainable.** I could have kept writing both books forever if I wanted to. At some point, you have to draw a line in the sand and publish the book. As soon as you finish it there will be some new research, some new story, or some new perspective that you should have covered. Don't worry about it; just use it for your next book.

AUDIOBOOK

WHAT AN AUDIOBOOK IS

Book-length content you listen to rather than read is an audiobook. When sponsored by a brand, it's a great way to capture the attention of podcast-downloading, iPod-carrying listeners or, when it is distributed via CD, to get a share of commuters' drive-time listening.

THREE KEY PLAY POINTS

1. Vocal talent has to be as strong as the written content.
2. Consider complementing the text with music.
3. Get people to sample the content by giving away portions or chapters for free.

VIRTUAL TRADE SHOW

WHAT A VIRTUAL TRADE SHOW IS

Current technology and high-speed Internet connections enable the creation of lifelike happenings (complete with "lounges" and "exhibit areas"). Event managers can create Internet-based virtual trade shows to generate leads, increase event participation, drive revenue, and improve communications with current and future customers.

THREE KEY PLAY POINTS

1. Most virtual shows use the "trade show" metaphor as the navigation model for the virtual show site.
2. Just as live shows sell booths, you can sell sponsored presences at your virtual site.
3. For content, consider a mix of live, scheduled events and prerecorded seminars that can be launched at the visitor's convenience.

VIRTUAL TRADE SHOW EXAMPLE

Cisco Next Generation Virtual Summit. Cisco brings together thought leaders from both its own organization and others, such as AT&T and XO Communications, to present both live and on-demand presentations, tackling some of the toughest issues in network communications.

COMIC BOOK

WHAT A COMIC BOOK IS

Here's what a comic book is not: a gimmick just for kids. By reinforcing text with vivid pictures, comic books communicate in a fun, fast, and memorable way to readers of all ages.

THREE KEY PLAY POINTS

1. For instructional content, comics may be one of the very best tactics available.
2. Memorable comic books can certainly generate buzz.
3. As an alternative to a comic book, consider an online comic strip that appears every week. Tom Fishburne (the Marketoonist) creates new posts almost every day in the form of a cartoon (see Figure 16.16). Tom has become a worldwide expert in visual content because of his cartoons.

Source: Content Marketing Institute

Figure 16.16 Tom Fishburne has become an expert in visual content strategy because of his cartoons. This one is from the February 2013 issue of *Chief Content Officer* magazine.

ROAD SHOW

WHAT A ROAD SHOW IS

Road shows are mini-conferences or tours that are typically conducted by a single organization, although related companies that don't compete will often participate. Usually, individual events last for a day or less and are conducted in cities where there is a high concentration of prospective customers.

THREE KEY PLAY POINTS

1. Concentrate on the takeaway: what will participants get by attending?
2. Coordination of event planning and promotions is crucial; both have to roll out on schedule.

3. You may need to train internal talent to maximize their effectiveness as speakers and presenters.

ROAD SHOW EXAMPLE

Lennox. Every year, Lennox, the heating and air-conditioning manufacturer, travels around the country to hold educational seminars with its dealers to talk about the latest technology and to get a chance to meet and thank dealers in person. The Lennox dealer meetings are critical to the company's entire marketing campaign.

PUBLIC SPEAKING TIPS THAT ROCK

Over the past 12 months, I've made public presentations more than 50 times and another 50 online presentations by webinar or webcast. Since 2007, I've presented well over 300 times in person or online.

I've also had to sit through another thousand presentations by other individuals over that time. Not that I'm perfect by any means, but I honestly don't wish that on anyone.

After my blog and my books, public speaking events have probably led more to growing the business than anything else I've done. Frankly, there are not enough businesses that take presenting in public as a serious driver of revenue. As a business owner or a marketing professional, it is your responsibility to start cultivating evangelists within the company who can spread the content mission of your organization.

The following are some of my presentation speaking tips that I try to integrate into every presentation I do (in no particular order). I hope they are helpful to you.

Put your Twitter name on every slide. Even at the least social media–savvy events, there are always multiple people tweeting. Putting your Twitter handle at the beginning of the slide deck usually doesn't do the trick. (What if someone comes into the room late?) Since I've added my Twitter handle to every slide, tweets have more than doubled. What a great way to expand the reach of your message!

Be prepared with tweetable messages. I learned from my friend Jay Baer to come prepared with tweetable sayings. It's best practice to put them on the slide (no more than 140 characters) and repeat them at least twice for maximum impact.

Prepromote your speech using the event hashtag. The day before and the morning before your presentation, be sure to let people know you are speaking, what you are speaking on, and what time the event is using the event Twitter hashtag (such as #cmworld, the hashtag for Content Marketing World). I can't tell you how many more people I get to my speeches who were undecided about which session to attend.

Never have more than 20 words on a slide. If people have to read your slide, you'll lose them. Use headlines and text to cue your stories and pictures to amplify your point. My goal is to someday take the advice of Seth Godin and have all my slides with no words, just pictures.

If you use words, make them at least 30-point type size or larger. If you do have text on a slide, make sure it's actually readable. Thirty points is the smallest I would go.

Don't stand behind the podium. A podium places an unnecessary barrier between you and your audience. Talk *with* the audience, not *at* them.

It's okay to walk around. You're a human and you have legs: use them. Find a few spots on the stage where you can walk back and forth. Hold your spots for five seconds, and move to the next spot. Every time you start on a new topic, move.

Get a speaking wardrobe. In order to be remembered, you need to use everything at your disposal. A wardrobe is key. Find something that people will remember. I personally always wear an orange shirt. I haven't done a presentation in five years without an orange shirt. People expect it and always comment on it. My friend Mari Smith uses turquoise and sometimes decorates the stage and seating area with special turquoise items. People always remember Mari, in part because she puts on a great show. When people see that color somewhere else, they think of Mari.

Smile a lot. It's contagious. Always start the presentation with a big smile, and set cues for yourself to smile at least every five minutes. The more people smile, the more positive they will be in general (and with your reviews). It also helps to keep people awake.

Use short links as calls to action. In every slide presentation, I include a number of short links for people to get additional information about something I'm discussing. I've had well over 5,000 people download one of my presentations directly from one of my sessions. I use bit.ly links to track the content.

Give away something for participation. I almost always give a signed copy of my book away to reward participation. It helps with questions later and always gets you talking with someone after the presentation (to deliver the book). That encourages more questions and opportunities to network. This tactic has delivered two new customers over the years.

Have one main call to action for the presentation. You want the attendees to do something, right? Don't give them too many options. Give them one thing you really want them to do from each presentation, and include a coupon code or short link to track it.

Use lists. Most of my speaking and presentation titles include numbers in the titles: "8 Content Marketing Tips to Initiate Now," "6 Keys that Separate Good to Great Content Marketing," and so on. Numbers keep people focused on where you are in the presentation.

Switch the flow, and tell a story every eight minutes. Your audience can only pay attention for so long. Every few minutes, stop the flow of your presentation by pausing and telling a story somewhat related to your point. They will remember the stories the most, which will keep them engaged and help drive your overall mission for the speech.

Take heed from Aristotle. When I first started teaching public speaking, I always used Aristotle's advice on speeches: tell them what you are going to tell them (the intro), tell them (the body), and then tell them what you just told them (the conclusion). Much of public speaking and getting things to stick is repetition. This type of setup does the trick.

BRANDED CONTENT TOOL/APPLICATION

WHAT THE BRANDED CONTENT APPLICATION IS
An electronically enabled service, the branded application gathers information from prospects and customers, then produces in return a customized analysis, assessment, report, or plan. By virtue of its quality and/or uniqueness, the branded application has the potential to go viral fast.

THREE KEY PLAY POINTS
1. Plan a coordinated launch strategy to give your application widespread distribution and publicity.

2. Make it easy for users to share the application with associates and colleagues.

3. Test, test, and test: the application experience will become a stand-in for the quality of your company. Get loyal customers to try it in beta before the full launch.

BRANDED CONTENT TOOL EXAMPLE

Marketing score. Powered by PR agency PR 20/20, the Marketing Score free online assessment tool and marketing intelligence engine (see Figure 16.17) helps business rate their online marketing on such things as marketing performance, lead sources, marketing team strength, marketing technology utilization, and content marketing. The tool has helped PR 20/20 drive into new business areas and uncover new revenue opportunities.

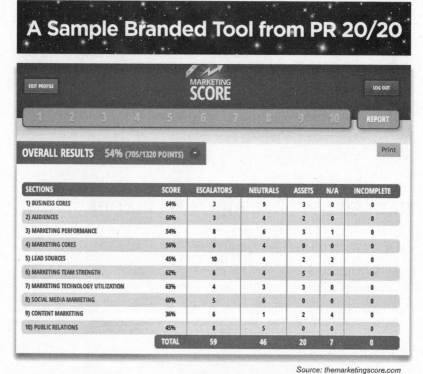

SECTIONS	SCORE	ESCALATORS	NEUTRALS	ASSETS	N/A	INCOMPLETE
1) BUSINESS CORES	64%	3	9	3	0	0
2) AUDIENCES	60%	3	4	2	0	0
3) MARKETING PERFORMANCE	54%	8	6	3	1	0
4) MARKETING CORES	56%	6	4	0	0	0
5) LEAD SOURCES	45%	10	4	2	2	0
6) MARKETING TEAM STRENGTH	62%	6	4	5	0	0
7) MARKETING TECHNOLOGY UTILIZATION	63%	4	3	3	0	0
8) SOCIAL MEDIA MARKETING	60%	5	6	0	0	0
9) CONTENT MARKETING	36%	6	1	2	4	0
10) PUBLIC RELATIONS	45%	8	5	0	0	0
TOTAL		59	46	20	7	0

Source: themarketingscore.com

Figure 16.17　The Marketing Score online assessment is a branded tool from PR 20/20.

ONLINE GAME

WHAT AN ONLINE GAME IS

An online game is an electronic game like any other except it's brand-ed—by you.

THREE KEY PLAY POINTS

1. Games should work without burdensome software downloads.
2. They must run across multiple browser types and operating system platforms.
3. Game experience should reinforce favorable experience of the brand.

GAME EXAMPLE

Traveler IQ Challenge. TravelPod's Traveler IQ Challenge (see Figure 16.18) reinforces the blog's position as the smart web destination for savvy globetrotters.

Source: travelpod.com

Figure 16.18   TravelPod's Traveler IQ Challenge online game.

INFOGRAPHIC

WHAT AN INFOGRAPHIC IS

As the name suggests, an infographic represents information or data visually, in a chart, graph, or other form of illustration. But the power of an infographic goes beyond its immediate visual appeal; unlike a mere list, an infographic can expose the relationships among disparate pieces of information, delivering insight, not just raw data.

THREE KEY PLAY POINTS

1. Everyone's confusion can become your opportunity—where can you deliver value by providing clarity?
2. Think metaphorically to find a guiding image or idea that frames your information.
3. Make your resulting infographic easy to share online for maximum reach and distribution.

INFOGRAPHIC EXAMPLES

The History of Content Marketing. CMI released *The History of Content Marketing* infographic (Figure 16.19), which was immediately shared by thousands of marketers and has become a staple of Wikipedia's entry about content marketing. The goal of the infographic was to promote CMI's growing annual event, Content Marketing World.

Eloqua's *The Blog Tree*. You've seen lists of top blogs before. But Eloqua, an Oracle company, wanted to go both broader and deeper. *The Blog Tree*, created in collaboration with JESS3, reveals the technological roots of successful marketing blogs, the main branches of the blogs' subject areas, and the relative popularity of the individual blogs themselves (Figure 16.20). As a result of publishing *The Blog Tree*, Eloqua boosted its average blog views by a factor of 40, collected 175 inbound links, inspired more than 700 tweets and 2,500 Facebook page impressions, and turned at least *49 viewers into sales opportunities or closed deals*.

The History of Content Marketing

Source: Content Marketing Institute

Figure 16.19 *The History of Content Marketing* infographic for Content Marketing World.

Figure 16.20 *The Blog Tree* from Eloqua.

ONLINE SURVEY RESEARCH PROJECT

WHAT AN ONLINE SURVEY RESEARCH PROJECT IS

Poll your customers, visitors, or colleagues with paid or free online survey tools from providers such as SurveyMonkey.

THREE KEY PLAY POINTS

1. What do C-suite executives want to know most? What other C-suite execs are thinking. Anything you learn will be eagerly devoured by other execs.
2. Potential survey audiences include blog readers, Twitter followers, LinkedIn and Facebook colleagues, conference attendees, and e-newsletter readers.
3. Keep 'em short! Any more than 10 questions (and that's pushing it) and you'll lose participants.

RESEARCH EXAMPLE

Content Marketing Benchmark Study. CMI and MarketingProfs have been producing their annual industry benchmark, the Content Marketing Benchmark Study (see Figure 16.21), for four years. It has

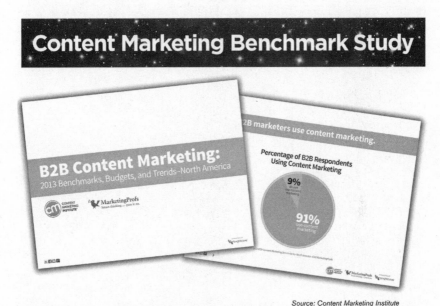

Source: Content Marketing Institute

Figure 16.21 Content Marketing Benchmark Study.

become the de facto research for the industry, has been downloaded well over 50,000 times, and has led to a number of six-figure opportunities for CMI.

DISCUSSION FORUM

WHAT A DISCUSSION FORUM IS

A discussion forum is a simple "bulletin board" online site where customers and prospects can post thoughts and make comments on your products and services.

THREE KEY PLAY POINTS

1. Make the interface simple; no one should struggle to participate.
2. Once it's up and running, the discussion forum can resolve many issues without imposing demands on your staff.
3. Treat forum participants as "insiders" entitled to breaking news about new products, new releases, and so on.

DISCUSSION FORUM EXAMPLE

Bottlehead Forum. Long before *content marketing* and *social media* became business buzzwords, the good people at Bottlehead created a forum for tube audio enthusiasts that remains one of the best audio sites on the web—and a brilliant way to encourage prospects to take the leap and buy their products.

CHAPTER 17

Finding Your Content Assets

Searching is half the fun: life is
much more manageable when
thought of as a scavenger hunt as
opposed to a surprise party.

JIMMY BUFFETT

You've done it. You've developed why you need the content, created and vetted the audience personas, and identified the buying stages where this essential content will impact the business. As you start to dig into your content marketing channel and workflow strategy, you realize that you simply don't have enough brand stories to meet the demands of the content marketing initiative.

In many content marketing programs, the core brand stories deal with transforming an employee's, customer's, or stakeholder's passion and expertise into one or multiple stories. How many times have you heard the following that stopped you in your tracks?

- Our [CEO, executive, or engineer] doesn't write; in fact, no one in our organization writes. (This one is almost certainly not true.)
- Our [CEO, executive, or engineer] can't write. (Okay, maybe this one's true.)
- How are we going to get all this content created? I just don't have the resources. (This one is almost always true . . . to an extent.)

Now, before exploring some of the following ideas, you need to realize that almost **no company** *has a shortage of raw material for content marketing.* What's usually missing is that the content is not in storytelling form or that a process has not been created to extract the information in a way that works with the content marketing plan.

THE VISUAL CONTENT AUDIT

Marketing executives are like most people: they like to learn by example. Having them engage in the following test will help.

1. Gather all your marketing content, both print and electronic (make printouts), and place it on a conference table. Include brochures, newsletters, blog posts, reseller information, and so on.
2. Get your marketing executives in a room.
3. Ask them, "Is our content more about our customers' pain points or more about us and how great our products or services are?"
4. Then ask them, "Will people share and spread this information in social media? Will they talk to their colleagues about it? Will they search for it? Will they become so engaged in it that they will friend or follow you?"

The purpose of the visual content audit is twofold. First, it starts a good discussion about what kind of content the company has been creating and whether it is helping or hurting the business. Second, it gives you a good sense of what content you'll need to develop to fit the gaps in your engagement cycle.

THE CONTENT AUDIT

Before you can ever determine what kind of content you need, you first need to figure out what you have. In addition, you need to determine whether what you have is any good at all or, better yet, whether you have some raw content that is still incredibly valuable that you can leverage throughout your customers' buying cycle.

Chris Moritz, senior content strategist at agency Campbell Ewald, has a very simple way for you to track your content. Putting the answer to your current content assets into some sort of spreadsheet is probably the best method. This is critical for tracking purposes and would include these things:

- Unique ID (1.0, 1.1, 2.0, and so on; every document/images/video should have a unique identifier that makes sense to the organization)
- Page title (or the name of the document)
- Web address (or location, if it's not digital)
- Document type (web page, PDF, Word document, video, and so on)
- R.O.T. (redundant, outdated, or tired?) score
- Notes (anything you might want anyone else reading the document to know, including who the target audience might be, who the original author is, or possibly when it was created)

This is your basic content inventory. Keep it safe, and refer to it often.

Why is this so critical? I've worked with dozens of companies that launched new e-books and white papers and hired freelancers and editors, only to find out midway through the process that much of the content initiative had already been created. This simple content inventory will save you time and money.

TAKING AUDITS TO THE NEXT LEVEL

Ahava Leibtag, owner of Aha Media Group, believes that a content inventory or audit is just the first step. While there is no one right way to look at the content you have, the following are some sample inventories that might work for you.

COMBINING YOUR ANALYTICS AND CONTENT AUDITS ON A SPREADSHEET

Your spreadsheet might look like an Excel document that has the following columns:

- Page title
- Page name
- Notes
- Page views [total]
- Page views [last month]
- Absolute unique visitors

Having this on hand will give you some insight into performance. For example, if a certain piece of content has received no page views in the last month, it's either not working, not marketed correctly, or not in the right spot.

COMPARING YOUR MOBILE AND DESKTOP ANALYTICS

See if there are major differences in the way people consume that content. Are certain pieces viewed at a much higher rate on a mobile device than on a desktop? Why do you think that is the case?

COUNTING THE TOP TYPES OF CONTENT YOU POST REGULARLY

Use a separate spreadsheet, or even present the information visually in a PowerPoint presentation, about how much of each type of content is created during a period of time, say, a quarter. What types perform the best: videos, PDFs, SlideShare presentations, and so on?

Ahava states the purpose of these exercises the best: "The goal of a content audit is not to simply collect data but to have the information you need to make good decisions."

A PRACTICAL APPROACH TO CONTENT ANALYSIS

By Patricia Redsicker, Owner, PR

> Your web content will never take care of itself.
> KRISTINA HALVORSON, *CONTENT STRATEGY FOR THE WEB*

If you tell your boss or client that the web content has issues, he or she will want to know what kind of issues you're talking about and why they are issues in the first place.

Knowing the answer to the question, "How do you know if your content is any good?" may not be easy. But it's important if you want to:

- Retain your audience
- Understand how your site measures up against the competition
- Know where your content needs improvement

In order to diagnose problematic content you should *analyze it periodically (at least every six months) and measure it against specific content qualities.* Those qualities are:

- Usefulness and relevance
- Clarity and accuracy
- Completeness (of sentences, thought, ideas, and logic)
- Influence and engagement
- Findability (SEO)

- Branding consistency
- Intended audience
- Consistency with business priorities
- Maintaining your content

Perform a content analysis of your website every six months.

Content must be maintained to be successful, and that takes a lot of hard work! However content problems arise precisely because owners don't take the time to do maintenance.

In fact if you haven't performed a content analysis of your website in the last six months, chances are high that there are content issues that need fixing. Some of those issues include:

- ROT (redundant, outdated, or trivial content)
- Broken links
- Missing meta descriptions
- Policy changes that might affect content
- Inconsistency with branding style
- Weak calls to action

THE PROCESS OF CONTENT ANALYSIS

To do a content analysis of your site, start with a content inventory to figure out what your web content currently looks like. The easiest way to do this is to use a simple spreadsheet that looks like Figure 17.1.

Go through every single page on your website and record what you find using the above format. Be sure to *make careful notes* and to add more columns as needed. Keep in mind too that *content is not only text but also video, photo images, audio, infographics, and everything else that lives in your website.*

DEDICATED OVERSIGHT

Once you have performed your content inventory, you'll have all the information you need to manage your site accordingly.

Unfortunately, when your main focus is to consistently create content that engages your audience, it is an enormous task to go back and evaluate what was created in the past to ensure that it is still relevant to your audience.

But as Arnie Kuenn says in his book *Accelerate*, "Responsible content delivery includes dedicated oversight." It is very important to have high-quality content on your website, not only to optimize user experience but also to ensure that your brand is consistently held in high regard.

Content Analysis Spreadsheet

ID	PAGE NAME	DOCUMENT TYPE	LINK	KEYWORDS	META DESCRIPTION	INTERNAL LINKS	PURPOSE	NOTES
1.0.0	ABC Company	Home Page	domain.com	content marketing services, custom content	content marketing solutions for B2B brands	About 1.1.0, Services 1.3.0, Blog 1.5.0	Sell/Market	Only 10% of pages here
1.1.0	About ABC	About Us Page	domain.com/about	content marketing solutions	We help you develop content that attracts and retains customers	Blog 1.5.0	Brand/PR	Staffing changes/needs updating
1.3.0	ABC Services Listing	Services Page	domain.com/service	content marketing strategy, social listening services	Our content marketing solutions are designed to help you create content that is compelling, relevant and consistent.	Home 1.0.0 Downloads 1.4.0	Sell/Market	Pricing Structure Confusing

Figure 17.1   Sample content analysis spreadsheet.

208

The last thing you want is for your credibility to be undermined simply because a user came across a broken link on your site. So if it means hiring someone to perform content maintenance or having to take the time to do it yourself, make sure that your site receives dedicated oversight.

QUICK TAKEAWAY

Of all the things that impact user experience on your website, content is the most important factor. Make sure that it is always *updated, organized, and relevant.* Yes, it's a lot of hard work, and the more content you generate the more content you will need to maintain. But the quality of your content is not something that you want to compromise.

EPIC THOUGHTS

- Before you create any new epic content, figure out first what you have to work with.
- Figure out a process to coordinate the content you have, and start thinking about when content will need to be updated. Assigning someone to this task will help.

EPIC RESOURCES

- Chris Moritz, "How to Start Your Content Strategy: The Discovery Phase," ContentMarketingInstitute.com, June 1, 2010, http://content marketinginstitute.com/2010/06/content-strategy-discovery/.
- Ahava Leibtag, "Why Traditional Content Audits Aren't Enough," ContentMarketingInstitute.com, January 24, 2011, http://content marketinginstitute.com/2011/01/content-audits/.
- Patricia Redsicker, "Content Quality: A Practical Approach to Content Analysis," ContentMarketingInstitute.com, February 21, 2012, http://contentmarketinginstitute.com/2012/02/content-quality -practical-approach-to-content-analysis/.
- Arnie Kuenn, *Accelerate*, CreateSpace Independent Publishing Platform, 2011.
- Kristina Halvorson, *Content Strategy for the Web*, New Riders, 2009.

CHAPTER 18

Extracting Content from Employees

What helps people, helps business.

LEO BURNETT

Some CEOs love to write, but most like to talk. If it's a challenge to get your C-level executive to produce thought leadership content, capture his or her thoughts in a different format. Interview that person using Skype, and record the conversation. *Your managing editors can turn that into other content marketing pieces* (for example, blog posts and white papers). Or if the content quality is good enough, you can use it in the captured format. Or if the CEO can't really write but is willing to simply type an e-mail, tell him or her to just write a long e-mail to you.

In other words, *don't block the process by forcing the person into something he or she isn't comfortable with.*

When you're at industry events, be sure to capture photos and video. Mix and match them with pieces of content that you may or may not produce. Perhaps the video gets used in a customer interview.

Another thing to do is just sit down with the person. If there's a product manager who is shy or doesn't feel as though she can write 500 words on a particular topic, interview her. Take her to lunch and record the conversation. Again, reuse that content in multiple formats.

HELP EXECUTIVES TELL STORIES

When talking with executives about writing and creating content, you have to begin by simply teaching them what "writing" is. The act of writing is just transferring what's in your head to words. As the famed sportswriter Red Smith used to delicately put it: all you have to do is "sit down at a typewriter and open a vein."

Of course the real magic in turning writing into a story or something worth reading happens in the editing process. Relieve your team of their worries by assuring them that the copy will be "polished up" during editing. Then get them rolling by offering the following tips:

- **Write it out.** Just write blind—get it out. Writers are usually surprised by how much structure and genuine goodness comes out by just opening up and not letting their mental "editor" get in the way. Tell your prospective contributor to just spend half an hour typing out his or her thoughts.
- **Storyboard it out.** If the person is having trouble getting anything going or opening up, tell him to just visualize what he wants to say and write down key phrases or concepts onto sticky notes. He can even draw what he's thinking on sticky notes. This is an especially great way to organize thoughts for a longer piece. (Mind mapping may help as well.)

USING FREEWRITING TO SOLVE WRITER'S BLOCK

I had an outstanding conversation recently with Mark Levy (who among other things is author of *Accidental Genius*).

Mark gave me a crash course in something called "freewriting." Freewriting, also called stream-of-consciousness writing, is a writing technique where the person writes for a set period of time without regard for spelling or even the topic. Mark uses this technique with his clients to unearth the raw content at the heart of the content creator.

Freewriting is a staple of creative writing programs around the world. According to Natalie Goldberg, author of the *True Secret of Writing*, the rules of freewriting include:

- Give yourself a time limit. Write for a set period, and then stop.
- Keep your hand moving until the time is up. Do not pause to stare into space or to read what you've written. Write quickly but do not rush.
- Pay no attention to grammar, spelling, punctuation, neatness, or style. Nobody else needs to read what you produce.
- If you get off topic or run out of ideas, keep writing anyway. If necessary, write nonsense or whatever comes into your head, or simply scribble: do anything to keep the hand moving.

- If you feel bored or uncomfortable as you're writing, ask yourself what's bothering you, and write about that.
- When the time is up, look over what you've written, and mark passages that contain ideas or phrases that might be worth keeping or elaborating on in a subsequent freewriting session.

I took my first stab at freewriting, a five-minute period where I first thought about the idea of integrating content into the marketing process. Here is my cleaned-up version:

- Problems with integrating content into marketing plan
- How to measure content marketing as part of the overall marketing plan?
- How do I integrate social media as part of the marketing plan?
- What tactics work the best, depending on the buying cycle?
- What internal resources are needed to achieve content marketing effectiveness?
- How do I tie in listening through social media with new content topics?
- What department should oversee the content process?
- How do I get the sales team to help develop content?
- How much freedom should employees have to be content spokespeople for our brands?
- When should I outsource versus insource content marketing? Is there an assessment?
- What's the difference between outsourcing $25 articles and outsourcing $500 articles? Is there a difference?
- How do I educate my CMO on the benefits of content marketing?
- What if our CMO wants to sell too much in our content?
- Should we start a blog?
- How actively do we need to participate on other sites?
- Do we participate on our competitors' content sites?
- What about content curation?
- When do we decide whether to develop the content ourselves or curate the content?
- How do I communicate what we are doing with our content across the enterprise?
- Is there a worksheet that will help me construct my content marketing plan?
- Is print still relevant in content marketing?
- What's the minimum amount I need to segment my customers regarding content?
- Do I need buyer personas? For all my buyers?

What I have as a result of this exercise is more than 20 possible blog articles for the near future. I'm sure I didn't do it perfectly, but it was a great start.

So, the next time you or your key employee content providers get writer's block, try this freewriting exercise. You could use this exercise with customer service, sales, engineering, or any other customer-facing staff member.

HELP EMPLOYEES BECOME AWARE OF CONTENT OPPORTUNITIES

In one technology company CMI worked with, much of the customer service happened through back-and-forth e-mail. When colleagues and I did an initial content analysis, we realized that a large portion of the client's possible blog and article content was happening through direct customer e-mail. It took only one customer service rep to notice this, and now everybody in the organization looks at the content he or she creates each day as part of his or her business. Now, customer service reps, as well as sales reps, are more routinely aware if one of their e-mails should be used as a FAQ on the website or expanded in a blog post.

In my experience, sometimes getting an outside perspective on this process can really help the marketing department get pointed in the right direction. Also sometimes it takes someone from the outside to side with an employee to get the C-level executives to open their eyes to the power of content marketing.

EPIC THOUGHTS

- In any employee content program, don't start by forcing staffers into processes that leave them discouraged and unmotivated.
- Stuck on content thoughts? Try a freewriting exercise by writing down all the questions your customers ask you on a continual basis. I'd be surprised if you don't come up with at least 50.

EPIC RESOURCES

- Mark Levy, *Accidental Genius*, Berrett-Koehler Publisher, 2010.
- Mark Levy's website, accessed on March 18, 2013, http://www.levyinnovation.com/.
- "Free Writing," *Wikipedia.com*, accessed July 9, 2013, http://en.wikipedia.org/wiki/Free_writing.
- Natalie Goldberg, *The True Secret of Writing*, Atria Books, 2013.

CHAPTER 19

The Content Platform

Expect the best. Prepare for the worst.
Capitalize on what comes.

ZIG ZIGLAR

Michael Hyatt, author of *Platform: Get Noticed in a Noisy World*, says, "Without a platform—something that enables you to get seen and heard—*you don't have a chance*. Having an awesome product, an outstanding service, or a compelling cause is no longer enough."

Of course, your content platform can be built a number of different ways: as a website, blog, Twitter presence, Facebook page, a print book, an e-newsletter, and more. Although some may disagree with me, I believe there is one true way to build your platform with content: by owning it.

Sonia Simone from Copyblogger says it best: "Don't build on rented land." Yes, you can create a following on Facebook, on Twitter, on LinkedIn, on someone else's blog, or as a guest writer on a popular media site, but you don't own anything on those channels; someone else does. Building your platform by focusing on, say, Facebook, is like building an amazing "rock star" home on leased land. While it's nice to live in, the owner can stop by at any time and sell it right in front of your nose and there is nothing you can do about it.

Just as with the important e-mail subscription (names that you own) versus followers or fans (connections that someone else owns), the magnet that draws people to you on a daily or weekly basis needs to be owned by you. You need both content you own and content spread around other platforms, but the focus should be on a platform you can control.

THE MEDIA COMPANY EXAMPLE

Look at the greatest media companies in our history, whether it's the *Wall Street Journal* or the leading trade publication in your niche. Their platforms used to be strictly print newspaper or the magazine. Today, every media company's platform starts on the web. And that's where you will start.

Take another look at *Inc.* magazine. Although, traditionally, its main platform has been its monthly print magazine, the majority of its focus nowadays starts on the *Inc.com* site. It is where readers share daily stories, prospective readers find solutions to their problems through search, and the company acquires more e-newsletter subscribers.

THE HUB-AND-SPOKE MODEL

Lee Odden, CEO of TopRank Online Marketing and author of *Optimize*, preaches about the value of the hub-and-spoke model (see Figure 19.1). The hub (your blog or website) becomes the center of your content marketing universe, and the spokes are places to syndicate your content. Here are some of Lee's suggestions:

- Create a social hub, preferably a blog, to which to drive social traffic.
- Develop distribution channels and communities off the hub.
- Spend time creating, optimizing, and promoting great content on the hub and growing networks in the spokes.
- The exposure of content to communities empowered to publish creates editorial visibility and links back to your hub.
- Links send traffic and increase search visibility.

WORDPRESS

WordPress, an open-source content management platform, is the most popular content management system (CMS) in the world. The WordPress code is free to use, but you need a WordPress developer to create a site for you.

I've used a lot of CMS platforms in my day. Today, our entire CMI organization runs on WordPress. Honestly, I don't care what type of plat-

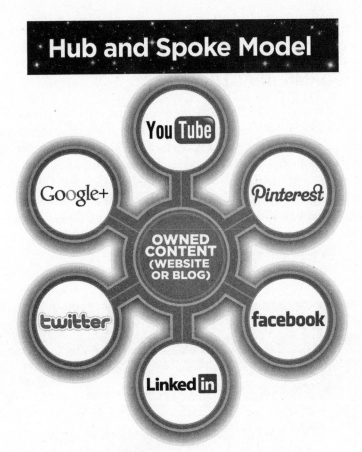

Figure 19.1   The hub-and-spoke model.

form you use, as long as you own it and host it yourself. If your website is hosted by someone else (for example, blogger.yoursite.com instead of www.yoursite.com), you are missing out on an opportunity to own your platform.

I say this often: "If your company does less than $50 million in revenue, you probably won't need any more than WordPress for your CMS." WordPress is used by CNN, the Rolling Stones, and Best Buy Mobile.

When choosing which CMS platform to use, be sure to select one that can be easily edited and maintained, includes simple publishing tools, and can be modified for a great user experience. (If you can't go in and modify your website or blog content right now, you have problems.) Besides WordPress, there are literally hundreds of other CMS possibilities for you to choose from (see http://en.wikipedia.org/wiki /List_of_content_management_systems).

PLATFORMS IN ACTION

BeingGirl.com, produced by Procter & Gamble, targets teen girls who have questions about their bodies and the changes happening during puberty and adolescence (see Figure 19.2). In an independent study by Forrester, BeingGirl.com was found to be four times more effective than any traditional advertising program run by P&G to that target audience.

P&G is able to use BeingGirl.com as the hub for the majority of its Facebook updates and Twitter stories, generating attention on outside platforms to drive traffic to BeingGirl.com.

Source: beinggirl.com

Figure 19.2 **BeingGirl.com from Procter & Gamble.**

Bettery magazine is the content platform for Smart, where it updates readers on the latest happenings in urban life (see Figure 19.3). Here is part of *Bettery*'s content marketing mission statement:

Bettery Magazine brings together two pioneers from different disciplines to discuss the problems, solutions and opportunities in urban spaces. "Change of View" pairs two photographers— one local, one visiting—to share their portraits of world cities. In "Interviews", the Bettery Magazine editors portrait the people behind exciting projects and concepts. "Events" promotes forums for creative exchange, happenings and exhibitions that foster a tangible dialogue among different communities. "News" provides tips and reviews on the urban lifeblood: design, architecture, food, music, street art, sports and film.

Source: betterymagazine.com

Figure 19.3 *Bettery* magazine from Smart.

Data software company Monetate developed a resources section that is the best in the industry (see Figure 19.4). Monetate hired a former traditional media editor, Rob Yoegel, as content marketing director. Rob developed a series of useful e-books and research reports, and he oversees two blogs as part of Monetate's platform.

There is no one right way to position your platform. You may choose to go the way of P&G with BeingGirl.com or Smart with *Bettery* magazine and have a small presence of your brand on the site. Or you could look into what Monetate is doing, where its platform is clearly a part of its main website and includes major branding on the top navigation. Both types of positioning can work, and as you go through your content strategy, you should start to see which platform direction will work best.

Source: monetate.com

Figure 19.4   Monetate's content platform resides on the Monetate.com website.

EPIC THOUGHTS

- Build platforms on Facebook, LinkedIn, Twitter, and other places where your customers are hanging out. But focus first on the content platform you own. Don't build on rented land.
- Your platform may be either separate from your company's website or integrated. There is no one right way, so give it some thought and choose the path that makes the most sense to your customers.

EPIC RESOURCES

- Michael Hyatt, "Why You Need a Platform to Succeed," MichaelHyatt .com, 2013, http://michaelhyatt.com/platform.
- Sonia Simone, "The 10-Step Content Marketing Checklist," Copyblogger, accessed July 9, 2013, http://www.copyblogger.com /content-marketing-checklist/.
- Lee Odden, "Social Media & SEO at Search Congress Barcelona," *TopRank*, accessed July 9, 2013, http://www.toprankblog.com/2011 /03/social-media-seo-search-congress-barcelona/.
- WordPress, http://wordpress.org/.
- Lee Odden, *Optimize*, Wiley, 2012.
- BeingGirl.com, accessed April 3, 2013, http://www.beinggirl.com/.
- *Bettery* magazine, accessed April 3, 2013, http://betterymagazine .com/.
- Monetate, accessed April 3, 2013, http://Monetate.com.

CHAPTER 20

The Content Channel Plan in Action

It is impossible for a man to learn what he thinks he already knows.

EPICTETUS

Now that content marketing has been explained, the content niche and strategy delineated, and specifics of content management and process worked out, it's time to examine content distribution.

Many organizations actually start with channels (for example, Twitter and Facebook) instead of first focusing on what goes in those channels. If you start with channels, there is little possibility you'll be able to measure true impact without first developing the content strategy.

I've seen a number of channel plans, and almost all of them are confusing. For this part of the book, I want to make sure that you have a visual idea of how to develop and execute a content marketing plan. All the ingredients are in front of you: your goals, your niche, your audience, content types, and the assets you have. Now you need to mix these together to make something worth your customers' time.

Again, depending on how many personas and content strategies you actually have, you'll need more than one of these, but let's start with one.

To put a content plan in action, you need to bring back the following components:

- The channel
- The persona
- The content goal
- Primary content type
- Structure
- Tone
- Channel integration
- Desired action
- Editorial plan

THE CHANNEL

This is not the content type but the core channel on which you are focusing for a content initiative. For this example, let's use the blog.

THE PERSONA

What audience are you targeting from your initial persona development? This is important because some channels are good for targeting certain personas and others are not. For example, at CMI, magazine distribution is the channel we choose to target senior marketing executives. Our blog is the channel we use to target the marketing doers, which would be Susan and Ben if you looked at our personas (see Chapter 10).

THE CONTENT GOAL

This is the point where you want to be clear about what your goals are for the content project. For example, after one of my speeches I talked with a senior-level marketer for a leading gas station chain. She said that the company had thousands of "fans" on Facebook and wanted to know how she could use content to get more fans. I simply asked her, "What is the purpose of you being on Facebook?" She didn't have an answer.

For each channel you use, *be specific about your purpose*. For CMI, even though we accomplish many objectives through our blog, such as brand awareness and customer retention, our main goal is lead generation and customer acquisition.

PRIMARY CONTENT TYPE

With a blog, the primary content type can be textual stories, videos, infographics, or a combination of those. At CMI, our primary content type is textual stories with a graphic image. Every month, we also integrate embedded e-books or videos as part of our text stories.

STRUCTURE

The structure includes how the content type is built. Most companies use 500 words as a good, solid range for blog post length. Multiple headings should be used to capture attention, and if possible, bulleted and numbered lists work well for web readers. In addition, at least one image is used and links are scattered throughout to attribute sources. With CMI's blog, our stories range from 750 to 1,500 words because our posts go in depth on a how-to topic.We also have a goal of linking to at least three other CMI blog posts to help with search engine optimization and reader navigation.

TONE

What's the tone of your channel's content? Is it playful? Serious? Sarcastic?

At CMI, the tone for our blog channel content is highly instructional, like a teacher, and we try to use as many examples as possible.

CHANNEL INTEGRATION

Do you have an integration plan with other channels? If you use video, do you integrate that with YouTube by embedding the video into your blog? If you are promoting an e-book, do you leverage SlideShare as an embedded document?

For additional promotion, how are you using Facebook, Twitter, and other channels? For CMI's blog, we leverage a number of additional channels, including:

- The blog content is e-mailed to subscribers every morning at 10 a.m. (Eastern Time).
- We tweet (using different words) the post three different times during the day, and then set up our tweet schedule through TweetDeck

(a Twitter management tool) to promote the post at least three other times throughout the week.

- The post is promoted on CMI's Facebook channel, but the focus is usually on something related to the image, not the text.
- We promote the post on our LinkedIn page, as well as our LinkedIn group.
- If appropriate, the post is also promoted on our Google+ channel.

DESIRED ACTION

With as many channels as you already have working—and as your content marketing will inevitably overlap into your channels—metrics are what you want to track at this point. I use the word *metrics* here very specifically, as opposed to *key performance indicators* (KPIs) or *results* (see Chapter 24).

In this case, *metrics* are "goals" that will align with the stories you are telling. For CMI, we have very specific goals about subscription rates (currently, our subscription goal is 2,000 net subscribers per month).

EDITORIAL PLAN

Remember the content marketing mission statement back in Chapter 13? We want to keep this top of mind as we develop compelling stories through the multitude of content types (see Chapter 16). Leverage your editorial calendar to make sure that the story creation process you are employing is consistently delivered to your audience persona.

So there you have it—the content channel plan in action (see Figure 20.1). Keep in mind that you can create multiple channels. You're allowed to have more than one blog or multiple Facebook pages—and you don't have to launch them at the same time. For example, you may find that two different types of blogs are more appropriate than just one. Or you may find that you want to later add a Twitter account specifically for a subsequent "chapter" of your content marketing story (as Dell or Delta Assist does for customer service purposes). There is no one right way to do things, so experiment, get feedback, and continue to evolve your channel plan.

The content strategy defines the channel strategy, not the other way around.

Figure 20.1   The content plan in action.

EPIC THOUGHTS

- Don't make the mistake that most organizations make and start with your channel first. By going through the proper steps for your content marketing strategy, you'll begin to see what channels make the most sense.
- Different channels require different types of storytelling. Stay away from "spray and pray" and develop a thoughtful, and differentiating, approach to each content channel.

PART IV

Marketing Your Stories

CHAPTER 21

Social Media for Content Marketing

**If things seem under control,
you're just not going fast enough.**

MARIO ANDRETTI

Social media promotion is critical to online content marketing success today. No content marketing strategy is complete without a
strong social media strategy. As Jay Baer says, social media is the fuel
to set your content on fire.

According to a 2013 report from CMI and MarketingProfs, B2B marketers use an average of five social media channels to distribute content,
whereas B2C marketers use four. Whether you're just getting started
with social media or looking to fine-tune your plan, this chapter is for
you.

Over the course of this chapter, we'll examine:

- Social networks such as Facebook, Twitter, Google+, and LinkedIn
- Video channels such as YouTube and Vimeo
- Photo-sharing sites such as Instagram and Flickr
- Online communities such as Pinterest, Foursquare, and Quora
- Niche content sharing sites such as Tumblr, StumbleUpon, and
  SlideShare*

*A big thanks to CMI news editor Mark Sherbin for helping to put this together.

FACEBOOK

With more than one billion users, it's most likely that your customers are hanging out there. Here are some tips for improving your presence and content presentation on Facebook.

You need more than just an interesting subject. Even if your product category is interesting by its nature, execution is very important. Spend time posting well-edited photos and well-written copy. Volume certainly isn't everything on Facebook; consistent quality is much more significant.

It's good to be brief, but it's better to be good. Short messages stand out on Facebook, but long messages work if they're compelling. Communicate your message succinctly unless you absolutely need the extra words.

Use smarter targeting. Page Post Targeting (PPT) is a newer service from Facebook that enables you to handpick your audience, allowing you to deliver a clear message to a smaller group. For instance, you can direct your message to reach women between the ages of 25 to 35 who have liked your page. (For more on how to use PPT, go to the CMI website: http://bitly.com/epic-ppt.)

Look Out for Graph Search. Formally launched in July 2013, Graph Search allows Facebook users to examine their current relationships to find answers to questions that closely align with their network. For example, on Graph Search you could search for "friends who live in my hometown," "photos of my friends in Cleveland," "restaurants my friends in New York like," or "music my friends like." It's Facebook's idea of a Google killer.

CMI contributor Amanda Peters published six key considerations when preparing a business for Graph Search:

1. **Publish, and publish often.** A brand's editorial calendars should include a variety of formats, including photos and videos, to engage each audience. Note that photos and videos must be posted directly to the Facebook platform, rather than via links to third-party sites, such as YouTube.
2. **Include *keyword* rich tags and descriptions.** These should reflect the linguistic behaviors of the audience to increase the likelihood of appearing in a user's Graph Search results.

3. **Include the location** where photos and videos are taken to index for results in a particular city.
4. **Create or update Facebook pages that refer to your local area.** Do so if your brand's post has a physical location associated with it; also include your address and contact information.
5. **Consider contests or promotions.** Encourage users to submit photos and videos, and tag your brand in their submissions, further increasing the potential connections between your brand and the Facebook audience.
6. **Ensure that the "About" section of your brand's Facebook page is optimized.** Include the relevant names, categories, and descriptions.

In short: create content that is useful, usable, visible, desirable, and engaging—the cornerstones of building a socially connected brand.

WHO USES FACEBOOK WELL?

Pet brand *PurinaOne* represents Facebook marketing that uses phenomenal storytelling to stand out (see Figure 21.1). Here's a few reasons that PurinaOne is successful at leveraging Facebook:

- Longer posts, supplemented with a picture, tell compelling stories.
- Posts are well written and inspire hundreds of comments from fans.
- Each piece of content is highly relevant to the brand's audience.

TWITTER

Twitter has become the official broadcasting tool of the web. How do you make your story stand out on Twitter? Here are some tips to follow:

Tell a story through your tweets. Present a consistent voice to tell the story of your industry and your brand. Each post should be compelling in its own right, but be sure to take a consistent voice into consideration.

Make use of hashtags. Including one to three relevant hashtags with your tweet makes it simple for people to find your content. (For example, we at CMI use #cmworld for our annual event.) Creating an original hashtag and linking it to a specific campaign is an even better use of the tactic.

Use it as a testing ground. Tweet your original content, and keep tabs on which pieces of content get more shares. Use this information to direct your future content efforts.

Source: facebook.com

Figure 21.1 PurinaOne's Facebook strategy stands out.

Cover industry events. Tweet live coverage of events that are significant for your audience to offer insights in real time. That way, your brand can act as the eyes and ears for individuals who can't make it to the event.

WHO USES TWITTER WELL?

With 300,000+ followers, food chain *Taco Bell* has found a great social media niche for its nationwide brand (see Figure 21.2). Why does this work so well for Taco Bell?:

- Even followers with small influence get retweets and responses. The brand's voice is down to earth and (at times) hilarious.
- Events and promotions get great visibility.
- Hashtags, especially trending topics, ensure that even nonfollowers can find the brand's tweets.

Source: twitter.com

Figure 21.2   Taco Bell's Twitter page.

YOUTUBE AND VIMEO

Although you can store your videos using helpful platforms like Brightcove, YouTube and Vimeo should be considered to distribute your video to social audiences. Here are some effective tips:

Enable video embedding. Making sure embedding is enabled, allowing other users to post your videos to their websites.

Mix professional and homegrown videos. Just because you don't always have a professional videographer at your disposal doesn't mean you can't make great videos. Showcase professional videos alongside homegrown ones to help humanize your brand.

Show, don't tell. Demonstrating your products or services in action is a much more effective way to create compelling videos than talking about what you do.

Keep it short. Your audience's attention span can be measured in seconds, even for video content. Keep your content short—less than a minute long, if possible—to deliver a succinct message.

Think compilations, not long shots. If you do create long-form video, give your audience little snippets of content that piece together a coherent narrative. Developing a video with a single shot (like a speaker presenting for five minutes) can easily fatigue your audience.

WHO USES YOUTUBE AND VIMEO WELL?

Major insurance brand *Allstate* maintains a fully branded YouTube channel that capitalizes on the brand's multiple video campaigns. Here's what works for Allstate:

- Quick videos that show, instead of just telling, have contributed to more than 26 million views.
- Videos range from professionally shot commercials to homegrown compilations.*

---

*These videos can be found on the YouTube website at http://bitly.com/epic-allstatevids and http://bitly.com/epic-allstate-riggins, respectively.

LINKEDIN

LinkedIn is now much more than a repository for our business contacts . . . it's a full-fledge publishing platform. Here are some tips to make it work for you:

Spruce up your company page. Company pages offer a platform to share diverse types of content, yet many brands are notably absent on the professional network. Rope your page in, update the cover photo, add boilerplate information, and start sharing.*

Encourage staff members to stay plugged in. People who work at your organization (especially executives) can connect their personal profiles to your brand, creating a new source of content that your audience can follow. Companies such as Kelly Services give all employees a premium LinkedIn account and send them content on a regular basis to share via their networks. Since Kelly started instituting the process, traffic from LinkedIn to Kelly content has soared.

Think quality, not quantity. LinkedIn users tend to be overwhelmed when brands and individuals overshare. Make sure you're only sharing the highest-quality content you create for your brand.

Participate in groups. Participating in LinkedIn group discussions is a great way to demonstrate thought leadership and strike up conversations that could lead to new business. Share your content, and interact with other group members to establish a strong rapport.

Leverage user-generated content with recommendations. Bringing in a steady stream of recommendations from clients or customers provides a renewable source of user-generated content.

WHO USES LINKEDIN WELL?

Social enterprise software developer *Salesforce* maintains a clean LinkedIn company page, to which nearly 10,000 employees have connected (see Figure 21.3). What's done well:

---

*Some tips on creating your company page can be found at the CMI website: http://bitly .com/epic-litips.

Figure 21.3   Salesforce.com's LinkedIn corporate page.

- Page administrators typically post only two to three times a day.
- The company's 12 products include 914 recommendations.

GOOGLE+

Although sometimes forgotten in the social media sphere of influence, Google+ (as of May 2013) now boasts over 350 million active users. What works on Google+? Try these tips:

Offer a healthy mix of content media. Google+ gives you the ability to create an eye-catching page experience. Take advantage of it by posting more than just links and text. Mix in a variety of photos, videos, and infographics for a healthy-looking page.

Symbols like # and + are your friends. Hashtags help your posts get discovered through search, while using the + feature gets the attention of individuals and brands. Finding ways to use these tools helps your audience find *you*.

Share individual content from your staff. Highlight personalities by pulling in posts from individual staff members to create a social-friendly and personalized experience.

Get more mileage from archived content. Just because content is old doesn't mean it's outdated. In addition to posting brand-new content, share old and archived content that may be trending or relevant to a timely topic.

Use longer-form content for commentary. Experiment with expanded posts that feel like mini–blog posts. You may want to do this when you're sharing third-party content that could benefit from your spin.

Leverage AuthorRank. AuthorRank is a concept where Google is trying to identify individual authors of a piece of online content. The more credible Google sees particular authors within your content, the better they will rank in Google. Basically, what you need to do is to tag all your authors to their particular content. To do this, check out this Content Verve article for all the details: http://bitly.com/epic-verve.

WHO USES GOOGLE+ WELL?

Computer hardware brand *Dell* produces a solid mix of content, including videos, pictures, and infographics with corresponding copy (see Figure 21.4). What's done well:

- Consistent updates include at least a few tags to enhance searchability.
- Long-form text helps put rich media in perspective by offering some background and commentary.

PINTEREST

Pinterest is an extremely popular photo-sharing site, where you can actively manage your own photos and share images and videos from others. It's been extremely popular in the retail space to date. Interested in seeing if Pinterest can work for you? Here are some ideas that will help:

Decide if the platform fits your audience before jumping in. As an interest-driven community, Pinterest is geared toward 18- to 34-year-old

Figure 21.4   **Dell leverages Google+ with a visual content strategy.**

women, but it's beginning to expand. If a good portion of your audience lands in this category, it's a good fit.

It's more than just images. Videos are powerful (and pinable). If you have a strong repertoire of video content, use Pinterest to drive traffic back to your website or YouTube channel.

Show your customers some love. Strengthen relationships, highlight success stories, and drive more traffic by creating a board showing off the achievements of your customers. It's a great way to illustrate your work without much braggadocio.

Share your reading list. Share book recommendations that are relevant to your audience to establish a stronger bond. Leveraging books that you've actually read helps demonstrate your brand's commitment to constant improvement.

Show your company personality. Instead of a lone product image or a posed staff picture, show your product or team in action for an image with more personality. Action shots help your audience imagine themselves as a customer or client.*

WHO USES PINTEREST WELL?

General Electric's "From the Factory Floor" board includes tons of behind-the-scenes content about the company's engineers and technology (see Figure 21.5). What's done well:

- The board mixes picture and video content with great calls to action to repin content.
- High-quality content points to other branded social media such as YouTube, Facebook, and Flickr.

Source: pinterest.com

Figure 21.5 GE's "From the Factory Floor" Pinterest board.

*Check out some action shots at the CMI website: http://bitly.com/epic-pinterest.

FOURSQUARE

Foursquare is a location-based social media site used primarily with smartphone devices. Should you be leveraging Foursquare? Here are some tips:

Encourage your staff to check in at the office and company events. Create incentives for staff members who check in at work. Do the same for company-sponsored events to highlight your work culture and establish the personal side of your brand.

Do research on your market to fuel content. Keeping a keen eye on where your audience checks in is a great way to collect data on your target market.

Check in at client and partner meetings. In addition to company events, encourage executives and other staff members to check in at client and partner meetings to showcase the brands you work with. Some of them may even repay the favor when they visit your office.

Create a badge. For a fee, Foursquare offers brands the ability to create their own badges. Check-ins and achievements—coupled with users following your brand page—unlock your badge for users trying to win it.

Share tips that are relevant to your audience. After you've created a brand page, you can share tips with your audience as they're out exploring. When users follow you on Foursquare, they'll have the opportunity to view those tips, creating a compelling content marketing connection.

WHO USES FOURSQUARE WELL?

With nearly 65,000 followers, the *New York Public Library* is a very active organization on Foursquare, sharing tips, specials, and more. What's done well:

- The library shares tips, behind-the-scenes content, and special promotions for events.
- Unlocked by 12,000+ people, the Centennial badge is accessible to library followers.

INSTAGRAM AND FLICKR

Instagram, recently purchased by Facebook, is now the web's dominant image sharing site. Flickr, owned by Yahoo!, hosts more than six billion images. Is image sharing part of your content marketing strategy? If so, here are some ideas:

Post images that accompany your content with a link to the piece. Coupling images with blog or other website content adds a call to action to your visual stimuli. In this way, picture-sharing sites become viable directors back to your content.

Share unique behind-the-scenes and personal content. Get personal with your audience; give followers an insider view of the inner workings of your organization. A "behind-the-scenes" feel comes with an exclusivity factor.

Tie promotions to images. Add promotions to visual content to help with engagement and conversions, and create a call to action that leads followers toward more content.

Turn followers into sources of content. Ask your followers for pictures that represent your brand, and reward the best contributors with recognition. Offer them a sense of ownership to strengthen the relationship.

Offer high-quality peripheral content. Even if a topic isn't directly related to your product, service, or brand, if your audience finds it interesting, it's worth sharing. Because Instagram and Flickr are picture-driven, they can open up a whole world of visual possibilities. Also, Instagram recently added the capability to distribute short videos, so testing that may work for your brand as well.

WHO USES INSTAGRAM AND FLICKR WELL?

With around 450,000 followers, *Red Bull* takes advantage of its extreme sports sponsorships to keep followers engaged (see Figure 21.6). What's done well:

- Red Bull posts visually stimulating pictures of skaters, snowboarders, and other athletes, reinforcing its brand with the occasional can of Red Bull.

Source: instagram.com

Figure 21.6   Red Bull's Instagram home page.

- Hashtags like #givesyouwings are frequently coupled with pictures for better visibility and trending opportunities.

STUMBLEUPON

Stumbleupon is one of the web's original discovery engines. Users can set preferences and then be shown content that is of interest. Here's what works:

Only sign up if you have time to stay active. Staying active on StumbleUpon is the way to gain more authority for your links. To get organic traffic, sign on, and stumble and rate often.

Use the "paid discovery" service. StumbleUpon's paid discovery program starts at 10 cents per click, putting your content in front of a targeted audience on the cheap. For a more professional version of this, try Outbrain, Taboola, Disqus, nRelate, or OneSpot.

Add a StumbleUpon button to each piece of content you create. Place a Stumble button on your content. A few shares from active users could translate to new, targeted traffic for your content.

Make it easy to share older content too. When you add new social channels, it's easy to think of them as part of a new phase in content marketing. But remember, content in your archives can benefit from sharing buttons too.

Find inspiration for your own content. Using StumbleUpon often will deliver more relevant content to your doorstep, introducing you to new websites, channels, and brands. As such, you'll find new inspiration for your own content around every corner.

WHO USES STUMBLEUPON WELL?

Financial management software developer *Mint.com* (owned by Intuit) signed up for paid discovery with great results. What's done well:

- Mint.com used layered targeting based on gender and topics such as financial planning and self-improvement.
- The company's paid discovery campaign returned a 20 percent increase in site traffic, logging 180,000 monthly visits through StumbleUpon.

TUMBLR

Tumblr, recently purchased by Yahoo!, is a microblogging platform that enables efficient usage of multimedia and imagery. As of July, 2013, Tumblr now hosts 125 million blogs. Here are some tips to making Tumblr work for you.

Use your tags. Tag content to help with searchability. Include descriptive tags on each piece of content to give your page much stronger visibility.

Post snippets of content. Snag an eye-catching quote from a popular post on your blog, include the link and tags, and share the preview. Other snippets (like pictures) work well to offer a preview of your content before the viewer makes the jump.

Reblog, comment, and "like" often. Use these features to share content from other Tumblr users. That way, you reduce some of the burden of content creation while still getting the attention of influencers. You can also create relationships that may result in more people sharing your original content.

Link back to your page. Attach a link to your Tumblr on every piece of content you post. If content goes viral, users can easily trace it back to your page. Without that link, your content may spiral off, giving you very little ability to track sharing.

Focus your content. Make sure your content fits a tight niche to help you dominate search results and focus in on the top ways your audience finds you.

WHO USES TUMBLR WELL?

IBM's "A Smarter Planet" Tumblr page (see Figure 21.7) is a well-designed, branded feed of how organizations are spurring innovation. What's done well:

Source: tumblr.com

Figure 21.7   IBM's "A Smarter Planet" Tumblr page.

- IBM Tumblr administrators do a lot of reblogging, establishing relationships, and reducing the burden of content creation with a curatorial approach.
- Each post includes a handful of tags to get more search visibility, drawing in more visitors and notes.

SLIDESHARE

Simply put, SlideShare, a division of LinkedIn, is the "YouTube for PowerPoint presentations." SlideShare now boasts more than 50 million unique users. Here are some tips to making it work for you:

Share your e-books. SlideShare offers simpler viewing than a PDF in Adobe Reader, doesn't require a download, is easy to track and measure, and offers a better organic search presence that's independent of your website.

Recycle old content. Find old PowerPoint presentations and start uploading them. Sales, branding, marketing, and conference presentations are all fair game here. Just make sure to update any outdated content.

Embed your slides on other sites. Like YouTube, SlideShare gives you the ability to upload a collection of slides to any website. This can be a great way to enhance a blog post or offer a preview of an executive's upcoming conference appearance.

Spend time on your title slides. The first thing users see is your title slide. Take great care in creating eye-catching, valuable ones to keep viewers from bouncing to another website.

Create lengthy, data-driven presentations. Longer content tends to perform better on SlideShare. This channel targets a select group of professionals, so keep your content on their radar by driving your presentations with data. (Bonus: Check out Todd Wheatland's *The Marketer's Guide to SlideShare* for the best instruction on how to leverage this platform.)

WHO USES SLIDESHARE WELL?

Support desk software developer *Help Scout* has an active SlideShare presence that uses e-books to drive traffic back to its website (see Figure 21.8). What's done well:

Figure 21.8   A sample SlideShare presentation from Help Scout.

- Presentations include sleek title pages with phenomenal design throughout.
- Slides are numerous and include lots of data to whet the appetites of analytical readers.

QUORA

Quora is a socially enabled question-and-answer site (Figure 21.9). Think of it as a forum open to the world, where experts from a variety of areas can "show their stuff." Here are some tips for making Quora work for you:

Create a comprehensive profile. A complete profile enhances the credibility of your questions and answers. It's also a tool that helps point visitors in the right direction when they visit your profile for more info about you and your brand.

Follow topics, and find influencers. Follow the topics that make the most sense for your brand and your audience. Identify major influencers by viewing who has submitted the most answers.

Ask and answer questions. This is how you create short-form content that could eventually point back toward your website. It's also a great way to find inspiration for new blog posts, e-books, videos, and other content topics.

Show your appreciation. Click the "upvote" and "thank" buttons at the bottom of the post. You'll stay engaged, make a few friends, and help make your content more valuable by identifying high-quality answers.

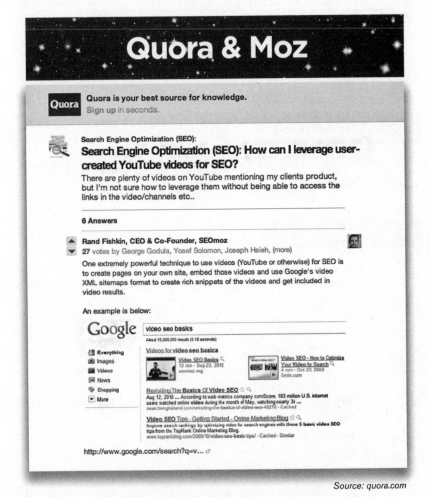

Source: quora.com

Figure 21.9   **Moz CEO Rand Fishkin leverages the Quora Q&A board to answer questions from the community.**

Develop a board to showcase Q&As your audience may find useful.
Post content to a board of your favorite questions and answers. You
can even invite other users to add content to your board, enhancing
relationships by collaborating on content.

WHO USES QUORA WELL?

Moz founder Rand Fishkin is an extremely active Quora member who
garners attention for his business through the site. What's done well:

- Rand maintains a complete profile that highlights his achievements.
- He follows topic, answers questions, and upvotes answers he likes,
  building relationships and keeping his feed fresh.

These are the main social channels that I believe, at this point, are worth
your time to at least consider some kind of resource investment. Focus
on the social channels where you are best able to find your audience, and
remember: quality before quantity at all costs.

EPIC THOUGHTS

- You have many social channels to choose from. Yes, create an identity
  in each one, but decide which one to apply resources to. Consistency
  counts, so focus on what you can actually do in those platforms.

EPIC RESOURCES

- Joe Pulizzi, "2013 B2B Content Marketing Research: Benchmarks,
  Budgets, and Trends," ContentMarketingInstitute.com, October
  24, 2012, http://contentmarketinginstitute.com/2012/10/2013-b2b
  -content-marketing-research/.
- Joe Pulizzi, "2013 B2C Content Marketing Research: Benchmarks,
  Budgets, and Trends," ContentMarketingInstitute.com, November
  14, 2012, http://contentmarketinginstitute.com/2012/11/2013-b2c
  -consumer-content-marketing/.
- Purina ONE's Facebook page, accessed March 24, 2013, http://www
  .facebook.com/PurinaOne.
- Taco Bell Twitter account, accessed March 24, 2013, https://twitter
  .com/TacoBell.
- Mayhem campaign (Allstate Insurance Company), YouTube, accessed
  July 9, 2013, http://www.youtube.com/user/Allstate?feature=watch.

- "John Riggins Honored as Hometown Hall of Fame in Centralia, Kansas," YouTube, October 19, 2012, https://www.youtube.com/watch?feature=player_embedded&v=M2jnRzPRYf0.
- Constance Semler, "New LinkedIn Company Pages: A Step-by-Step Guide for Content Marketers," ContentMarketingInstitute.com, April 19, 2011, http://contentmarketinginstitute.com/2011/04/new-linkedin-company-pages-a-step-by-step-guide-for-content-marketers/.
- Salesforce.com's LinkedIn page, accessed March 24, 2013, http://www.linkedin.com/company/salesforce.
- Amanda Peters, "6 Keys to Creating Engaging Using Facebook Graph Search," ContentMarketingInstitute.com, March 14, 2013, http://contentmarketinginstitute.com/2013/03/creating-content-facebook-graph-search/.
- Henrik Bondtofte, "Understanding Google's Author Rank and How to Use It in Your Content Marketing," ContentVerve.com, December 4, 2012, http://contentverve.com/understanding-googles-author-rank-in-content-marketing/.
- General Electric's "From the Factory Floor" Pinterest board, accessed March 24, 2013, http://pinterest.com/generalelectric/from-the-factory-floor/.
- New York Public Library page on Foursquare.com, accessed March 24, 2013, https://foursquare.com/nypl.
- Red Bull page on Instagram.com, accessed March 24, 2013, http://instagram.com/redbull.
- IBM's "A Smarter Planet" Tumblr page, accessed March 24, 2013, http://smarterplanet.tumblr.com/.
- Todd Wheatland, *Marketer's Guide to SlideShare*, Content Marketing Institute, 2012.
- Help Scout on SlideShare.com, accessed March 24, 2013, http://www.slideshare.net/helpscout.
- Rand Fishkin's page on Quora, accessed March 24, 2013, http://www.quora.com/Rand-Fishkin.

CHAPTER 22

Alternative Content Promotion Techniques

Successful organizations make habits of things others don't like to do, or don't find time to do.
DON HOUSE

It still amazes me how many marketers and businesses create their content, send out a few tweets about it, and then stop. As you develop any pieces of content, part of that plan needs to be how you are going to get that content into the hands of new and current customers—how to market it. The marketing of your content is perhaps the most important part of the content marketing process. Why? As Gilad de Vries from Outbrain always says, "If you create great content, but no one reads it, did you create great [epic] content?"

Content is created to be consumed. If it is not and it doesn't accomplish your objectives, start looking for a new role in the organization. So before you create any more epic content, *first* figure out how you are going to market it.

Like all things in content marketing, there is no wrong or right, including content promotion. Content marketers experiment, test, learn, and eventually find what works. This chapter is chock-full of content promotion tips and tricks.

SEARCH ENGINE OPTIMIZATION

Content and search engine optimization are inextricably linked and, although not new by any means, some companies don't put enough resources against this area (especially as search engines continue to change their algorithms). For the longest time, we at CMI believed that if we understood the basics of SEO and created epic, shareable content, that would be enough to get us found in the organic search rankings. Although we had respectable traffic coming to our site from search engines, when we became serious about SEO in the last year, we more than doubled that amount.

CREATE A "HIT LIST" OF KEYWORDS

In working with Mike Murray, our SEO expert (and the author of the article that follows), we now target a rolling list of 50 keywords. Every month, Mike updates the spreadsheet (see Figure 22.1) so we know how we are performing against last month and against our key competitors.

FOCUS CONTENT ON A SEARCH PHRASE

Every piece of blog content CMI creates targets a keyword phrase such as "native advertising" or "content marketing agencies." When you

Sample Keyword "Hit List"

Keyword	Searches	Google Rankings				Bing Rankings				Yahoo Rankings			
		Dec	Jan	Feb	Mar	Dec	Jan	Feb	Mar	Dec	Jan	Feb	Mar
b2b content marketing	480	1	1	1	1	3	3	2	1	3	3	2	1
b2c content marketing	46	4	1	1	1	1	1	1	1	1	1	1	1
best content marketing	140	1	1	1	1	1	3	1	1	1	3	1	1
brand storytelling	880	1	1	1	5	6	4	5	4	6	4	4	4
content calender	1000	18	17	16	23	3	2	2	1	3	2	2	1
content engagement	140	2	2	2	1	2	3	1	1	2	3	2	1
content marketing	40500	2	2	2	2	2	2	2	2	2	2	2	2
content marketing best practices	46	4	3	5	5	2	2	2	1	2	2	2	1
content marketing blog	210	1	1	1	1	1	1	1	2	1	1	1	2
content marketing book	36	2	2	2	2	2	2	2	1	2	2	2	1
content marketing guide	36	8	8	4	2	4	5	7	1	4	5	7	1
content marketing news	58	15	20	13	10	26	26	-	2	26	27	-	2
content marketing process	28	1	1	1	1	1	1	1	1	1	1	1	1
content marketing roi	36	5	4	2	4	2	2	2	8	2	2	2	8
digital content marketing	210	14	10	-	30	5	3	5	14	5	3	6	14
effective content marketing	22	1	1	3	3	23	1	1	1	27	1	1	1
engaging content	480	1	2	2	3	1	1	6	1	1	1	6	1
how to curate content	91	16	16	18	12	1	1	1	1	1	1	1	1
measuring marketing effectiveness	260	1	1	1	1	4	3	4	4	4	3	4	4
successful content marketing	36	2	3	2	1	2	2	8	7	2	2	8	7
what is content marketing	880	1	1	1	1	1	1	1	1	1	1	1	1

CMI keywords & rankings | 25-former-and-Top

Ready

Source: Content Marketing Institute

Figure 22.1 CMI's "hit list" spreadsheet targeting SEO keyword performance.

develop a piece of online content, try to think of the most likely keyword phrase someone would type into a search engine.

12 TIPS FOR KEYWORD SELECTION TO GUIDE YOUR CONTENT MARKETING SEO

Mike Murray, CMI's SEO Specialist

Some content marketers play fast and loose with keyword selection for natural search engine rankings. They shirk proper research and analysis, or they merely take wild stabs at whether a keyword phrase is worth pursuing in the first place.

If you constantly create Internet content without thinking through search engine optimization (SEO) and keywords, you will rank for something (content does resonate with search engine algorithms). Yet, you will consistently run the risk of shortchanging your SEO strategy—and your company's ability to grab its fair share of relevant search engine traffic—for branding, conversions, and more.

Every piece of content on a website or in a blog post isn't necessarily going to take a company to number one on Google [or any search engine] for a keyword phrase that people use 15,000 times a month. But you can get more out of search engine optimization—with just a bit more effort.

To the degree that time and your skills allow, you should consider the following questions and factors that affect content marketing and SEO in every piece of online content you create and distribute. To make the process easy, I've created a short checklist that you can reference when thinking through keyword possibilities for your website or blog content.

Ask yourself the questions in this checklist as you begin your SEO efforts—you can learn a bit more about the details involved in each point below.

1. HAVE I MINED KEYWORD RESEARCH RESOURCES?

It's not uncommon to run right to Google for ideas (though your AdWords account provides more in-depth data than this free tool), but Keyword Discovery, WordTracker, and other tools can provide additional insights. I'm partial to SEMrush, which suggests possible keywords that you may have overlooked in your own pages and posts. (It analyzes more than 95 million keywords.) You can also tune into the words people use at Social Mention. I've even checked the index at the back of a book for ideas.

Within a few minutes of entering some keyword phrases at SEMrush, I had an Excel spreadsheet filled with 30,000 keyword ideas from a Fortune 100 company. Despite some high rankings, clearly the company has plenty of opportunities to rank better.

Even if you find keywords among the data that's available, you still need to know whether people are really searching for those things. Your list might look suitable, but search counts matter. Yes, sometimes you should target a keyword phrase with 1,000 monthly searches. Quite often, you may want something less competitive. I don't rule out keyword phrases with 50 searches a month, but I also don't jump at ones with 30,000 searches. If I do go that high, it's because the keyword phrase is relevant and the website has much going for it, especially in terms of inbound links.

2. IS THE KEYWORD PHRASE RELEVANT?

Does the keyword phrase really match what your business does or whom it targets? Years ago, someone told me he wanted to rank for "e-commerce." It never occurred to him that this term might be a little broad. In a case like this, he should have considered "e-commerce" as part of a keyword phrase, like "e-commerce solution provider."

Remember, though, that the keywords you choose must look like a natural part of what you're writing. Also, keep in mind that spelling can make a difference. "Swing set" may be the preferred term for playground equipment, but many people search for "swingset." You don't want to use the "wrong" word and appear like you can't spell correctly. (Though with something as common as "swing set," you could probably go with a version on one page and another spelling on a different page.)

3. ARE WE BUYING THIS KEYWORD PHRASE THROUGH PAID SEARCH?

Paid search, including buying ads on a search engine, is another source of keyword research that your company may already have on hand. But many companies settle for performance from paid search and skip SEO to their detriment. If you're buying a keyword for paid search, you ought to make sure it's also a viable candidate for SEO and content marketing.

For example, a large specialty retailer may invest in the keyword "GE dishwasher." If it's working because the paid search conversions are acceptable, then it may also be worth pursuing with SEO.

Conductor, which released "Natural Search Trends of the Fortune 500" in 2010, found that Fortune 500 companies spent $3.4 million a day on paid search with nearly 100,000 keyword phrases. However, only 2 percent of their websites and keywords made it into the first 30 organic (nonpaid) results on Google.

Sure, you can buy your way to the top of the paid results, and outstanding natural search engine rankings may not come easily. But if you're paying for the keywords, that should be a signal that an SEO strategy ought to be considered. It's not just about ranking so high that you can stop paying for a keyword phrase. Depending on the conversions and ROI goals, maybe you will keep a keyword phrase with both paid and natural search.

4. AM I ALREADY RANKING FOR THE KEYWORD PHRASE?

As you start writing, it would be good to know how well you're ranking for the topic you are covering. Are you in the top 10, top 20, top 30, or all the way out at 199? You can use tools such as Web CEO, BrightEdge, and Moz to get ranking data. (To learn more about tools like these, get *Enterprise SEO Tools: The Marketer's Guide*, which explores different platforms that can help you manage, track, and optimize thousands of keywords. This free report is available here: http://bitly.com /epic-seo.)

5. WILL MY NEW PAGE ADEQUATELY MENTION THE KEYWORD PHRASE?

You can write some incredible content that goes into great detail about a topic with examples and fresh perspectives. But be sure to incorporate your most strategic keyword phrases along the way. You can't get by with just one reference in the thirteenth of fifteen paragraphs.

Keyword density "rules" have long been debated. But a top priority should always be to look for natural opportunities to mention keywords. If you're using your target keyword phrase every 150 to 200 words, you're probably on track. And don't sweat it if you use them more often—as long as it doesn't look like you forced the keyword phrase in where it doesn't necessarily belong. You can always scale back the references after you check on your rankings (which will also be heavily influenced by the page title, page header, website age, inbound links, and many other factors).

6. HOW MUCH TRAFFIC IS MY WEBSITE RECEIVING FOR THE KEYWORD PHRASE?

As you peer into your own website analytics, you should see a wealth of keyword data. You can dive deep a couple of ways, including analyzing the initial keywords used to reach your website and your internal site search data when users arrive. For example, you might discover that someone searches for "construction loan financing," but that may prompt you to look at some options like "construction loan requirements" or "how construction loans work." You may also need to adjust your content strategy to work the new keyword phrases into existing or new pages.

Don't be discouraged if you find that a keyword phrase isn't searched that often; it may still hold a lot of value. I look at keyword traffic in light of rankings. For example, a keyword phrase may have only 20 searches a month, but that 20 may rank poorly only because no one gave the keyword a boost with serious SEO. On the other hand, a keyword phrase might rank as number 2 on Google and still bring only a couple dozen visitors. But this would be okay if the keywords are a good match for the services or products you sell. You don't need 1,000 visitors to connect with good prospects.

I keep an eye out for multiple keyword phrases on a web page that rank highly on search engines. You may find that a single page could support "free online checking account" and "free checking accounts online." However, sometimes you can't get both phrases to rank among the top three positions (maybe one keyword phrase ranks number 7 and the other ranks number 14). You may need a new priority page that focused on just one of the phrases in order to get it to rank better.

7. AM I GETTING WEBSITE TRAFFIC FOR SIMILAR KEYWORDS?

I constantly check website analytics to see what relevant keywords people are searching for that I didn't even include on my list of the most strategic keyword phrases. Existing and new content created in conjunction with SEO efforts can give life to a wide assortment of related keywords and phrases. For example, I may have originally targeted "laptop computer" for a given piece of content, but the way you write your content may give rise to a number of other keyword phrases like "buying a laptop computer." You can take credit for the impact by charting search engine traffic growth for those keywords, pageviews, and more.

8. IS THIS KEYWORD PHRASE (OR SIMILAR PHRASES) ALREADY CONVERTING?

You can track keywords through your website analytics and conversion funnels, including e-commerce (associating keywords with product sales). Some companies gain additional insights with call tracking services such as those offered by Mongoose Metrics, Marchex, and others. Call tracking technology has many benefits. For example, at a keyword level, when someone uses a keyword phrase on a search engine and then reaches a website, a unique phone number temporarily appears in the content (replacing the regular website phone number). The phone call, which is tied to the keyword phrase, can be tracked and recorded.

9. ARE THERE CALLS TO ACTION ON THE PAGE?

It is particularly important that you target keyword phrases in your content by including effective calls to action. What is the offer? What does it look like? Is it buried? If you drive traffic through SEO, you don't want the visitor to have to struggle to figure out what you want him or her to do as a result of viewing your content. Make it apparent that readers should call a toll-free number, request a demo, download a guide, or request more information, and then make sure you've made it easy for them to do it. It's also critical that you test the placement and colors of forms, phone numbers, and assorted offers. Many people think of SEO only in terms of keywords, but website usability and conversion opportunities can also help ensure that the SEO traffic pays off, rather than being wasted if too many people leave moments after they arrive at a website.

10. ARE THERE RELATED PAGES THAT COULD SUPPORT AN INTERNAL LINK STRATEGY?

You can achieve high rankings for a single page, but your content marketing strategy will get a boost through SEO if you have related pages created to support internal cross-linkage. In other words, make sure you create opportunities to cross-link the strategic keywords in the anchor text on several of your pages or posts to improve your odds of higher search engine rankings. And don't forget to include the targeted keyword phrase within your links (or at least near the link). For example, maybe one page mentions "low-cost car insurance" in passing, but those words could be included in the text of a link to another page on your site or blog that goes into more detail about the pros and cons of low-cost car insurance policies.

11. HOW WILL THIS KEYWORD PHRASE CHOICE FIT INTO FUTURE CONTENT?

Your keyword selection options for SEO and content marketing should be based on planned content for the weeks ahead, not just the content you're dealing with today. With a content calendar, you can start thinking about keyword possibilities even before someone writes an article, describes a service, or creates a blog post. If you have a primary set of keyword phrases, your content planning strategies should reflect your keyword phrase priorities and deficiencies. For example, if you're already ranking exceptionally high for "riding lawn mowers," maybe that doesn't need your attention, but you may be ranking poorly for "self propelled lawn mower," and want to create content to address this in the near future. Your keyword plans should keep this in mind.

12. IS THE KEYWORD PHRASE IN OUR DOMAIN NAME?

Google in 2012 announced that it would crack down on low-quality exact match domains (EMDs) for websites that want to rank primarily on the merits of their domains. I'm sure Google wanted to deal with obnoxious domains and small websites (such as this pretend domain: seocontentmarketingtipsideasforonlinemarketers.com). However, for respectable websites, the domain name still seems to influence search engine rankings.

CONCLUSION

I'm sure you will want to weigh some other factors as well before selecting keywords, but the above list gives you a good starting point. At a minimum, leverage the keyword research tools available to see whether people are actually using the keyword phrase you're targeting. Inevitably, you're going to create content that people aren't searching for at a rate of 10,000 times a month. (Maybe you'll need to settle for 100 in some instances when you look at alternative keyword phrases.) But any new content can be a good opportunity to include your most strategic set of keyword phrases and cross-link them with your existing content.

CONTENT SYNDICATION

Are there sites out there looking for epic content in your industry? If so, there may be an opportunity to syndicate your original content on their site. CMI does this with a site called Business2Community.com. Business2Community gets about 500,000 unique visitors to its site each month, and many of those people are interested in content marketing. That's an audience we want to reach. Here's how it works.

- About two weeks after CMI publishes a piece of content on our site, we allow Business2Community to "republish" the content on its site. (We wait a few weeks so that Google knows for sure that CMI was the original publisher.)

- Inside the content, we at CMI include educational links back to relevant blog posts on the CMI website, as well as receiving an "author's link" at the bottom of the page.

If you are looking for additional exposure leveraging your current content, seeking out content syndication partners may be an option.

CONTENT 10 TO 1

Continuous algorithm updates in search engines mean that credible individuals that share your content are more important than ever to being found in search. Since our customers are completely in control of how and when they engage in our content, this means we have to think from the beginning about how each of our stories will be produced and shared.

So, think 10 to 1. Can you reimagine your stories in 10 different ways? Can that blog post become a white paper series, an e-book, or even a printed book? Can that video story be transcribed into a blog post, broken apart and shared via a social network, or transformed into a podcast? Think about these things up front:

- **How will you preactivate the content in all situations?** (Get the community involved in the content.)
- **How will you share the content?**
- **What can the base content offering** (blog, video, and so on) **become?**

Todd Wheatland at Kelly Services has a goal of 20 pieces of content per content story. In the past, Kelly would create a white paper, which might be promoted on a blog, associated with a distributed press release. Today, that one white paper becomes individualized white papers for each persona, is split up into e-book chunks for easier consumption, becomes multiple blog posts, and is transformed into a series of infographics (which is shared on LinkedIn and SlideShare). This method works for Kelly because it plans for it up front as part of the company's overall content strategy.

London-based Velocity Partners calls this process "content atomization" (see Figure 22.2).

ADD IMAGES TO EVERYTHING

Skyword research has found that business-oriented web pages *with images* have performed 91 percent better than those pages *without*

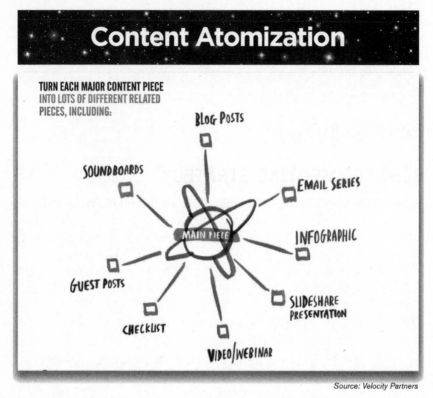

Figure 22.2   **Content atomization example from Velocity Partners.**

images. Skyword has examined the performance of tens of thousands of posts in performing the study, and it has been able to segment the value of images for business purposes (excluding entertainment and news and sports posts, among others).

So images don't just make *a little* difference, they make *a lot* of difference. Adding a little commentary and common sense to the study, it seems reasonable that posts with images both *perform better in search results* and *are shared at a higher rate* than those posts without images.

Of course, this should come as no surprise. People in the magazine business had a saying that "the cover of a magazine serves just one purpose: to be opened." Design has mostly been responsible for that happening.

What are the next steps?

- Define the role of your content producer, and the mix between original art and stock photography.

- Include images in all your blog posts.
- Review all your content to make sure that it is *visually appealing*.
- Tag all your online images with meta-tags and captions when possible (millions of searches per day are image searches).

And last but not least . . .

- Build time into your content process so that design doesn't become a last-minute operation. Integrate design into the process up front.

BLOG COMMENTING STRATEGY

In building my business, I thought about all the relationship building it took that helped make us one of the fastest-growing private companies in the world. Frankly, it was a combination of a number of things that made it happen. What really amazed me, however, was the *first step* to the majority of our relationships with the leading content thinkers around the world.

COMMENTING ON BLOGS

What opened the door to the majority of my relationships and friendships with the key industry influencers was commenting on their blogs and sharing their content.

How did I first make contact with David Meerman Scott? I commented on his blog. The same thing with Mike Stelzner as well as Brian Clark, Jay Baer, Bernie Borges, and Drew Davis (all these individuals are well known in the content marketing space).

THE FORGOTTEN SKILL OF BLOG COMMENTING

I was recently at a large marketing conference where I asked the audience how many of them had corporate blogs. About 50 percent of the room had a blog. Then I asked how many of them had a blog commenting strategy. Only about 10 percent of those bloggers had a commenting strategy. What a shame.

Great content alone is not enough; you have to work it.

You could be the greatest content creator on the planet, but if you don't work the channels, no one will know about it *and* your business won't be positively impacted. At the top of your list of distribution techniques should be commenting on the right blogs.

Not sure how? Here's a handy list:

- Find out where your customers and prospects are hanging out. Use tools such as Google Alerts and Twitter (or a reputation management system) to find out what blogs are making an impact on your customers.

- Develop a list of at least 10 to 15 key blogs in which you are going to be engaged.
- Make an informative comment on each of those blogs at least once per week.

Realistically, this should only take an hour or two per week, but the payoff will be tremendous. Each of those influential industry leaders will know you. After a while, some will start sharing your content. At some point, you may even become friends with them. And, over the long term, it will positively affect your blogging and online marketing goals.

FREE YOUR CONTENT

I've had the pleasure of listening to David Meerman Scott, noted author and speaker, many times (including CMI's own conference, Content Marketing World). According to his own personal statistics, a white paper or e-book of his will be downloaded 20 times and up to 50 times more *without* a gate in front of it. This means there is no lead form in front of the content.

You may be asking, "Why is this topic a part of this chapter?" Simple. So many times we marketers have epic content, but we put a barrier in front of it, making it almost impossible for people to share and spread our message. Of course, there is always a time to put a form in front of one's content, but you need to understand the implications of a form or a gate. There is a trade-off.

Ask yourself, "What is my objective?"

Most people gate their content for lead or customer management purposes. This means they want the prospects' information in order to sell them something or they want more information about the customers in order to sell to them more precisely. That makes sense, doesn't it?

This is a solid marketing objective, but is it the *best* or even the *right* one?

Shouldn't your goal with the creation of branded content be to spread your ideas? Doesn't it make more sense from a marketing perspective to have 50 people engage in your content instead of 1?

And here is a key point that David made clear: who are the customers you have who will actively share your content? Bloggers and social media influencers. What customers do you have that usually *do not* download gated content? Bloggers and social media influencers.

So people who gate their content are not only limiting the people who will get access to our content, they are cutting off those customers who will actively share it with their audiences.

THE POSSIBILITIES

Let's say you received 1,000 leads via your white paper download. From David Meerman Scott's numbers, let's even take a more conservative 10 times more downloads if we remove the gate. This would give us 10,000 downloads with no lead data. Of all those people, let's say that 1 percent would share this with their blog audiences (with a very conservative audience of 100 people, although most blogs get much more).

With those numbers, the total possible content reach for gated content would be 2,000 people. Nongated content would be 20,000 people.

And take this note to heart: I haven't seen one piece of content marketing from a brand "go viral" and massively spread that was gated. If you have seen this, please let me know. What's more important to you: lead information on the few, or the opportunity to spread your brand to decision makers with whom who you are not talking right now?

There are times and places to get customer information. Is the time or place to do so in front of the content you want shared actively? Note: using this strategy doesn't mean you can't "ask" for an e-mail address for prospects to subscribe to your content (see Chapters 9 and 23 for more).

BRANDSCAPING

Andrew Davis's book *Brandscaping* discusses how content partnerships can work. Essentially, a brandscape is a *collection of brands that work together to produce great content*. I'm starting to believe that this is critical to the evolution of content marketing, as more brands struggle to manage the content marketing process.

It's true that many brands struggle with coming up with the funding for content marketing projects. Why not work with noncompetitive partners to develop amazing and compelling content for a similar customer?

CMI has been doing this with a Cleveland organization called Positively Cleveland. The goal of Positively Cleveland is to get more people to visit and stay in Cleveland. Since CMI holds its largest event, Content Marketing World, in Cleveland (where we bring in over 1,500 people from outside the area), we were approached by Positively Cleveland to promote the city. This meant that yours truly was featured in a number of advertisements in local magazines, talking both about our event and why we decided to hold our event in Cleveland. This was a win-win for both organizations. It worked so well in fact that we are looking to partner with more local organizations that have similar goals and target audiences.

EPIC THOUGHTS

- Although organic search doesn't drive the traffic it used to, it's still at the top of the content promotion list. Pay heed.
- Most organizations repurpose after the success of one content product. A better plan is to plan for repurposing up front. Imagine what your stories can become and what channels make the most sense to your customers and your objectives.

EPIC RESOURCES

- Keyword Discovery: http://www.keyworddiscovery.com.
- WordTracker: http://www.wordtracker.com.
- SEMrush: http://www.semrush.com/.
- "Natural Search Trends of the Internet Retailer 500 / Q2 2010," www.Conductor.com, accessed July 9, 2013, http://www.conductor.com/resource-center/research/natural-search-trends-internet-retailer-500-q2-2010.
- Web CEO: http://www.webceo.com/.
- BrightEdge: http://www.brightedge.com/.
- Moz: http://moz.com.
- "The Content Marketing Strategy Checklist," Velocity Partners, accessed April 10, 2013, http://www.velocitypartners.co.uk/wp-content/uploads/2012/06/Content-Marketing-Strategy-Checklist-Velocity-Partners.pdf.
- Google Alerts: http://www.google.com/alerts.
- "Positively Cleveland," Cleveland Meetings: http://www.clevelandmeetings.com/champions/pulizzi/.

CHAPTER 23

Leveraging a Social Influencer Model for Content Marketing

**If it ain't broke, break it
(or someone else will break it for you).**

TOM PETERS

As of February 2013, the Content Marketing Institute site averaged 130,000 unique visitors per month, almost 300,000 pageviews, and over 40,000 e-mail newsletter subscribers (both daily and weekly). In each category, this is double our performance from 2012, and almost all of our revenue at CMI, in one way or another, can be traced to a CMI blog post.

CMI's daily blog content deserves the lion's share of credit for these results. For the past year, CMI published one blog post per day, seven days a week, every day of the year. That's 365 total pieces of content. Three hundred of those pieces of content have come directly from bloggers and writers who do not work for CMI (whom we call our "community").

CONTENT MARKETING INSTITUTE: A CASE STUDY

In May 2010, my partners and I had the crazy idea of launching CMI. With minimal resources and budget, we looked at all available options to creating content. After looking at the competitive landscape and audience need (our audience is marketing managers and directors in mostly enterprise organizations), we believed there was an opportunity for daily instructional posts about the practice of content marketing.

We started with a budget of $6,000 per month to cover five posts per week (we didn't start weekend posting until 2012). Those funds were needed to cover raw content costs, editing costs, proofreading, uploading into our WordPress content management system, and any images for individual posts. It goes without saying, but this was not much to work with.

The only feasible way we (Michele Linn, our content director, and I) thought we could make this work was to reach out to outside contributors, without paying them, in exchange for promoting them on our site.

THE INFLUENCER LIST

Luckily, we had a head start with a defined influencer list. We defined an influencer as a blogger, competitor, or media organization that was creating content of interest to our target audience. We actually rated our influencer list quarterly in something called the "Top 42 Content Marketing Blogs." (This can be found at the CMI website at http://bitly .com/epic-cmibloggers).

Initially, this list was made up of influencers we found by tracking keywords (like "content marketing") in Google Alerts, authors in industry trade publications, those that were talking about the topic on Twitter, and other bloggers that we just found interesting. Although the main list included 42 people, there was a secondary database of over 300 people that we tracked in one way or another.

GETTING THE ATTENTION OF INFLUENCERS

Influencers are important people. They generally have real jobs and are extremely active on social networks, spending their time sharing content and blogging. Getting on their radar is not easy. So, to get their attention, we gave away content gifts. We did this in a few different ways.

SOCIAL MEDIA 4-1-1

Originally coined by Andrew Davis, author of *Brandscaping*, Social Media 4-1-1 is a sharing system that enables a company to get greater visibility with social influencers. Here's how it works.

For every six pieces of content shared via social media (such as Twitter):

- Four are pieces of content from your influencer target that are also relevant to your audience. This means that 67 percent of the time you are sharing content that is not yours, and calling attention to content from your influencer group.
- One piece can be your original, educational piece of content.
- One piece can be your sales piece, such as a coupon, product notice, or press release.

While the numbers don't have to be exact, it's the philosophy that makes this work. When you share the content of influencers, they notice. And you should share without asking for anything in return so that when you do need something someday the influencers are more likely to say yes.

BIG CONTENT GIFTS

As we at CMI tracked our "top content marketing blogger" list, we decided we could get better visibility with influencers by actually ranking them and sharing the rankings with the masses. This was an incredible success.

We hired an outside research expert to put together a methodology of how to rank the top bloggers, looking at areas such as consistency, style, helpfulness, originality, and Google PageRank (this is a ranking Google gives to the credibility of a website). Then each quarter, CMI would publicize the list, showcase the top 10, send out a press release, and try to make a big deal out of it. Needless to say, the top 10 and the honored top 42 loved the list. Not only did most of this influencer group share the list with their audiences, approximately half of the top 42 influencers placed our widget (with personal rank of that particular influencer) on their home page, linking back to our site. So not only were we building long-term relationships with these influencers, we were getting credible links and traffic as well.

In addition to the top bloggers list, CMI started to put together large educational e-books showcasing the influencers' work. For example, in 2009 and again in 2011, we launched the *Content Marketing Playbook*. The playbook included over 50 case studies about content marketing, with many coming directly from our influencers. We made sure to note in the playbook which examples came from which influencers.

When we released the playbook and let the influencers know about the e-book, those we highlighted in the playbook eagerly shared the content with their audiences.

BACK TO THE BLOG

Because we at CMI didn't have the resources to pay for raw, educational content about content marketing, we knew exactly where we needed to turn: to our influencers. When we announced the original CMI blog, the first group to whom we reached out was our database of social influencers. Dozens of these influencers were more than happy to help us out, as we had promoted them for years without ever asking for anything in return.

Michele Linn served as our content editor, organizing the editorial calendar and topics with each of the influencers. It was Michele's job to heavily edit the influencer content we received. Yes, most of them were already pretty decent writers, but we wanted their content to really shine. Why? We believed that if we presented them as true rock stars on our site, with amazingly helpful content, the influencers would be more likely to share the content with their audience. This step was critical, because at the time we had very little reach and following online; we needed to leverage the influencers' networks in order for us to build our own.

THE IMPORTANCE OF THE THIRD CIRCLE

So often, organizations think only of the databases they own to distribute their content. Today, the power of social media gives us an opportunity to leverage the databases of others to further distribute our messages. You know your network, whether that's through e-mail, your mailing lists, or your social media connections. But the growth of media properties such as *Mashable* and *Huffington Post* have come on the back of social sharing. This is a strategy you need to consider for your business.

In the book *The Book of Business Awesome*, Scott Stratten wrote a chapter that discusses the "Three Circles of Content Sharing." They are:

- **The first circle.** These are the connections that are closest to you—and the strongest. These are people who share your content simply because they know and trust you. You can think of these people as your "brand fans."
- **The second circle.** These are the friends of those in your first circle. They see your content on a regular basis because your first-circle connections share it.

- **The third circle.** These are the connections of your second circle—ultimately the most valuable if you are seeking maximum content reach.

According to the third-circle theory, there are some rules to understand and live by:

- Your first-circle connections will share anything because they are blinded by their love for you, so you can't put a lot of weight into what this group shares.
- The second circle is where most brands fall down with their content. Just one or two bad impressions of your content from those in your first circle, and you'll lose them forever. This means that your content must be truly epic to keep them interested. The second circle will initially look at your content solely based on their connection with the people in your first circle. Once you get them to open the content, it's up to you to keep them engaged.
- The Holy Grail lies in the third circle. According to Stratten, "this is the group you need to be thinking about when you're creating content." If you reach the third circle, people there most likely have no prior connection to your brand in any way. If people in the third circle share your content, they will do it solely because it is amazing information that they feel is worthy of being shared.

There are three keys to making it to the third circle:

- **Focus on slow and steady progress.** The big content hit is extraordinarily rare. One such example is Dollar Shave Club (see Figure 23.1), whose viral content as of April 2013 has approximately 10 million views. Normally, viral content hits happen after a slow, continuous stream of awesome content. For example, I developed a blog post on Coca-Cola Content 2020 that has been seen by over 200,000 unique visitors (lots of sharing by the third circle). But it wasn't immediate; this success happened after over 500 pieces of regularly scheduled content were published first.
- **Capture (and captivate) your first circle.** Many brands worry about their followers on social networks such as Twitter and Facebook. Of course, those are great, but reaching the third circle should start with e-mail. I'm amazed by the number of blogs and pieces of web content that don't have "getting the e-mail address" as a primary purpose of the blog. Social sharing often starts and ends with e-mail. This does not mean gating the content, where readers have no chance of seeing the content without giving their information.

Figure 23.1 The viral launch video from Dollar Shave Club, 10 million views strong.

You can ask for the e-mail address in multiple ways, but still give them free access to the content. So first get them to opt-in to your content, and then continuously send them the best information for your niche on the planet.

- **Become the leading information provider for your niche.** When I give a speech to brand marketers, I often ask this: "Who here has the goal of being the leading information provider for your buyers?" Rarely do hands go up, and this is a big problem. Why should your customers and prospects engage in your content? Because it solves their pain points in some way. There are simply too many choices out there where they can avoid your content altogether. So you have to set up the processes and talent internally and externally to make sure that your content is epic, mind-altering content. I really think most brands feel that mediocre content that can fill the social gaps is just fine.

"Just fine" will never get you beyond the first circle. Third-circle content requires industry domination. At a minimum, set this as your goal, and then set out to make it happen.

INFLUENCER PROGRAM RESULTS

CMI started to see positive traffic patterns almost immediately simply because of the amount of social sharing from the network. That, in turn, led to more social sharing and some amazing SEO results. (We soon dominated the search rankings for anything around the topic of content marketing.) The CMI blog platform has enabled us to launch multiple events, a magazine, two webinars per month, and every other revenue-generating activity we have.

While you may or may not launch a blog that has outside contribution like ours, committing to maintaining a social influencer list is a critical component to your social sharing program.

One outside benefit I wasn't expecting? A number of people on our social influencer list are now good friends of mine. How's that for social media magic?

EPIC THOUGHTS

- For social to work, you need to share. But it needs to be content that is right for your audience and from people that are influential in your industry.
- You know your network. The goal is to have your network share with their network and that network to share with theirs. That's where the magic happens.

EPIC RESOURCES

- "Top 42 Content Marketing Blogs," ContentMarketingInstitute.com, http://contentmarketinginstitute.com/top-content-marketing-blogs/.
- Scott Stratten, *The Book of Business Awesome/The Book of Business UnAwesome*, Wiley, 2012.

- DollarShaveClub.com, "Our Blades Are F***ing Great," YouTube .com, accessed July 9, 2013, http://www.youtube.com/watch?v= ZUG9qYTJMsI.

PART V

Making
Content Work

CHAPTER 24

Measuring the Impact of Your Content Marketing

Never give up. Never surrender.
TIM ALLEN IN *GALAXY QUEST*

A year from now, what's different?

When I used to sell custom publishing services for large B2B brands, that is the last question I asked before the agreement was signed. The answer to that question was the most critical element of the final agreement. That answer told me everything about how the clients were going to measure the content project my company was about to create for them.

That's the exact question I want you to ask yourself when you think of measurement. Before we get started into the meat of the chapter, let's take a look at what CMI experts have to say about the subject.

> First, go to bat knowing what your business objectives are. If your content answers first to your business objectives, you can measure its impact where the client or executives need to see impact. Retweets, "likes," and comments don't matter to business objectives. Design your content measurements around sales, revenue, and costs and you'll keep executives and clients happy.
>
> JASON FALLS (@JASONFALLS)

First off, engaging customer advocacy around a brand is a long-term initiative, so this has to be stated up front. But audiences speak with their time, so ensure that you report on follower numbers, unique visitors, and anecdotal kudos for reaching out. Put those up against sales lift after three or four quarters to demonstrate performance (taking into account the dozens and dozens of other elements that drive brand performance during the same time, of course).

TOM GIERASIMCZUK (@GIERASIMCZUK)

I often tell clients, "Have the capability to measure everything—and then don't." You have to create a great atmosphere of measuring what's right, rather than measuring what you can. Measurement has long been about a "proof" that something works rather than providing an insight into how to improve a process. This is why I sometimes refer to analytics as WMDs—or Weapons of Mass Delusion. We can become so myopic about making sure that the graph is always going up and to the right that we become fearful about trying anything new. So, building an atmosphere of delivering the *right* analytics to the *right* manager at the *right* time becomes key. Reports of "likes," and "followers," and "pageviews," and other "engagement" metrics are not only not critical to the C-Suite, they are pointless. If we're approaching our analytics and measurement programs with the right mindset—and using them as ways to improve our process to reach our ultimate goal—then we will have alleviated much of that concern to begin with.

ROBERT ROSE (@ROBERT_ROSE)

I don't take on clients unless they're willing to use better analytic tools than Google Analytics. Something like a HubSpot or another platform is a must for me and, I think, any content marketer. I once wrote an article entitled "My Blog Made 2 Million Dollars in Sales." How's that for ROI? When people read that, they were shocked at just how much ROI could actually be measured with the right tools. And frankly, this is a huge problem we've all got to fix—*it's time to measure ROI!!*

MARCUS SHERIDAN (@THESALESLION)

Realistically, there have never been effective ways of measuring most traditional advertising and marketing except at the end of the fiscal year, when you know whether you made a profit or not. Only then could you surmise that something must have worked in your communications strategy.

Comparatively, we're presented with a veritable cornucopia of ways to measure success through content marketing.

The most important thing to identify from the outset of the content marketing initiatives is the metric sought for each content asset or approach utilized. Every metric—from video views, to e-mails opened, to tweets retweeted, to wall posts shared, and, yes, to products and services sold—can then be woven together into a narrative of how well the initiative is (or is not) working.

RUSSELL SPARKMAN (@FUSIONSPARK)

There is no magic silver bullet. Remember, this is marketing and it is organic—it takes time. Traditional advertising dies on the vine and is very hard to measure. Content marketing is totally measurable, but it takes time to get real data. Unless you are willing to launch a program for at least six months, there is no reason to do anything. You need time to gather data!

MICHAEL WEISS (@MIKEPWEISS)

Content marketing success takes time. Just because you develop a couple of really great articles or blog posts or videos doesn't mean you'll convert a lead to a sales opportunity tomorrow. Give it enough time to make a difference. For example, if your sales cycle is typically nine months, deploying a content marketing pilot across one quarter will not demonstrate the results the program can achieve. Content marketing is not a campaign with a start and stop date.

You also need to look at what you measure. Clicks and opens are fine, but they are not the true measure for content marketing success. Content marketers must look past initial response to measure sustained levels of engagement and impact to length of sales cycle. Ultimately, contribution to downstream revenues must be quantifiable in relation to content marketing strategy. And that takes time and commitment.

Figure out how to measure incremental success that shows content marketing is headed in the right direction toward that ultimate goal.

ARDATH ALBEE (@ARDATH421)

This is not about measuring, because you can only measure so much. But it is about setting realistic expectations. All clients expect their video to go "viral," and they think that means millions of views. You have to show them that perhaps a few thousand views is realistically the highest that can be hoped for. This takes a level of trust between the clients and the person telling them, but it is crucial.

C.C. CHAPMAN (@CC_CHAPMAN)

Measurement is absolutely critical to the success of a content marketing program, and the biggest mistake I see is not agreeing up front on what the initial key performance indicators (KPIs) will be, why they are important to the business, and how we will track and grow them. Many novice content marketers focus on less meaningful leading indicators (pageviews, followers, and so on) and lament client and C-suite focus on actual revenue. Getting to that revenue number may be challenging, and it may not be immediate, but in most cases it's going to be necessary in order to continue to justify the investment. So make sure to set up your measurement out of the gates with those systems in place—sourcing leads, tracking conversions, and so on—to ensure you can demonstrate the ultimate ROI.

WILL DAVIS (@WILLDAVIS)

The consensus is clear: measure behavior that matters to your business.

In the rest of this chapter, I've included a couple of different ways to show return for your content marketing. Why not just one? As said many times in this book, I don't believe in just one way to show return on objective. Different strokes for different folks. I've included all of them here so that you can integrate a measurement system most in line with how you currently measure your marketing. *This is key! Do not* plug in a brand-new formula to measuring your entire marketing effort because you are now a content marketing believer. Instead, take the best points of this chapter and insert them into what you already do. This will make it much easier to get buy-in from the entire organization.

Jason Fried, cofounder of the software company 37signals, said in his *Inc.* magazine column, "I don't care if the ultimate ROI on a particular project is 18 percent or 20 percent or even 25 percent—as long as it's not negative." With content marketing, you want positive return. Once you can measure the return on your content projects, the first key thing to do is make sure it's positive. The rest will come in the fine tuning.

WHAT THE C-LEVEL WANTS TO KNOW ABOUT CONTENT MARKETING

Please don't show an analytics report to your CXO. (In this case, CXO refers to the senior executive in charge. This could be the CEO, COO, CMO, or whomever is in charge.) That person doesn't care and probably will end up asking questions that will simply waste your time. Your CXO only cares about three things when it comes to your content marketing measurement and ROI:

- Is the content driving sales for us?
- Is the content saving costs for us?
- Is the content making our customers happier, thus helping with retention?

The reports you show the CXO need to answer these types of questions; otherwise, why show them anything at all? Content marketing is all about developing content that maintains or changes a behavior. That's the focus.

RETURN ON OBJECTIVE: PART ONE

Sales lift, impact, retention, and the like are key measurements to any return on objective (ROO) program. (*Note*: I like to use ROO instead of ROI because it focuses the content marketer on the real objective.) The "measurement picture" comes into play when sales data are missing or challenging. Sometimes ROO can be determined with one metric, and other times four or five are needed to show an impact on the organization's business goals.

ROO measurements come in all shapes and sizes; they usually include multiple items to give you the complete answer to your question. The important aspect to remember is, it's not measurement for the sake of measurement. The tools and tactics in the paragraphs that follow are used to answer directly what the project's objective is. If you keep that in mind, you'll get your ROO.

Here are a few measurement initiatives to get you started:

- Tracking sales lift of those who receive the content program versus those who do not
- Tracking conversions for online content products or e-mail subscriptions and measuring new or increased sales from that group

- Online readership studies to determine the impact of the content project as well as the acquisition of customer informational needs and trends (Are readers engaging in the right behaviors?)
- Measuring engagement (time spent) through online research or by using analytic measures on e-newsletter or web portal products
- Preawareness/postawareness study to measure the impact of the program

THE CONTENT MARKETING PYRAMID

Robert Rose and I have been working on the Content Marketing Pyramid for measurement for some time. In short, our pyramid includes three separate sections.

- **Primary content indicators.** Primary indicators are the types of measurements that the CXO wants to know about (sales, costs savings, and retention rates).
- **Secondary content indicators.** Secondary indicators are the types of measurements that help make the case for primary indicators (lead quality, lead quantity, shorter sales cycles, and so on).
- **User indicators.** These are the types of measurements that the content "doers" need to examine to help drive the secondary indicators (web traffic, "likes," page views, and search rankings).

It may be easier to create an analytics pyramid for each of the goals you are trying to achieve. Everything you measure needs to start with an objective; for example:

- Build brand awareness or reinforcement.
- Create more effective lead conversion and nurturing.
- Increase customer conversion.
- Achieve customer upsell or cross-sell.
- Create subscribers to our content.

So let's say you're putting together an initiative to generate more leads for your company. Your pyramid might look like Figure 24.1.

The pyramid is divided into three sections. Here's how to go about building it.

Step 1: Segment your pyramid. Segment your pyramid into three divided lines. The bottom, widest part of the pyramid will be your user indicators. These are the metrics that are audience based and are meant

The Content Marketing Pyramid

GOAL: Increase Leads 10% with No Increased Cost

Primary Indicators
(For C-Suite Reporting)

Converted Leads
Total Cost Per Lead

Secondary Indicators
(For Managers Reporting)

Blog Subscribers
E-mail List Subscribers
Incremental Leads
Lead Source %

Lead Quality
Cost Per Lead
(each stage)
Cost Per Visitor

User Indicators
(For Analytics Team)

Page Views
Visitors
Visitor Trending
Top Content
Keywords
Top Landing Pages
Referrers

A/B Tests
Conversions
PPC Bid Mgmt
Page Rank
Ad Quality Scores
Lead Scores
Comments

Engagement
Blog Traffic
Content Shares
Email Subscribers
Followers/Likes/+1's

Source: Managing Content Marketing

Figure 24.1   The content marketing ROO pyramid.

to measure activity. You will slice, dice, add to, subtract from, and change these metrics on a frequent basis.

The second level of the pyramid will be your secondary indicators. These will be the metrics that you associate with team members and specific processes that help you reach your goals. These are generally what we think of as short-term goals.

At the top of the pyramid are your primary indicators, or the key performance indicators (KPIs) for the goal. These metrics will be very few in number and will be the dashboard that you present to your manager or CXO. These metrics change very rarely, if at all, and are fed by the insights, interpretation, and data from below (as well as some gut feel). The goals are what you report (and nothing more).

Step 2: Map the segments. Say that your goal is to "increase the number of converted leads by 10 percent without raising costs" and you've created a new instructional blog to help you accomplish this goal.

There are a few ways you can get to that number. You can either improve the conversion rate of the existing number of leads by 10 percent or you can increase the actual number of leads by a percentage so that the number of converted leads naturally goes up by 10 percent.

To build your primary indicators you'll only want a handful of numbers in that top dashboard:

- The number of converted leads by week/month/quarter
- The total cost per converted lead by week/month/quarter

Those two numbers are the only KPIs for that particular goal that matter to the CXO.

Then, for your secondary indicators, you may want to monitor a number of metrics; these will give you great insights and help your team improve the process in order to reach your goals. Examples include:

- E-mail list subscribers vs. goal
- Total number of leads by week/month/quarter
- Incremental leads from the new blog
- Lead source (for example, organic search, Twitter, Facebook)

Lastly, you have your user indicators at the bottom. These are the day-to-day metrics that will help you understand and get the insight to improve the process of your secondary indicators. Examples include:

- The number of visitors to the blog
- New visitors vs. returning visitors
- Pageviews on the blog
- The number of blog comments
- Blog subscriptions
- Conversion rate from subscribers to leads
- The number of shares through social media (most shared posts)
- SEO metrics for keywords
- Twitter followers
- Facebook likes
- Social media reports (both internal and external)
- Blog comments and responses (qualitative)
- Most popular blog content/category
- Persona measurement (if you're trying to attract targeted personas)

Tracking User Indicators

Content Marketing Institute 2013 Marketing - Monthly KPI Tracker	2012 12/31	1/31	2/28	3/31	4/30	5/31	2013 6/30
Increase email signups							
Laura/Angela							
Total daily alert signups - GOALS	13,628	18,389	16,717	18,046	19,374	20,702	22,030
Total daily alert signups - ACTUAL	13,628	15,389	17,201	18,327	18,655	20,984	22,312
New daily alert signups this month	1,551	1,761	1,812	1,887			
Unsubscribes (average per month)				159			
Signups from eBooks (daily)	738	826	711	653			
Sign ups from pop up (daily)	2,018	1,081	1384	1298			
Daily from CF only	152	261	217	250			
Sign ups from Join Over Box (daily)	Pulled into "Daily from CF only" - do we need to separate?						
Total weekly newsletter signups - GOALS	24,299	26,082	27,802	29,522	31,241	32,961	34,681
Total weekly newsletter signups - ACTUAL	24,299	26,082	27,887	30,631	32,351	34,071	35,790
New weekly newsletter signups this month	3,552	1,783	1805	2459			
Unsubscribes (average per month)				226			
Weekly from CF only (EMUDHOME)	395	512	475	459			

Source: Content Marketing Institute

Figure 24.2 A sample of the user indicators tracked by CMI on a monthly basis.

At CMI, we visit our user indicators on a monthly basis. Figure 24.2 gives an example of what that looks like.

The purpose of these metrics is to help improve your process. If you find that you're putting a lot of time into, say, Facebook but are not getting any visitors or subscribers out of it, you can alter your strategy and experiment with other social networks.

User indicators will be your finger on the day-to-day pulse of how your content is doing. Because you've taken the time to map your blog content to your personas and your engagement cycle, you'll also know where these visitors are coming into the engagement cycle.

BRINGING THE PYRAMID TOGETHER

If you spend the time to do this the right way, you will have *a lot* of tools to answer some extraordinarily complex questions about your content marketing as well as your overall marketing strategy. You may find some interesting things, for example:

- Social media channels are producing the most qualified leads.
- E-mail subscribers stay longer as customers than as nonsubscribers.
- You're attracting way more of Persona One (let's call him Danny), but Persona Two (let's call her Suzie) makes up a much higher percentage of your qualified leads.

And this is where you'll earn your keep. Once you can show certain trends with your content, then you can start to do more of what's working and less of what's not.

MORE CONTENT, MORE FIBERGLASS POOLS

Let's go back to our friend Marcus Sheridan from River Pools and Spas (see Chapter 6). River Pools became the unquestioned leader in fiberglass pools by creating consistent, epic content targeting homeowners in its area. As Marcus began to analyze the return of its content marketing, he found some interesting results:

- If somebody reads 30 pages of River Pools' website and goes on a sales appointment, that person will buy 80 percent of the time. The industry average for sales appointments is 10 percent.
- Some customers engage in hundreds of pages on the River Pools site (see Figure 24.3). Those customer visits tended to close faster than the others.

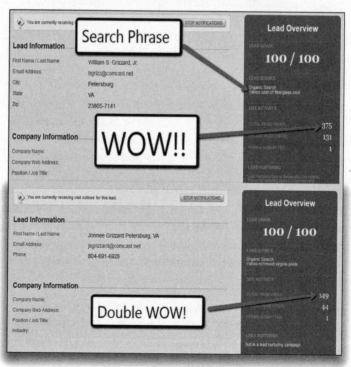

Source: Marcus Sheridan

Figure 24.3 A husband and wife (separately) engage in over 100 pieces of content about fiberglass pools on the River Pools and Spas website. Shortly after, they called, made an appointment, and quickly became customers.

This is the key. What is different about people that engage in your content? Do they become better customers? Do they close faster? Do they stay longer as customers? Are they more likely to give you referrals?

With anything you do for measurement, that's what to focus on.

ANALYTICS AND TRACKING

Marcus Sheridan is asked by other small businesses all the time how he tracks who engages in what content. The answer: a marketing automation system. Once someone completes a subscription form or "contact us" form on his site, Marcus can track exactly what content that person engages in and then integrate that information into the customer relationship management (CRM) system (Salesforce.com, Zoho CRM, Highrise, and so on).

All companies should have an analytics program such as Google Analytics that tracks visitors and visitor behavior, but analytics can only go so far. While we marketers can track general trends of all users, we cannot track the individual user without more powerful technology. There are a number of marketing automation systems available for companies of all shapes and sites, including:

- Act-On
- Marketo
- HubSpot
- Eloqua
- Silverpop
- Pardot
- Sales Engine International
- Infusionsoft

Be prepared to spend between $12,000 and $50,000 per year (depending on your needs) for a marketing automation system. While you don't need one to get started, you'll quickly learn that without one you can't answer all the questions about how your individual subscribers are consuming content and what makes them different from one another. That said, the plan must come first, then the technology to support the plan.

A DEEPER LOOK AT CONTENT MARKETING METRICS

Convince & Convert (and CEO Jay Baer) and the Content Marketing Institute partnered on our own bit of brandscaping. In this case, it was about the four main types of metrics that content marketers need to focus on (consumption, sharing, lead generation, and sales). Although this falls in line with our pyramid approach above, there is enough differentiation that I wanted to include it here. (Remember, there is no silver bullet.)

Too often, content marketers tell themselves that they can't accurately measure their results, that a tactic isn't measurable, or that they don't feel comfortable measuring content.

These statements hang over your content marketing like a dark cloud. If you find yourself falling into this camp, don't worry: you still have time to get on the right track.

As with the Content Marketing Pyramid indicators, looking specifically at different kinds of metrics—four of them, in this situation—helps to make the business case:

- Consumption metrics
- Sharing metrics
- Lead generation metrics
- Sales metrics

CONSUMPTION METRICS

Typically the easiest measurements to set up and understand, consumption metrics answer the question "How many people viewed, downloaded, or listened to this piece of content?"

These are some of the more prominent consumption metrics:

- **Pageviews.** These are easy to measure using Google Analytics or a similar web analytics program.
- **Video views.** YouTube Insights and similar data work best here.
- **Document views.** Platforms like SlideShare give you access to this data.
- **Downloads.** When a website is ungated (no subscription forms), measure downloads through your CRM platform or Google Analytics and other web analytics software.
- **Social conversations.** Services like Mention.net, Salesforce.com Marketing Cloud, Sysomos, and Viralheat are all viable options for measuring chatter.

This is the phase of measurement where some content marketers quit. But don't stop here—you've only just begun.

Revealing new questions. The consumption metrics you collect should raise a number of questions:

- Do people consuming this content engage in other, more desirable behaviors on my site (such as filling out an inquiry form)?
- Do they do so at a ratio different from site visitors overall?
- Do people consuming this content come back for more?
- Do they do so at a ratio different from site visitors overall?

Consumption metrics aren't everything, but they are important. To find the social impact of content consumption, let's turn our attention to sharing metrics.

SHARING METRICS

Of all the places your content could reside, your site may have the least amount of traffic. (For example, with CMI, we see a much larger percentage of content downloads coming from sites like SlideShare than from our own website.) Fortunately, the web has bred a culture of sharing, and this is totally measurable (if you look at the right metrics).

Sharing metrics answer the question: "Is the content working, and how often is it shared with others?"

Your sharing metrics may include:

- **Likes, shares, tweets, +1s, and pins.** Sharing tools typically keep track of these, with Google Analytics (and similar web analytics programs) offering additional insights.
- **Forwards.** Your e-mail provider and Google Analytics can help you track e-mail forwards.
- **Inbound links.** Tools such as your blogging software Open Site Explorer, Raven Tools, and Majestic SEO simplify how you measure these.

Measuring sharing metrics is important for every organization. But keep one thing in mind: sharing metrics are overvalued because they're measured publicly, in full view of prospects and competitors. Assigning an internal business value to sharing metrics is crucial to your content marketing. Otherwise, you may get caught up in a competition that has no real impact on your bottom line.

That said, you can tell very quickly if there is something wrong with a piece of content. For example, if a Content Marketing Institute daily blog post doesn't receive at least 100 tweets in the first 24 hours and

200 tweets in the first seven days, something may be wrong with the content. Once we see that, we can dig into the content to see whether it was the title, the copy, or the image, or perhaps we may have been too sales focused.

Boosting sharing. With a clear understanding of how sharing metrics affect business goals, your next step is to make sharing easy to help boost your numbers. You accomplish this by doing things:

- Place easy-to-use sharing buttons on every piece of content. Configure them to focus on channels your audience uses most often. (At CMI, we place sharing buttons just under the title and also at the end of the online content, to maximize sharing.)
- Make sure any infographics you create are easy to embed into customer or influencer content (or on Pinterest).
- Enhance your use of social proof by, for example, embedding positive Twitter comments on your website or clearly showing how often your latest e-book has been downloaded. (*Note*: CMI states clearly on its call-to-action forms how many other people have subscribed to receiving the company's content; for example: "Join 40,000 of Your Peers.")
- Create content that's worth sharing. Every time you create a piece of content your team needs to ask, "Will our customers share this content?"

LEAD GENERATION METRICS

Measuring lead generation metrics helps you answer the question: "How often does content consumption result in a lead?"

These are a few crucial metrics in this category:

- **Form completions and downloads.** Through your CRM and URL tracking, measuring how often visitors access gated content is simple. You can also measure this by setting up goals in Google Analytics.
- **E-mail subscriptions.** Your e-mail provider or CRM tracks how many visitors sign up to receive your e-mails. (Using a program like MailChimp or AWeber, or perhaps ExactTarget for larger enterprises will help.)
- **Blog subscriptions.** You can measure blog subscriptions through services like FeedBlitz or your CRM system.
- **Blog comments.** A strong comment platform (like Disqus, Livefyre, or one built into your blogging software) helps here.

- **Conversion rate.** How often do visitors who consume content become leads?

  Your conversion rate is key to viewing lead generation from the highest level. It comes in handy if you're comparing your overall website conversion rate to that of an individual piece of content. For instance, if your overall conversion rate is 2 percent, the e-book that's converting at 1 percent isn't working as well as you might think. But before you give up on the e-book, determine: do prospects that download that e-book do more positive behaviors such as becoming customers more quickly or spending more when they do buy?

Measuring indirect lead generation. Of course, not all of your content produces leads directly. However, all of your content can contribute to lead generation behavior. Therefore, set goals in Google Analytics or a similar data program to measure how content contributes indirectly to lead generation:

- For key behaviors that don't produce revenue immediately (such as e-mail sign-up), assign a specific dollar value. At CMI, a new e-mail subscriber is, on average, worth $21 per year to us as a business (when we take our total subscribers and divide that into the revenue generated from those subscribers).
- Set custom analytics reports to show goals for each piece of content. (Perhaps you may want to measure that white paper download separately.)

Tip: Social platforms with their own custom URL shorteners (such as Argyle Social and HubSpot) are adept at tying social media posts to landing pages so you can track indirect lead generation values. For CMI's online e-books, as well as our print magazine, we set up unique "Bitly URLs" (bit.ly is a trackable URL shortener) for each piece of content, so we can track the individual performance of each piece of content and its origin (for example, a blog post or print magazine article).

SALES METRICS

The ultimate goal of your content marketing is—and always has been—to grow the business.

Measuring your sales metrics answers the question: "Did we actually make any money because of this content?"

The metrics you need to understand these include:

- **Online sales.** Typically, you measure these through your e-commerce system (for example, Authorize.net).
- **Offline sales.** You track these through your CRM and unique URLs measured by your analytics program. Robust systems such as Eloqua, ActOn, Marketo, and InfusionSoft will record which pieces of content your customers consumed, which allows you to put a dollar value on each component.
- **Manual reporting and anecdotes.** Yes, it's even important to record those handshake deals. In your CRM system (such as Salesforce .com), be sure you have your sales team report on where leads originated so you can track this. In some cases they may not know, but do your best.

Remember: if you're going to track leads and sales, you have to do something trackable. To understand the impact of one blog post, you should include a call to action that is unique to that piece of content. *ThinkMoney* from TD Ameritrade inserts unique calls to action throughout the print magazine so the company can make a solid case that the magazine is performing.

Keeping in mind customer retention. Your most important content audience is your current customers. Smart companies use sophisticated CRM systems to track what content is consumed by customers and measure the impact of individual content components on retention and renewal rates. When you have a new piece of content, make sure your current customers get special access to it first.

Even though customer retention is the grandparent of all goals for content marketing, most people tend to default to customer acquisition and lead generation goals first. Don't make that mistake. If you are taking your content program to the next level, start with your current customer base. Goals to keep customers longer, happier, and/or spending more are the most noble content marketing objectives.

RETURN ON OBJECTIVE: PART TWO

Content return on objective should be calculated at the program level first. There is no inherent ROO of "content marketing." Rather, you have an ROO for each program that can then be rolled up to determine an overall return. *To understand the business impact of your content marketing, start out by calculating the investment.* Then, calculate the return and use these numbers to find the ROO. Here's an example with a hypothetical blog.

Step 1: Calculate the investment.

- Multiply the hours per month needed to create the content by the hourly pay rate of the employees or contractors used to create the content.
- Multiply the result by the overhead factor. (This accounts for rent, insurance, utilities, and so on. So a $30-per-hour [$57,000-per-year] employee should really be a $45-per-hour employee when overhead is factored into the equation. So to whatever your hourly rate per employee is you can add a 50 percent upcharge to cover miscellaneous expenses.)
- Add all other costs, such as design fees, hosting fees, subscriptions, and software. Allocate them to a content program specifically, or amortize them monthly and spread the costs evenly across each content program.

Example: Assume 20 hours per month at $50 per hour to produce a corporate blog, multiplied by a 50 percent overhead factor. Add in $1,000 per month for design, $50 per month for hosting, and $200 per month for miscellaneous fees.

The true monthly blogging cost = $2,750

Step 2: Calculate the return. Multiply your leads per month by your lead conversion rate, average lifetime customer value, and average profit margin.

Example: You collect 40 leads per month from the corporate blog (determined by lead form, CRM system, and so on). At a 10 percent lead conversion rate, you'll generate four new customers. Assume a $5,000 average lifetime customer value and a 30 percent average profit margin.

True monthly blogging return = $6,000

Step 3: Calculate ROI. Subtract the investment from the return. Then, divide by the investment.

Example:

$6,000 - $2,750 = $3,250

3,250 ÷ 2,750 = 1.18

Return = 118%

Sometimes, you just can't close the loop on ROI because you may not have all the data to do the above formula.

To use this measurement strategy effectively, you must:

- Track everything over a long period of time.
- Take note whenever anything changes, including PR coverage, website updates, or new radio campaigns.
- Track multiple revenue data points, including total leads, new customers, average order size, churn, and total revenue.
- Look for patterns that indicate your content is working; for example: "When revenue went up, content consumption and sharing metrics also went up."

The correlation approach isn't an exact science, but it gets businesses farther than doing nothing at all, making it an important alternative.

WHAT IS THE VALUE OF YOUR TIME?

Do you know the value of your time? If not, you should.

In my early days of consulting, I took certain jobs at around $50 to $75 per hour. After those particular projects were completed, it felt like a lot of work for not a lot of payoff. When I started doing the math (like the previous analysis), I realized that for our small company to truly be profitable, I needed to charge at least $125 per hour. The result was fewer but more profitable jobs—and a better use of my time.

Now let's look at the same kind of scenario, but for the content you create. Let's go back to a blogging example. Let's say that you spend two hours creating a blog post (any epic blog post should take you at least one hour) and your marketing director spends another one hour editing it and inserting key links and images. You've calculated your time at $200 per hour and your marketing director's time at $100 per hour (all costs in).

Then the hard cost of creating your blog content is $200 × 2 + $100 = $500 per blog post. With that knowledge, now you can start maximizing the process. For example, what if you spent 15 minutes talking to a freelance writer who writes and prepares your blog post for distribution? The freelance writer's time is an even $50 per hour, and he takes two hours to write, edit, and link to other key documents. This also focuses your marketing director on more strategic activities. So instead of $500 per blog post, now the formula is .25 × $200 (your time) + $50 × 2 = $150 total. How's that for ROI?

The key is knowing what the pieces of the content process actually cost you and then determining if they are the best way to produce and distribute content. If you are just getting started, give it a few months and see how things go. At first, it's always better to develop hard-hitting, epic content, and then figure out how to be more efficient after the fact.

BRINGING IT ALL TOGETHER: THE CONTENT MARKETING VISUAL PLAN

All this information—from content niche, to audiences, to measurement—is a lot to absorb. Putting it into picture form might help you to conceptualize it.

Considering all your planning as you moved through the first 24 chapters of this book, you could easily break down your strategy (and ultimately how you are going to measure your content marketing) in something like the visual framework in Figure 24.4.

You will find it helpful to work through your strategy, using all the spreadsheets and tools, but then take a deep breath to build this visual representation of your plan. Print it out. Share it with your team. It will help get everyone on the same page and set clear objectives for your content marketing moving forward.

CALCULATING THE VALUE OF A SUBSCRIBER

What we've found at the Content Marketing Institute is that subscribers to our content are better customers. Subscribers are more likely to attend our events and buy our training; in fact, 80 percent of our consulting customers were first subscribers to our daily blog post. In addition, subscribers close faster and stay longer. Epic content does that. The goal with your content is to find out why having subscribers helps you attract and/or retain customers.

This is the method used by brands for over 100 years. There has never been a better opportunity than now for you to become the leading informational expert in your niche. By doing so you will definitely grow your business.

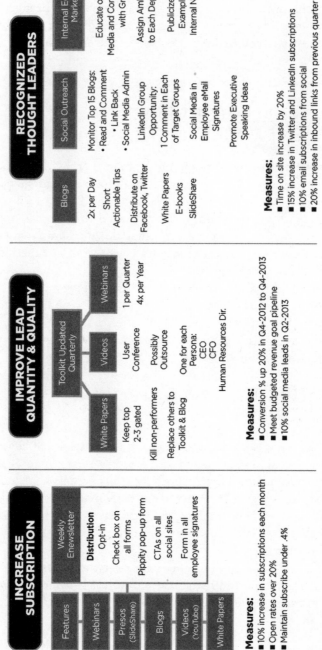

INCREASE SUBSCRIPTION

Features
Webinars
Presos (SlideShare)
Blogs
Videos (YouTube)
White Papers

Weekly Enewsletter

Distribution
Opt-in
Check box on all forms
Pippity pop-up form
CTAs on all social sites
Form in all employee signatures

Measures:
- 10% increase in subscriptions each month
- Open rates over 20%
- Maintain subscribe under .4%

IMPROVE LEAD QUANTITY & QUALITY

Toolkit Updated Quarterly

White Papers
Keep top 2-3 gated
Kill non-performers
Replace others to Toolkit & Blog

Videos
User Conference
Possibly Outsource
One for each Persona:
CEO
CFO
Human Resources Dir.

Webinars
1 per Quarter
4x per Year

Measures:
- Conversion % up 20% in Q4-2012 to Q4-2013
- Meet budgeted revenue goal pipeline
- 10% social media leads in Q2-2013

RECOGNIZED THOUGHT LEADERS

Blogs
2x per Day
Short Actionable Tips
Distribute on Facebook, Twitter
White Papers
E-books
SlideShare

Social Outreach
Monitor Top 15 Blogs:
- Read and Comment
- Link Back
- Social Media Admin
LinkedIn Group Opportunity:
1 Comment in Each of Target Groups
Social Media in Employee eMail Signatures
Promote Executive Speaking Ideas

Internal Education Marketing
Educate on Social Media and Communication with Groups
Assign Ambassador to Each Department
Publicize Great Examples via Internal Network

Measures:
- Time on site increase by 20%
- 15% increase in Twitter and LinkedIn subscriptions
- 10% email subscriptions from social
- 20% increase in inbound links from previous quarter

Figure 24.4   A simplified visual representation of the content marketing plan.

EPIC THOUGHTS

- What are the behaviors you need to see that lead to accomplishing your business objectives? "Likes" and tweets are indicators and can help us tell the story, but that's where the story should end.
- Remember, owners and senior marketing executives only care about revenue, cost savings, or happier customers. Focus your objectives on those three things and only show the CXO reports that can help tell that story.

EPIC RESOURCES

- Jason Fried, "Against Maximizing," *Inc.*, April 2013, p. 43.

CHAPTER 25

The Evolution of Your Epic Story

We've only just begun . . .

THE CARPENTERS

There are so many additional concepts I'd like to cover in this book, but as we've discussed with content marketing, there is no perfection and, as Seth Godin says, shipping the product is the most important.

I've left this last chapter for those critical questions that I receive on a regular basis and feel the book would be incomplete without. And then I leave you with a bit of motivation at the end of this chapter.

EXAMPLES FOR INSPIRATION

Although there are dozens of case studies already in the book, you can never have a shortage of content marketing examples. Below are some epic examples of content marketing collected throughout the years. Enjoy!

IBM. In IBM's business simulation game, called *CityOne*, players solve problems in four key areas: banking, retail, energy, and water. Each scenario offers opportunities to understand real-world implications of business decision making in a *SimCity*-style simulation. To date, *CityOne* has racked up over 20,000 players from more than 130 countries since its launch in 2010, proving simulation gaming may be a powerful new content initiative that can engage, educate, and influence. (http://bitly.com/epic-cityone)

Indium. Seventeen engineers from materials supplier Indium have discovered content gold with their *From One Engineer to Another* blog. Through it, they produce valuable content, videos, and answer questions about a variety of engineering topics (for example, how to set up and operate the Indium sulfamate plating bath). Even if you don't know what that means, you can appreciate what they are striving for: to bring ideas to life through interactive conversations. According to Indium's marketing director, they've seen a 600 percent jump in leads since the launch of the blog. (http://blogs.indium.com/)

Ford. A successful online community not only shares your company's messages but also allows your customers' voices to be heard. Ford's user community achieves this by combining Ford content with user stories, images, and videos. The emphasis on the community is clearly on the visitor, as categories such as "Your Stories" and "Your Ideas" weigh prominently on the community's home page. This approach creates a loyal band of community followers who are motivated to contribute content in support of the community, and it creates a powerful user experience as well. (http://social.ford.com/)

Caterpillar. The Caterpillar online community is an online forum where professionals who work with Caterpillar equipment and engines can exchange information, find answers, and get expert advice from their peers. (https://caterpillar.lithium.com/)

Intuit. Intuit Labs is an open collaboration platform that asks entrepreneurs to help solve the company's latest product challenges and rewards winners with cash. Intuit designs challenges for both code-writing techies and tech-challenged entrepreneurs, serving as a great way to foster innovation and engagement while gathering user-generated content as well. (http://intuitlabs.com/)

Zenith Infotech. MSPtv is an educational community for managed service providers. The steady flow of useful content on the community, which includes podcasts, webinars, videos, and more, helps resellers position and troubleshoot their products, allowing Zenith Infotech to educate customers in a new, interactive way. (http://www.msptv.net/)

General Electric. GE is using its site, Ecomagination, to familiarize consumers with different aspects of its business by discussing science, innovation, and great challenges that will better the future. With a mix of bright visuals, videos, and cutting-edge articles, it's a "go-to" for anyone interested in the latest environmental issues and acts as a "forum for fresh thinking and conversation around clean technology and sustainable infrastructure." (http://www.ecomagination.com/)

General Mills. The Tablespoon community is an attractive, interactive site for people passionate about food and entertaining. The site gathers the best of the best, and uses a clean categorization technique for its content, splitting it up by topics that matter most to its core audience: Quick Dishes, Taste for Adventure, and Rock UR Party. Depending on the type of cook you are or event you're hosting, these categories help you find content easily and quickly in a more innovative way than traditional websites. And, with help from the company's newsletter, readers can also stay in the know on the latest recipes and inspirations. (http://www.tablespoon.com/)

Sherwin Williams. *STIR* magazine for iPad targets a very specific audience that includes interior designers, architects, and people who are simply passionate about decorating their homes. The online magazine combines high-quality articles, videos, interactive tools, blogs, events, and "chatter" (comments from its social sites) into a comprehensive resource for people seeking ideas, inspirations, problem-solving tips, and more. (http://bitly.com/epic-stir/)

Roberts and Durkee Law Firm. Epic content solves problems. Boring brands have the same opportunity as everyone to share information that improves customers' lives or helps them to do their jobs better. For example, in 2008, Roberts and Durkee, a law firm, used content marketing to become the de facto consumer advocate for victims of the Chinese drywall problem that hit the U.S. market toward the middle of the decade. The firm created a website/blog called Chinese Drywall Problem to help thousands of Florida homeowners whose homes were built with toxic drywall. This content strategy established Roberts and Durkee as the expert in Chinese drywall problems and resulted in tremendous business opportunities for the firm. (http://www.chinese drywallproblem.com/)

Agilent. Agilent Technologies produces measurement instruments that help scientists, researchers, and engineers measure variables in chemical analysis, life sciences, and electronics. Going completely against type, Agilent resisted the typical dry technicalities in favor of the truly unexpected: a video puppet show. This technique proved to be highly successful for Agilent, increasing traffic to its website and encouraging more prospects to click through in search of more information. (http://puppetchemistry.com/)

Lauren Luke. In 2007, Lauren Luke began selling makeup products on eBay in an effort to subsidize her modest day job as a taxi dispatcher in Newcastle, England. In an effort to improve her eBay sales, Lauren began creating practical makeup application videos and distributed them on YouTube. Five years later, Lauren has her own brand of makeup distributed exclusively by Sephora, she has a series of teen books called *Lauren Luke Looks*, and she's built a bigger brand than Estée Lauder on YouTube. Most impressively, Lauren Luke hasn't spent a dime on traditional advertising. (http://laurenluke.com/video/)

Guitar Center. Guitar Center's innovative, fun, and unique videos speak to a very targeted audience in the ways they want to converse: through music. The Guitar Center TV Channel on YouTube also seamlessly integrates with the company's website, provides an open forum for discussions from passionate players, and features company promotions. (http://www.youtube.com/GuitarCenterTV)

Urban Martial Arts. The *Urban Martial Arts* blog is an example of low-cost content marketing. The blog is run by a small martial arts dojo in Brooklyn, New York, and is used to highlight the character-building activities and recreation enjoyed by its students (especially children). The blog incorporates a good mix of multimedia to appeal to various audiences, including videos, social media integration, and articles. (http://urbandojo.com/blog/#)

NLB. NLB, the largest Slovenian bank, wanted to break the mold of cold, distant financial institutions and get closer to its customers and prospects. To do this, NLB launched Financial Advice, a new content marketing project that uses a mix of digital media and live customer engagement to reposition itself in the market. In addition to a new web portal, a print magazine, and an iPad app, NLB has opened a new branch in capital Ljubljana where customers can get free personal financial advice, pick up free coffee, read educational materials, and stay for daily presentations on personal finance. (http://bitly.com/epic-NLB)

Unilever. Unilever jumped into the content game with The Adrenalist, a website that provides great content for adrenaline and adventure junkies, tied to promotion of its Degree Men deodorant. The site's themes, Bravery, Excitement and Thrills, are all demonstrated through various content avenues such as adventure blogs, videos, and even grooming tips for the modern man on the go (with subtle reminders of who is sponsoring the thrilling content: your oh-so-mandatory deodorant). (http://www .theadrenalist.com/)

Liberty Mutual. Liberty Mutual uses content to help associate its brand with "responsible thinking, preparation and doing the right thing." Its site, The Responsibility Project, tackles issues pertaining to ethics, politics, and economics, and much more, to support its theme of "being responsible" in all aspects of your life. The site features interactive polls, videos, articles, and a blog that do very little to communicate the company's products and services, demonstrating how good content that serves a broader purpose is often much more effective than promotional content. (http://bitly.com/epic-liberty)

Nightmares Fear Factory. This haunted house in Niagara Falls, Canada, catches terrified customers on camera and publishes the photos on its Flickr photo stream. The campaign got huge publicity and certainly makes anyone looking at these pictures want to head up to Canada and find out what's so scary. (http://bitly.com/epic-fear)

RCI. RCI, the largest timeshare vacation network in the world, has embraced the future of content marketing and focused on creating the great content that its readers want, helping the brand own the travel category. What was once a custom-published magazine available only in print, RCI's *Endless Vacation* moved beyond the boundaries of glossy paper and onto the iPad. The application allows readers to delve deeper with interactive articles, photo galleries, alternate covers (just shake it!), panoramas, and more. (http://bitly.com/epic-endless)

U.S. Navy. Navy For Moms serves as a community for a very niche audience. Now people don't have to rely on just the promises of military recruiters, because they can hear the authentic voices of real Navy parents. On the community, parents share concerns, stories, ideas (such as how to send Christmas packages overseas), and more in an interactive setting. (http://www.navyformoms.com/)

Lexus. *Lexus Magazine* is a custom print publication, meaning that the brand has become a true publisher by offering sponsored content that's produced and distributed by the company. The magazine isn't about only Lexus cars but also about the Lexus lifestyle; it features articles about travel and other luxury experiences, localized to be relevant for each reader. (http://bitly.com/epic-lexus)

Google. *ZMOT*, or the "Zero Moment of Truth," is a phrase used to define the key activities online consumers take before making a decision to purchase. Google developed *ZMOT* as multiple e-books, research reports, and videos about the changing nature of consumer purchase patterns. Today, this research is quoted in almost every online presentation given around the world. (http://www.zeromomentoftruth.com/)

Society of Fire Protection Engineers. *Fire Protection Engineering* magazine is the official publication of the Society of Fire Protection Engineers (a 60-plus-year-old society with over 4,000 members dedicated to the practice of fire protection engineering). The key to success for the magazine? Using content that's been vetted by an editorial advisory board, which is a surefire way to align messages across multiple online, print, and in-person initiatives. Take a tip from the Society of Fire Protection Engineers and have people on your board who are either readers of the magazine or members of your association to make sure you're hitting the mark. Readers of *Fire Protection Engineering* magazine can find all the latest articles online in an easy-to-read list, or get the print version depending on their reading preferences. (http://magazine.sfpe.org/)

MORE EPIC EXAMPLES

Intel. *iQ* by Intel is an employee-crafted digital magazine about innovation. Currently 200 Intel employees help curate the site. Intel has the goal of leveraging thousands of its employees as the project continues. (http://iq.intel.com/)

Social Media Examiner. Launched in 2009 with one daily "how-to" post about social media, the online media magazine now boasts over 200,000 subscribers, helping to drive the small company into a multimillion-dollar event business. (http://socialmediaexaminer.com)

Pinsent Masons. The U.K. law firm developed Out-Law.com well over five years ago in its quest to be a true legal resource for customers and prospects. The site has over 100,000 visitors a month in traffic and drives new business for the international law firm. (http://www.out-law.com/)

Marketing Automation Companies. Some of the best content marketing in the world comes from marketing automation software firms such as Eloqua, Marketo, and HubSpot. I recommend spending some time on their sites to get a feel for their content creation and distribution. (http://eloqua.com; http://marketo.com; http://hubspot.com)

Rockwell Automation. The Asia Pacific division of the global manufacturing company has been using a unique blend of corporate content marketing and localized stories to distribute quarterly online and print news to its customers. Check out the Australia and New Zealand version of the company's magazine, *Automation Today*. (http://bitly.com/epic-atap)

Louis CK. The popular comedian is taking out the middleman. His stand-up special "Live at the Beacon" made over $1 million in 12 days by selling access for $5. Louis CK has now applied this business model to his ticket sales. For more on the model, see the *Forbes* article "Comedian Louis CK Is the King of Direct-to-Consumer Sales." (http://bitly.com/epic-louisck)

Kraft. One of the best-known branded apps, Kraft iFood Assistant puts delicious recipes at your fingertips with its handy smartphone app. Need recipes? How about a built-in shopping list? Well, Kraft has you covered in this mobile app, now available on all smartphone platforms. (http://www.kraftrecipes.com/media/ifood.aspx)

Konecranes. The 80-plus-year-old crane company is getting into the media business. With its magazine *Way Up*, cutting-edge infographics, and case studies, Konecranes' website Resources section is something to behold. (http://www.konecranes.com/resources)

Patagonia. Patagonia, the high-end retailer dedicated to *doing no harm* to the environment, developed *The Footprint Chronicles* to show an environmental friendliness report of every textile factory and supplier it works with. What is great about the blogs and reports is that they detail *both the good and bad* with each of the suppliers and what they need to improve upon. (http://www.patagonia.com/us/footprint/)

Lifetime Fitness. *Experience Life* is the lifestyle print and online magazine developed by Lifetime Fitness, the billion-dollar health and fitness company with over 100 centers around the United States. *Experience Life* is now published 10 times per year and has a circulation of more than 600,000 subscribers as well as newsstand distribution. The magazine has evolved to serve both members and readers to grow the Lifetime Fitness brand. (http://experiencelife.com/)

Zappos. *Zappos ZN* is Zappos's digital magazine dedicated to sharing the latest fashion trends. Over the past few years, Zappos has been moving toward selling more than shoes (as this magazine clearly shows). Kudos to Zappos for integrating compelling stories with reviews, and the ability to purchase directly from the iPad (a great example of content to commerce). (http://www.zappos.com/d/zn/)

LCBO. The LCBO, located in Ontario, Canada, is one of the world's largest buyers of beverage alcohol, with more than 600 retail locations in Canada. *Vintages* is the LCBO's member-driven publication specifically targeting wine enthusiasts. The magazine is distributed both through the mails and online in digital book format. (http://www.vintages.com /index.shtml)

Cleveland Clinic. The Cleveland Clinic has dedicated editorial resources to its comprehensive blog, Health Hub. From questions about autism to what to feed babies, the clinic is working to answer all patient questions in one convenient location. (http://health.clevelandclinic.org/)

Four Seasons Hotel and Resorts. According to Pace, Four Seasons produces over 3,000 pieces of content through 392 channels. Eighty percent of online readers take an action, and regular readers spend an average of 30 percent more on bookings than customers that don't engage in Four Seasons content. (http://magazine.fourseasons.com /magazine/about-us)

State Farm. Insurance giant State Farm partnered with actor William Shatner to produce a series of humorous educational videos about deep frying a turkey. Reportedly, year over year State Farm saw $3 million less in claims due to deep-frying turkey accidents. (http://bitly.com /epic-shatner)

Maersk. The global transportation company boasts over one million Facebook fans by sharing engaging images and questions on a consistent basis. (https://www.facebook.com/MaerskGroup)

Whole Foods. The organic foods leader publishers a Tumblr page called Dark Rye (an extension of its online magazine *Dark Rye*) that tells stories of regular people trying to create sustainable lifestyles. While the online magazine publishes monthly, the Tumblr blog operates on a daily schedule. (http://dark-rye.tumblr.com/)

Jeni's Splendid Ice Creams. Jeni's, located in Columbus, Ohio, is one of the fastest-growing ice cream brands. Jeni's developed *Jeni's Splended Ice Creams at Home* as a print book in June 2011. The book has been incredibly successful, garnering reviews from such publications as the *Wall Street Journal,* helping to accelerate Jeni's growth internationally. (http://bitly.com/epic-jenis)

Credit Suisse. The global financial services company has developed *The Financialist*, a digital magazine with insights into breaking news, as well as in-depth reporting on the issues, trends, and ideas it sees driving the markets and the economy. (http://www.thefinancialist.com/)

Sun Life Financial. Sun Life developed the Brighter Life microsite to target a family audience who have questions about money, healthcare, and other family financial issues. Its financial content includes a variety of timely articles and videos with tips and tools for personal finance and retirement planning. (http://brighterlife.ca/)

Colby College. The Maine liberal arts college has developed a site called Inside Colby, specifically "for students, by students." Students use the site to blog with photos, video, and even podcasts about their on-campus experiences. (http://www.insidecolby.com/)

Altair Engineering. For 10 years, this product development company has been producing *Content to Reality*, an award-winning print magazine delivered to over 50,000 design engineers. The magazine has help Altair "cut through the clutter" and gain relationships with prospects who previously were unaware of Altair. (http://bitly.com/epic-altair)

KINVEY'S CONTENT-DRIVEN APPROACH TO GROWTH

For its first 15 months, Kinvey marketed like most companies market. It blogged—typically about itself. It collected names—by asking visitors to sign up for an unspecific "newsletter." As a result, the pattern of sign-ups was lumpy. When the company launched its product or closed a round of funding, registrations surged.

But those events are, of course, not scalable. The company was doing little to build its community in between these milestone moments.

Enter: a content-driven marketing program.

The first step was to fix the easy stuff. Change the substance of the blog from self-referential to genuinely helpful. And incorporate "learn more"–type links whenever appropriate. Agree internally to an essential set of nonbranded keywords, and make sure every contributor knew the terms, anchor text, and optimized page.

The next step was more challenging because it required resources. In parallel select a marketing automation platform, develop a basic lead nurturing process, and begin to develop content that was worth the "cost" of one's identity.

Building out the marketing automation system took longer than completing the first conversion-worthy content assets. So Kinvey published ungated content initially—to increase traffic and begin to earn the reputation of a company that publishes quality content. Once the technology infrastructure was built, it began publishing gated content, which the company distributed organically and through paid social media and display channels. It identified topics that converted well (e.g., anything Android related) and redirected content-creation efforts to those subject.

The Result: Kinvey grew the size of its user community by 600 percent in seven months, and the rate of growth is doubling every quarter.

Source: Joe Chernov, VP of Content Marketing, Kinvey

A REVIEW: TOP CONTENT MARKETING QUESTIONS ANSWERED IN 140 CHARACTERS OR LESS

Sometimes I just want quick answers. Don't give me the whole explanation; just give me an answer, and get me on my way.

In that spirit, I have put together a list of the top content marketing questions I have received on an ongoing basis and briefly answered them in (around) 140 characters.

If I missed any question that you'd like answered, please let me know.

1. What are some of the best B2C content marketing examples that you like to reference?

   Patagonia, Red Bull, Coca-Cola, and Kraft

2. How about B2B content marketing examples?

   Kelly Services, PTC, OpenView Venture Partners, and Cisco Systems

3. How do I integrate content marketing in my own company?

   Use the SAS model—get the leaders from each department (through e-mail, search, PR, and so on) and have them meet weekly to coordinate content activities.

4. Where do I start with my content marketing strategy?

   Develop your content marketing mission statement. There can you have impact as an authoritative voice. Do this before you develop any more content without strategy.

5. What's the most underutilized content distribution tool?

   SlideShare, and it's not even close.

6. How do I create more content?

   You most likely have enough content. First look at stopping some things that aren't working and reallocating those resources to quality content initiatives.

7. But my content is not in story-ready form?

   True, most companies have content assets, but they aren't in a compelling form. Hire or contract out a journalist, editor, or natural storyteller to help get those assets into shape.

8. Should I insource or outsource my content?

   Most companies do both. It doesn't have to be an either/or proposition, and there is no silver bullet. Find the resources necessary to get the job done. It will never be perfect, so don't wait.

9. Should I place my content behind a form or set it free?

It depends on the goal. If the metric you are using is a lead, there has to be a form somewhere. That said, if you use a form you might get less sharing and awareness . . . and that may be okay. As a rule, free your content!

10. Do I need an e-newsletter?

E-mail is possibly the greatest owned media channel for brands. To keep that channel alive, you need a consistent flow of amazing content. Blog-to-e-mail RSS or an e-newsletter works just fine.

11. Why in the world would I give away all our knowledge for free?

As the great Don Schultz has always said, communication is the only true competitive advantage. If you don't help your customers reach greater heights, who will? Your competitors?

12. Do I have to be on Facebook and Twitter?

No, you don't. But if you are, ask yourself why you are using those channels. In fact, ask yourself why you are using every channel.

13. How do you get all your content creators on the same page?

Make sure *every* one of your content creators has a copy of your content marketing mission statement. In most brands, content creators never know what the true reader or company content mission really is.

14. What is the best way to figure out my customer's pain points?

First, talk to your customers. Then, talk to more customers. Then, listen on Twitter and launch some surveys. Then talk to sales and customer service. Then talk to your customers.

15. How do I measure ROI?

You don't. Figure out what the specific content marketing objective is, and then measure your return on objective. Use the four types of content marketing metrics for guidance.

16. What kind of content works best?

According to Julie Fleischer (at Kraft): (1) have a purpose; (2) be captivating; (3) go where the customer is; (4) be aware that timeliness matters; and (5) know your metrics.

17. What is the difference between *content* and *content marketing*?

Content marketing must work to enhance or change a behavior. If it doesn't, it's just *content*.

18. How do I get C-level buy-in for my content marketing?

Prove it works. Start a pilot. For television shows to get approved, they need a pilot; you should do the same. Create a six-month pilot period using agreed-upon metrics.

19. What is the biggest reason why content marketing initiatives fail?

First, the brand stops producing the content (campaign mentality). Second, there's inconsistency. Third, it's not remarkable content.

20. How important is design in your content marketing?

What is the purpose of a magazine's cover? To get it opened. Much of that depends on design. If your design doesn't compel people to engage, what's the point? Invest in design.

21. What is a no-brainer issue that some marketers don't deal with but ought to?

Mobile content. There is no reason why your content shouldn't work on a mobile device. Fix it.

22. Will brands start doing content creation and distribution better than publishers?

In certain niches, some will. But publishers and brands are better together. Brands have more resources, but the media model is changing, I think for the better. Traditional publishers will always be needed.

23. Can't I just create one content platform for all my customers?

How are broad, horizontal news sources doing these days? Look at what Patagonia does and how many different content platforms it has for different editorial interests.

24. Should I stop everything else and just do content marketing?

Do you want to be fired? Content marketing works *with* your other marketing, not in replacement of it. Nowadays, the issue is that most brands are underdeveloped in content marketing and need to catch up.

CONTENT MARKETING COMMANDMENTS

I keep these printed and on my wall as a reminder of the content marketing revolution and the importance to my business. Enjoy!

- The content is more important than the offer.
- A customer relationship doesn't end with the payment.
- Printed marketing doesn't stop with the full-page advertisement.
- "Being the content" is more important than "surrounding the content."
- Interruption isn't valued, but engagement is.
- A blog can be, and should be, a core part of communicating with and marketing to your customers.
- Internal marketing always takes precedence over external marketing.
- A brand is a relationship, not a tagline.
- Focusing on what the customer wants is more important than what you have to sell.
- A news release isn't meant to be picked up by the press but rather to help customers find your great content on the web.
- Communicating directly with customers is the best choice.
- Marketers can and should be publishers.
- Today's traditional publishers are scared of marketers.
- Without content, community is improbable, if not impossible.
- The marketing brochure should be stricken from all strategic marketing plans.
- Content without design doesn't look appetizing (or deliver on marketing goals).
- Lead generation is only one small part of the marketing picture.
- Hiring an editor is not a want, but a must, for all organizations.
- No matter the medium or the provider, someone is always selling something.
- The long tail of search engine optimization is driven by consistent content on your corporate blog or website.
- Ninety percent of all corporate websites talk about how great the company or product is and forget about the customer.
- Ninety percent of all corporate websites are terrible.
- Buyers are in control; the traditional sales process has changed; and relevant content lets organizations into the buying process.
- Long-form branded content can be created anywhere your customers work, live, or play.
- The chief content officer is the CMO of the future.

- Customers want to be inspired. *Be the inspiration!*
- There is no one right way to do content marketing. Be willing to experiment.
- In-person events continue to be one of the best ways to connect with your audience.
- Never overlook the power of simplicity.
- Content marketing success in your organization means having the right process.
- There are no shortcuts to great content marketing; it takes a lot of elbow grease.
- Don't rely too much on search engines to bring traffic to your site.
- Content curation is important, but it is not a strategy. To be the trusted expert in your industry, you must create your own content.
- Don't wait for perfection. Great content doesn't have to be perfect. It will never be perfect.
- Outsource effectively, or be effectively outsourced.
- If you don't have scaling problems with your content, you aren't moving fast enough.
- Before you create your content masterpiece, first figure out how you are going to market it.

GO TELL YOUR STORY

I believe that you will do great things with content marketing. Hopefully after reading this book, you have the tools you need to create and distribute epic content that will transform your customers and your business. Go out, and be epic!

1. Develop and refine your content marketing mission statement.
2. Find one or multiple partners and launch a content marketing project together.
3. Consider that maybe *less* content will mean *more* impact.
4. Find at least three thought leaders in your organization and build them into your content plan.
5. Send each of those thought leaders to Toastmasters to work on his or her public speaking skills.
6. Define your most valuable audience, and consider a targeted print publication.
7. Assign one employee to SlideShare, and figure out how to leverage this tool as part of your content marketing.
8. Develop a series of stories for your industry on an aspect that has never been covered before.

9. Make sure that every content landing page you develop this year has only one call to action.
10. Spend 30 minutes dissecting Coca-Cola Content 2020.
11. Stop one content initiative this year.
12. Write your book.
13. Update your social media influencer list before the end of the year.
14. Compile a substantial piece of influencer content (for example, an e-book of influencer insights).
15. Get at least five employees who are not in marketing involved in your weekly content plan.
16. Make it a priority to personalize your content by persona.
17. Start a podcast series for executives.
18. Sit down with every salesperson and ask him what his customers' biggest pain points are.
19. Develop a list of the top 100 questions coming from your customer base.
20. Commission a piece of art from a local artist to use in your next content piece.
21. Target one traditional marketing initiative that can be enhanced with content marketing.
22. Set a goal this year to double the number of e-mail subscribers to your content.
23. Attend Content Marketing World. (Sorry, that's a blatant sales pitch.)
24. Read one nonmarketing book each month during the year. (It will open up new content marketing ideas.)
25. Develop a content marketing metrics plan for your CEO or supervisor that includes only those metrics that will make the case for company business objectives.
26. Stop doing the same old press releases and create them as engaging stories.
27. Find a way to work with the leading trade magazine in your niche on a joint content effort.
28. Commission a piece of research that is important to your customers.
29. Take research findings and use them to build a six-month campaign with at least 20 independent content pieces.
30. Commit to smarter usage of images in your content.
31. Do an audit of all your blog posts and determine which types of titles lead to the right reader behaviors.
32. If you have the budget, start identifying media companies in your industry that may be ripe for acquisition.

33. Make sure your content is easy to read on both smartphones and tablets.
34. Set up an editorial leader in each of your silos and plan to meet with that person at least once per week.
35. Develop a customer event that doesn't talk about your projects but rather educates customers on where the industry is going.
36. Create a piece of content this year that would be completely unexpected, and see what happens.
37. For every story idea you have for next year, plan on developing 10 pieces of content from it.
38. Send a videographer and journalist to the next industry event and cover it.
39. Give out quarterly awards to all internal content creators based on number of content shares. Make it public.
40. Choose 10 of the top bloggers in your industry and sponsor a one-day brainstorming session on how you can all help each other.
41. Ask whoever is in charge of customer service what her top 10 complaints were last year. Build a content program to help with answers.
42. Whatever you do this year, make sure you are telling a different story than everyone else in your industry, not just the same story told incrementally better.

THE FINAL WORD

You have made it to the end of this book. I've obviously said enough, but I wanted to say a final "thank you." I truly appreciate the time and effort you put into this piece of work.

Of course, your journey is just beginning, and content marketing continues to evolve. If you'd like to keep up with everything going on in the art and science of content marketing, I would like to urge you to subscribe to CMI's daily blog updates on ContentMarketingInstitute .com. You won't regret it.

Now go out and change the world by giving your customers the best storytelling on the planet. Be epic!

**Life is either a daring adventure
or nothing at all.**
HELEN KELLER

Index